The Death of the Book

The Death of the Book

MODERNIST NOVELS AND THE TIME OF READING

John Lurz

FORDHAM UNIVERSITY PRESS *New York* 2016

THIS BOOK IS MADE POSSIBLE BY A COLLABORATIVE GRANT
FROM THE ANDREW W. MELLON FOUNDATION.

Library of Congress Cataloging-in-Publication Data

Names: Lurz, John, author.
Title: The death of the book : modernist novels and the time of reading / John Lurz.
Description: First edition. | New York : Fordham University Press, 2016. |
    Includes bibliographical references and index.
Identifiers: LCCN 2015035229 | ISBN 9780823270972 (cloth : alk. paper) |
    ISBN 9780823270989 (pbk. : alk. paper)
Subjects: LCSH: Modernism (Literature) | Books and reading.
Classification: LCC PN56.M54 L87 2016 | DDC 809/.9112—dc23
LC record available at http://lccn.loc.gov/2015035229

Printed in the United States of America

18 17 16   5 4 3 2 1

First edition

To my parents (who else?)

CONTENTS

".... look, look. Look where your hands are. Now."

Toni Morrison, *Jazz*

Introduction

Opening the Book

I

In the end this is a book about reading books. Indeed it is about the end of book reading—or, as my title proclaims, about what is so often and so lightly called its "death." It examines the ways that the experimental novels of Marcel Proust, James Joyce, and Virginia Woolf imagine a particular relationship between literature and extraliterary "life" by exploring the dynamic between an embodied readerly subject and the physical object of the book. Analyzing the varied metaphorics mobilized by these novels to highlight the book's materiality, these reflections on the book's mediation of a literary text insistently involve a more serious meditation on transience and temporal progress than is implied in the glib forecasts of its demise. In doing so they trace a temporality of reading based less in the subjective experience of time than in an impersonal ephemerality with which both reader and book are bound up. As I reveal the determining role played by reading—and specifically reading books—in these novels' famed interrogation of the subject's status in the world, I cut across current debates surrounding aesthetic autonomy, modernist temporality, and the relation between literary and media studies. Ultimately developing a particularly modernist conception of literary experience not accounted for by either rigorously historicist or traditionally formalist accounts of the period, my project investigates a set of twentieth-century considerations of what it means that the texts we read are embodied in and mediated by the object of the book.

An early moment in Woolf's *Mrs. Dalloway* offers a preliminary illustration of the argument to come. As Clarissa is on the way to famously "buy the flowers herself," she passes a bookstore where a volume catches her eye and interrupts her urban reverie. Before she directs her attention to the unidentified Shakespearean quotation she finds there (whose own significance I will address in a moment), the narrative lingers over her encounter with the book. Woolf writes, "But what was she dreaming as she looked into Hatchard's shop window? What was she trying to recover? What image of white dawn in the country, as she read in the book spread open."[1] As the "white dawn" of Clarissa's recollection merges with her perception of the book, the "spread open" expanse of its page provides a physical, real-world materialization of the mental image that she is attempting to recall. On the linguistic level the fragmentary construction of the final sentence performs this coincidence grammatically as it runs "the image of white dawn" into the description of the book at which she is staring. These lines thus stage the act of reading as a visual encounter and an affective experience that blends the internal and the external: her mental visualizations dovetail with her perception of the world outside her own interiority. More than this the lines create this portrait of reading through a quiet appeal to the object of the "book spread open" and suggest the extent to which this novel views the mental work of linguistic deciphering and imagination as bound up with, indeed dependent on the physical or perceptual relationship Clarissa has with that language's material support.

This books focuses on just this kind of readerly physical attunement, one that finds its articulation and performance in the careful ways that the modernist novels in my study plot their own readerly consumption. In elaborating this book-based understanding of reading, my argument opens up new ways to consider key issues at stake in the novels of this period, including modernism's famous investigation of time and subjective experience. For if this moment from *Mrs. Dalloway* begins to indicate the place held by the book in this study, the narrative context of this moment, along with the Shakespeare quotation itself, addresses the other operative term in my title, namely *death*. As she comes upon the book, Clarissa is significantly thinking about her own mortality. Right before she looks into the shop window, she observes that "what she loved was this, here, now, in front of her," and wonders "did it matter that she must inevitably cease completely; all this must go on without her." She imagines "that somehow in the streets of London, on the ebb and flow of things, here, there, she survived" and envisions herself "laid out like a mist between the people she knew best, who lifted her on their branches as she had seen the trees lift the mist." While the vaporous immateriality of the arboreal mist allows her to dream that "it spread ever so far, her life, herself," the book's own "spread" is decidedly more concrete (9). It brings her back from this fantasy of subjective immortality to both the finite, material world of objects and to the inescapable march of time which the rhythm of "this, here, now" make so perspicuous. At the same time, the Shakespearean lines that Clarissa finds there— *Fear no more the heat o' the sun / Nor the furious winter's rages*— indicate that, far from sparking an existential crisis, the open spread of the book offers a sense of temporal forbearance, not exactly a consolation but a measured recognition of mortal finitude.

While it is Clarissa who is beginning to cultivate a stance of stoic endurance in the face of such finitude, it is *Mrs. Dalloway*'s reader who is asked to connect that cultivation with the attention paid to "the book spread open." If the narrative content places subtle emphasis on her experience of the book, the way the quotation from *Cymbeline* is also set off from the novel's otherwise continuous stream of text draws *our* attention, for a moment, to the format of the volume we are facing. And, though the page image from the Harcourt edition indicates that this kind of bookish attention occurs here only briefly, the other novels in my study use a number of comparable combinations of textual and material figures to expand and extend this awareness. The ways the works of Proust, Joyce, and Woolf not only work to develop such an awareness but also intertwine it with the sense of mortality and temporality suggested by this moment is part of what I'm alluding to in the figure of the book's "death" and constitutes my own book's intervention in our understanding of what reading entailed for these novels.

This was also, of course, the era when the more colloquial understanding of the phrase "the death of the book" was beginning to have some meaning. As a watershed moment in the development of media technologies that included the mass circulation of photography and the rise of film, not to mention the increasing use of telegraphy as well as the invention of the phonograph, the automobile, and the telephone, the early twentieth century presented these writers with an enlarged and diversified media landscape in which literature was no longer the undisputed cultural queen. Friedrich Kittler provides what life, herself. But what was she dreaming as she looked into Hatchards' shop window? What was she trying to recover? What image of white dawn in the country, as she read in the book spread open:

> *Fear no more the heat o' the sun*
> *Nor the furious winter's rages.*

This late age of the world's experience had bred in them all, all men and women, a well of tears. Tears and sorrows; courage and endurance; a perfectly upright and stoical bearing. Think,

Figure 1.   Virginia Woolf, *Mrs. Dalloway* (New York: Harcourt, Brace, 1925), 9.

is perhaps the best-known account of the effect that this meeting of diverse media forms had on literature, an influential reading that stands behind almost all subsequent discussions of modernism's place in the history of mediation. He describes how Edison's invention of the phonograph in 1877, his development of the kinetoscope in 1892, and the operation of the latter by the Lumière brothers in France and the Skladanowsky brothers in Germany in 1895 as the first exhibition of cinema proper "launched a two-pronged attack on . . . [the book's] monopoly on the storage of serial data."[2] As the gramophone and film bypass the signifier-signified dynamic of language with their respective capabilities to aurally and visually record experience in real time, the privilege of creating a vivid fictional world for a reader, which had been mainly accorded to literature, is suddenly transferred to the new media—a situation that leaves writers and readers in what seems like a newly circumscribed position.

Using a structure that plays directly into the "great divide" that so many inquiries into modernism have worked to break down, Kittler proposes either complicity or rejection as the "two options" by which literature responded to this "attack." On the one hand, literature could "join" the technological media by working to produce lyrics for "phonographic hits" and screenplays for films, while, on the other, it could "reject [the new media], along with the imaginary and real aspects of discourse to which they cater" (247–48). What results in this account is thus a split between writing for popular mass culture and a conception of "high modernism" characterized solely by what he calls "the rituals of the symbolic," which focus on a language that represents nothing but its own play. "Literature," he writes, "became word art put together by word producers" (248–49). One of the aims of this book is to take up what his view misses: Kittler's conception of the gramophone, film, and literature as specialized means of storing experience, each with its own specific (and exclusive) content, disregards the way that each also functions as a technology of *transmission* that works to communicate and convey as much as it documents and records.[3] Far from sequestering literature in an isolated realm of linguistic signification, the extreme experimentation of Proust, Joyce, and Woolf operates, in my argument, to renew our attention to the sensuous object on which the transmission of its writing relies. This perspective is at the heart of my introductory discussion of *Mrs. Dalloway* since it is what makes conceptual space for us to countenance the subject's evanescent encounter with the more concrete space of the page, which might—and often does—otherwise go unnoticed.

Such a seemingly trivial feature of Woolf's novel intimates how the novels I consider become aware of themselves as offering their own time-bound media experience, one that intertwines the register of the verbal with the object of the book in which the "rituals of the symbolic" unfold. Since reading is precisely the act in which this intertwining takes place, my ambition to draw out and illustrate these novels' media awareness motivates my argument's rabid reliance on close reading, as evidenced by my opening gambit with *Mrs. Dalloway*. By getting close to the texts of these novels, I show that they emphasize various aspects of their own bookish embodiment as part of an investigation of subject-object relations. In doing so I fill a glaring hole in accounts of modernism's meditations on mediation. Works like Sara Danius's *The Senses of Modernism*, Julian Murphet's *Multimedia Modernism*, and Mark Goble's *Beautiful Circuits* all focus on the analogical relationship among modernist literature and the new media of its moment and analyze how texts of this period begin to ape the formal and expressive resources of technological mediums that exceed the strictly verbal. As such they disregard the way these works are also thinking about the larger ramifications of literature's own traditional format and mode of access, namely book reading itself.

In a recent article on the history of media discourse as such, however, John Guillory offers terms that help me to emphasize the way these novels leverage the linguistic register to reflect on what it means that a physical support is transmitting that language. Describing a more general intensification of media awareness at this moment, Guillory proposes that "the development of new technical media perplexed thereafter the relation between the traditional arts and media of any kind. . . . The emergence of new media thus seemed to reposition the traditional arts as ambiguously both media and precursors to the media."[4] In this account our approach to literary art—and to representation itself—undergoes a fundamental shift as literature (which, Guillory observes in a footnote, "seems to be less conspicuously marked by medial identity than other media, such as film" [322n3]) suddenly finds itself regarded in a new light: not only as an art but as a medium. Guillory's argument brings literature's mediality into focus by suggesting that the change in the status of fine arts to media forms as a response to these technological innovations "demanded nothing less than a new philosophical framework for understanding media as such in contradistinction to the work of art" (347). That is, these new media forms exceed the paradigm of imitation or mimesis through which the fine arts had been considered since Aristotle's *Poetics*. Instead, as the category of the medium "directs our attention first and foremost to the material and formal qualities of different kinds of expression and only second to the object of representation" (346), it reveals the way mimetic representation of something like language also involves a multivalent process of mediation. From this perspective the linguistic play and formal experimentation for which a writer like Joyce is so famous become an implicit investigation of what is entailed in the communication of literature's message. Identifying "the entire problematic of mediation as the extrapolation of a communicative process from the physical medium," Guillory sketches the larger conceptual scaffolding that frames the way the novels in my study imagine the bodily relationship with the book on which the transmission of their texts depend (351).

My focus on reading's intersection with issues of mediation extends attempts at renewing and reinvigorating close reading as a critical practice. For instance, as part of her recent discussion of the aesthetic and cultural resources modernism offers to contemporary electronic literature, Jessica Pressman mines modernist textuality in order to elaborate a formalist approach to digital literature. Routing her argument through the figure of Marshall McLuhan, Pressman follows McLuhan's identification of modernism as the foundation for the first electronic age to show that the literature of this period and the New Criticism which it sparked were an integral part of the establishment of media studies itself. "Literary modernism," she points out, "invites media studies."[5] Accordingly by examining the ways the novels in my study project their own consumption, which range from descriptions of the interpretive process to embedded examples like Leopold Bloom's readerly doings during his trip to the outhouse early in *Ulysses*, I examine these works' meditations on the materiality of their own media platform. This is less in the service of developing a foundation for the consideration of electronic media and more to show that the format of the book offers resources for rethinking the very idea of literary experience. Though the end of this introduction and the concluding coda will more clearly gesture at the connections between my argument and current conversations in computer-based new media aesthetics, the close textual discussion necessary for me to track the subtle staging of these novels' bookish embodiments leaves little room for explicit discussions of new media themselves. Instead I develop the concern evinced by these novels for aspects of a book's transmission—like the spacing of the page or the appearance of print—and show that this concern contributes directly to their larger projects of understanding the place of a mortal readerly subject in the world of inanimate objects.

At the same time, the privileged place this argument grants to the object of the book is not meant to dismiss the other material objects and sensuous relationships that crop up throughout the novels I consider. On the contrary, for the works under discussion the book functions as an avenue—even a medium—to consider the rapport we have with the external world precisely because it is an object that transmits the textual systems by which this rapport is described. By repeatedly referring readers to the volume they are holding in their hands, these novels stage the book as the object on which the representation of all other objects depend and grant it an implicit precedence that my project's focus aims to make explicit. As this bookish epistemology of reading demands continual negotiations between the figures for the materiality of the book that so often set these novels into motion and the referent of the book facing the reader, my own argumentation moves back and forth between analyzing representations of materially sensitive reading in these narratives and demonstrating the concrete operation of such sensitivity on the part of readers themselves. In doing so I construct a portrait of modernist book reading that shows how deeply entangled the discursive and phenomenal domains of literary experience are for these early twentieth-century novels. My

investment in these questions influences my obvious, even aggressive
selection of canonical novels by Proust, Joyce, and Woolf since, more
than any other works of the period, their texts offer explicit portray-
als of the reading process and the entanglement between the body of
the reader and the object of the book. My departure from more contextualist discussions of twentieth-century culture in favor of a closer
reconsideration of the novel's embodied textuality is meant to develop
a modernist "implied reader" whose sensitivity to the physical book
is elided by other media-centered approaches.[6] Moreover my discussion of these particular novels locates the experience of book reading
in the very heart of modernism itself (rather than on the margins of
the period, where Leah Price locates it in her discussion of the Victorian book) and indicates the potential for considering moments, such
as Clarissa's experience at the bookshop window, which might otherwise seem to function rather peripherally within works less centrally
concerned with the specificity of their format.

II

When Clarissa dawdles in front of the shop window, her deliberations
help to clarify the singularity of her reaction to *Cymbeline* and to situate it in relation to a second important historical frame, namely the
almost fully industrialized book market that the twentieth century inher-
ited from the Victorian era. Just a few lines after Clarissa muses on the
open page, the narrative states that, in the window, "there were Jorrocks'
Jaunts and Jollities; there were *Soapy Sponge* and Mrs. Asquith's *Mem-
oirs* and *Big Game Shooting in Nigeria*, all spread open. Ever so many
books there were; but none that seemed exactly right to take to Evelyn
Whitbread in her nursing home" (10). Clarissa's somewhat exasperated
"Ever so many books there were" signals the skyrocketing number of
books available to readers on the day in June 1923 when *Mrs. Dalloway* takes place (not to mention the day in 1925 when the novel itself
appeared in bookshop windows). Part of this proliferation of printed
materials—newspapers, advertisements, and small literary magazines
as well as books proper—was due to the technological innovations in
papermaking and type-casting as well as to the rise in mechanized printing and binding, which decreased the cost and increased the yield of publishing throughout the nineteenth and into the twentieth century.[7]
    Leah Price has recently discussed the effect this flood of volumes
had on the Victorians themselves, who, she shows, maintained a

merciless opposition between *book* and *text* that privileged textual interior over bookish exterior.[8] This seems to be exactly the direction in which Clarissa moves: the gentle emphasis on the "book spread open" cedes to a focus on content as the attention she pays to the expanse of the page is usurped by the linguistic signification labeling these volumes. Moreover the rather cursory, almost rapid-fire enumeration of the diverse titles in the shop window effectively levels out the specificity of the individual books; each one seems just as good (or, in this case, just as inappropriate) as the next. This seemingly endless and undifferentiated supply of books leads to a mode of *inattention* that rather starkly contrasts with the lingering consideration Clarissa demonstrated in the earlier passage. While Price's project seeks to "excavate Victorian alternatives to the worship of the text that demonizes the book" and looks to "now-forgotten genres and subcultures" that remained sensitive to the materiality of the book (16), this scene in *Mrs. Dalloway* points to the notably less marginalized place that the book comes to have in the modernist literary imagination. In other words, whereas Price looks at moments of what she calls "nonreading," moments in the Victorian age when "the book's material properties trump its textual content," the aesthetic projects of the novels I consider galvanize *the connection between* accessing literary form and encountering bookish format (8). Indeed rather than being banished to the periphery of the literary world, the situation here seems to be almost the reverse: not only do the Shakespeare lines affiliate the format of the book with the pinnacle of "high literary culture" (as opposed to the more frivolous titles Clarissa dismisses), but the way they reverberate in her mind throughout the novel also suggests that their literary and affective impact is due, in part, to the material attention with which she approaches them.

Nevertheless I want to stress that the distinction I'm developing between these "high" modernist novels and less "serious" literature is rooted not in particularities of literary content or even of physical format—Jorrocks's *Jaunts and Jollities* is as much a bookish object as *Cymbeline* or *Mrs. Dalloway* itself—but in Clarissa's performance of two different and ultimately entwined readerly attitudes. We will see in fact that the novels in my study often illustrate the materially sensitive reading they're attempting to cultivate by appealing to deliberately ordinary and unexceptional texts. In a similar way my argument looks away from "special editions" or luxury first runs and focuses on how these five novels imagined themselves to be exploiting the everyday material affordances of an object made at once exceedingly commonplace and quaintly outmoded through advances in both mass production and technological mediation.

The close reading approach I take to develop the role played by the book's status as a material object also opens up the very concept of materiality as it's mobilized in studies of the book. The customary understanding of "materiality" concentrates on the historical, particularly the economic circumstances influencing a work of literature. In the burgeoning field of book history, for example, materiality has often been used to address the way a host of agents, including authors, publishers, printers, shippers, booksellers, and readers, contribute to a conception of the book as a cultural form; this approach has grown to include a consideration of such issues as circulation and reception to further enrich our understanding of what and how knowledge is disseminated at various historical moments.[9] From this perspective the book is as much a physical object as an abstraction figuring the historical forces that shape textual production and reception. As my focus on Clarissa's response to *Cymbeline* should suggest, however, materiality in this argument is functioning in a rather more concretely phenomenological way to explore the particulars of the physical relationship between a reader and a book object, a perspective on the book that draws from the conceptual modification of literature from "art" to "medium" suggested by Guillory. Just as Clarissa's more dilated encounter with the phenomenal materiality of the book occurs within but does not extensively scrutinize the kind of commercial space that might stand in for one of book history's main areas of investigation, so too does my discussion's interest in the experience of reading a physical book limit its consideration of the larger technological and socioeconomic contexts in which it nonetheless takes its place. As this orientation allows me space to attend to the more or less overt ways that these novels refer to their mass-produced volumes at the same time as they offer deep considerations of their own reading experience, we will see that it ultimately enables an account of reading as itself a specific kind of media experience that supplements more culturally focused accounts of the print medium.

If this framing of my project seems to play directly into the accusations of aesthetic autonomy leveled at the modernist period, the specific ways the novels in my study meditate on the book offers an alternative lens through which to understand the relationship between these texts and their extraliterary circumstances. Andrew Goldstone has recently worked to complicate our understanding of literary autonomy by excavating how various modernist claims for aesthetic autonomy figure particular modes of embedding literature in the historical world of the writer.[10] My focus on the attention placed by these novels on the object of the book complements his argument and reveals the no less particular way these novels imagine themselves intersecting with the external world of the reader. This approach finds a precedent in the project of N. Katherine Hayles, who has examined literary works from the digital age to address the "fantasies of unlimited power and disembodied totality" permitted by the late twentieth-century ability of information to circulate unchanged among different material substrates.[11] Though not strictly synonymous, her terms resonate with the independence from external circumstances and obligations that characterizes our understanding of autonomy, and accordingly her calls to reconsider phenomenological materiality frame my own turn to the book's object status as a similar remedial response. More precisely, as the five novels in my study combine a pointed awareness of their material aspects with a deep concern for temporality, they imagine a specific phenomenology of the book that tracks the inexorable passing of time in which literary experience necessarily unfolds. Even as my close reading approach might seem to assert the aesthetics of these novels as laws unto themselves, the very attention to their bookish dynamics is in the service of showing how insistently they take time itself as the determining condition that neither writer nor reader can escape.

As it becomes clear that these novels' investment in this phenomenological materiality has everything to do with the time of reading that they use their books to embody, we will see that the double-edged genitive phrase "the death of the book" expands beyond just a simple description of the book's fate in the face of other media forms. It also designates the sense of finitude and temporal passing that, as we read them, these books transmit *to us*. As such my argument makes a specifically object-centric contribution to Martin Hägglund's recent rereading of Proust and Woolf, in which, counter to the traditional understanding of their works' desire to transcend temporal finitude, he shows that their aesthetics seek "to render the radical temporality of life."[12] As I discuss more fully in chapter 1, my focus on the book draws out the temporality of objects implicit in the more subjective emphasis to which Hägglund's interest in formulating a new account of desire leads him. This allows me to approach significant modernist novels that don't figure in his study at the same time as it also broadens our understanding of time's role in this period by connecting it to other issues—such as the materiality of media forms—that held central importance at this moment. Even so the exceptionally lucid and nuanced account of temporality that Hägglund has developed sharpens the way time is working for my own argument about modernism's insistence on the "finitude" of both the book and the reader and helps me to continue to exfoliate the stakes of my close reading approach to these works.

One of Hägglund's major moves is to revise a simple understanding of linear chronology by reorienting temporality's structural horizon from a notion of immortality toward a notion of "survival," from the idea of an eternal timelessness to that of continuing on in a certain state. Doing so allows him to stress that time's very *passing*—which has little to do with the perpetuity of eternity—is what constitutes temporality as such, a condition that reveals a radical finitude inhabiting every temporal moment. He identifies a "structural relation to loss" as constitutive of temporal life and writes, "Every moment of living on necessarily involves a relation to what does *not* live on, and this negativity already constitutes a minimal relation to death" (8). Hägglund's argument here explicates the sense of finitude proclaimed in my emphasis on the book's "death." As it points to a nonsubjective and even nonhuman conception of time, it also makes space to consider the "continuity between life and non-living matter" implicit in the relationship between subjects and objects that, I suggest, these novels use the reader-book interaction to exhibit.[13]

Hägglund bases this continuity in what he calls the "'arche-materiality' of time," which helps to further emphasize that the "phenomenological materiality" of my argument by no means involves a naïve postulation of immediacy ("Arche-Materiality" 266). Rather, as I will repeatedly demonstrate, the novels in my study imagine the book to function according to the "co-implication of space and time" constitutive of materiality as such. To explain this complex line of thinking, which I am borrowing from Hägglund and his philosophical roots in Derridean deconstruction, let me briefly detour through his discussion of Lily Briscoe's painting in Woolf's To the Lighthouse. Commenting on her desire to capture the present in her painting, he writes, "When Lily experiences a miraculous moment and tries to seize its quality, it is because she senses how it is in the process of being lost and never will return" (*Dying* 58). Comparing this to a more abstract statement he makes about time itself indicates that the memorializing effect of Lily's painting is in fact only a more explicit illustration of the general condition of temporality. He points out that "the succession of time entails that every moment ceases to be as soon as it comes to be and thus negates itself. . . . Every temporal moment therefore depends on the material support of spatial inscription" ("Arche-Materiality" 269–70). Lily's painting thus offers what, following Derrida, Hägglund calls the "originary *becoming-space of time*" (270).

Yet Lily's painting also (and inevitably) exhibits the converse "becoming-time of space." For even as the painting is meant to preserve the moment, "the very form of preservation is itself temporal. The spatial painting that retains moments of time can only remain for a future that may obliterate it" (*Dying* 59). Hägglund's avowal of the painting's fragility in the face of an always uncertain future points to the fact that spatial objects necessarily involve a temporal dimension. As he emphasizes, the persistence of the spatial *is itself a temporal notion*, and the chiasmic relation between the phrases "becoming-space of time" and "becoming-time of space" grammatically expresses the way these two dynamics always involve and are implicated in each other. Their fundamental intersection thus begins to explain why the phenomenological materiality of the book explored by the novels I discuss does not (indeed cannot) entail an assumption of pure, fully available presence. As Lily's painting shows, time and space always slip away from themselves into the other, and neither is completely graspable. And we'll see how the novels in my study imagine their own bookish reading experience in strikingly similar terms. What's more, they do so in ways that place the readerly subject rather literally in touch with the very situation of ephemerality that they embody.

III

While the terms in which I have been developing my discussion make it seem, to put it bluntly, like a matter of life and death, the finitude and temporality to which these novels open our eyes ultimately describe the place that my account of book reading has within more specific conversations about media studies and modernism. On the one hand, critics such as Mark B. N. Hansen and Johanna Drucker, in addition to Hayles, have also made explicit claims for the importance of the phenomenological materiality of media, for a reinvestment in the body as an integral component in artistic experience, and for the need to consider the continuities between print and contemporary electronic media.[14] On the other, recent trends in the consideration of modernism, baptized the "new modernist studies," have focused on expanding our understanding of the temporal, geographical, and discursive boundaries of the field, the last of which emphasizes what we might call "book historical" questions of textual production, dissemination, and reception. Situating my argument and its methodology in relation to one particularly visible strain in this expanded field of inquiry, namely the rising interest in modernist "little magazines" sparked by their ongoing digitization in the online Modernist Journals Project (MJP), will articulate the ways my account of these novels can enhance both of these conversations.[15] Although the arguments I develop do not focus on new media as such, no discussion of the book today—not even an argument as thoroughly delimited as this one, with its explicit reliance on the way five canonical modernist novels imagine the format's significance—can forgo commenting on the relevance of its account for the revolution in media forms currently taking place.

Even as we read the proclamation on the MJP's homepage that "modernism began in the magazines," it is clear that it did not end there. Not only was the serialization of *Ulysses* ultimately superseded by the volume that readers as early as 1922 came to know, but we now access the original appearances of its chapters in the *Little Review* through their remediations on the MJP's website.[16] Glossing over the ramifications of transforming these magazines from print into electronic form, Sean Latham pits the magazine and the book *against* each other in an article detailing the powerful recuperative work of magazine studies. As he focuses on the role played by women editors in the birth of modernism (such as Margaret Anderson and Jane Heap at the *Little Review* itself), he writes, "Although women's roles as editors of cultural magazines have long been acknowledged, such work has often been marginalized by the long-standing primacy of the book in literary history." Advocating "not just new theories of authorship . . . but new models of reception, editorship, and textual interactivity adequate to the magazines" that work to shelve any claims for a modernist cult of the solitary genius, he takes up the cultural-historical approach that also characterizes the field of book history. In so doing he, like book history, considers the book as a cultural form—one, in his argument, exclusively allied with an ideology of aesthetic autonomy—that seems to make very little space to consider its status as a physical object.[17]

To resuscitate this aspect of the reading experience, my project takes its cue from the works I examine and considers figures and formal mechanisms that emphasize the physical relationship we have with our so-called reading material. Not only does this perspective allow me to paint a less antagonistic picture between the formats of the magazine and the book, but it is also the place in which my argument about the temporality of book reading speaks (perhaps surprisingly) to the computer-based new media that seems to be taking up more and more of our contemporary attention. Following Rita Raley, Hayles has pointed out how work in new media, such as Noah Wardrip-Fruin's *Screen*, "has redefined what it means to read, so that reading becomes . . . a kinesthetic, haptic, and proprioceptively vivid experience, involving not just the cerebral activity of decoding but bodily interactions with the words as perceived objects moving in space" (*Electronic* 13). With the novels in my project I will show how such a reconsideration of reading is not limited to electronic literature. Rather, as the book artist turned new media theorist Drucker has suggested, "many points of continuity exist between print and digitally networked artifacts and these don't have to depend on the seductive, special-effects, images of frictionless manipulation in holographic information spaces" ("Humanities" 18). Though Drucker consistently appeals to the language of new media—"We must create theoretical frameworks for discussing reading *as interface*," she writes—my argument about the mediation of these novels leads me to formulate my discussion in the less high-tech terms of the book around which they revolve ("Reading" 218).[18]

If both Drucker and Hayles mount arguments that, in Hayles's words, "us[e] electronic textuality to better understand print," my efforts in showcasing the commitment of these novels to exploring the mediating functions of their own material aspects *use print to better understand print* and, in so doing, expand our understanding of its continuity with the arguments about textuality that these new media critics draw from the electronic. With the particular concern they hold for their bookish embodiment, the novels in my study imagine a much more complicated account of their more traditional format than "the stability of print" that Hayles contrasts with the fundamentally processual nature of the electronic (*My Mother* 100). The fact that, as she points out, print persists "for (more or less) long periods of time" is precisely where these novels locate their mobility: in the very temporality tracked by and embodied in their volumes. As this bookish temporality puts the book into conversation with the flux more obviously associated with electronic media, it also addresses the little magazines, whose serialized publication schemes exhibit their own kind of temporal extension. Indeed if we open up one of the little magazines to Joseph Conrad's narrative of his early development as a novelist, which appeared in the *English Review* in 1908–9, we can get a sense of the way my argument about these novels and the temporal transmission of their physically material format almost literally unfolds within and has ramifications for cultural studies of print media as well as the digitally focused work of new media studies.

In the opening installment of his autobiographical musings "Some Reminiscences," Conrad describes the composition of his first novel, *Almayer's Folly*, and writes of the "idleness of a haunted man who looks for nothing but words wherein to capture his visions," terms whose exclusive appeal to an otherworldly language seems to divorce literary activity from more mundane circumstances (1: 40). The kind of cultural-historical questions that constitute so much of the work in periodicals studies and book history seeks to show up these fantasies of autonomy through a larger discussion of the conditions of production or the networks of writers and editors at the *English Review*, a monthly periodical begun by Ford Madox Ford in 1908 to awaken a cultural awareness that Ford found lacking in the British populace.[19] Conrad's further comments on novel writing, however, offer their own way of grounding his chosen genre in a specific moment, one that contorts the contextualist approach in its performance of the kind of subject-object relations I've been claiming for the books of these novels.

He describes the labor of a novelist "whose first virtue is the exact understanding of the limits traced by the reality of his time to the play of his invention. Inspiration comes from the earth, which has a past, a history, a future, not from the cold, immutable heaven" (5: 63). Distinguishing himself from the universalizing moralism of Rousseau, who, he points out, "was no writer of fiction . . . no novelist" (5: 62–63), he underscores the particular form and historicity of his work. Conrad's language, however, twists his point's resonance with Latham's assertion, made with Robert Scholes, that reading modernist magazines allows scholars to "investigate the ways in which modern literature and the arts connected to the culture of commerce and advertising and to the social, political, and scientific issues of the time" (517). While this is certainly implied, the tension here between terrestrial change and a transcendent stasis also suggests the more phenomeno-logical orientation in play, the extent to which Conrad views his nov-elistic work as limited by time itself. And it is no accident that, when external "reality" does break in and remind him of the passing time in which his novelizing is taking place, his descriptions figure that time in the "earthly" materials of his writerly composition.

Indeed the repeated, even compulsive way Conrad's manuscript pages function as the hinge between his subjectively focused imagina-tive work and the "real world" of objects in which he pursues it offers what we might punningly call a "mediating" alternative to the com-mercial or political aspects on which cultural studies of print media focuses. At the same time, taking a look at this insistent focus—which loosely echoes Clarissa's encounter with *Cymbeline*—also offers a way to consider the dynamism of print in terms that put it into a con-tinuum with the digital. Just a few paragraphs into "Some Reminis-cences," Conrad describes how a conversation with a fellow sailor causes him to break off from his writing. Not only does "the hallu-cination of the Eastern Archipelago" that made up the content of his narrative disappear from his mind at this moment, but he conflates the imagined story with its material support and writes, "The story of 'Almayer's Folly' got put away under the pillow for that day" (1: 38). Moreover the manuscript itself—whose visual, nonverbal aspects are described in terms of its "faded look and an ancient, yellowish com-plexion" (1: 44)—is a presence that threads throughout his reminis-cences to weave together and track the development of his work as a writer. Thus as he describes how Almayer's "memorable story, as if it were a cask of choice madeira, got carried for three years to and fro upon the sea" (1: 44), these autobiographical reflections become as much an objective "it-narrative" that progresses over time as they are an investigation of his own subjective history.[20]

The manuscript of *Almayer's Folly* comes to light when his cre-ative reverie is interrupted, and Conrad portrays the actual inscrip-tion of a few lines with a similar material sensitivity. After quoting the words he wrote, he further intertwines his imaginative invention with the phenomenal objects of his composition and describes how "these words of Almayer's romantic daughter I remember tracing on the grey paper of a pad which rested on the blanket of my bed-place" (1: 36). It should thus come as no surprise that Conrad's identity as a novelist crystallizes, almost without his knowing it, in the physical act of put-ting pen to paper: "Yet it stands clear as the sun at noonday that from the moment I had done blackening over the first manuscript page of 'Almayer's Folly' (it contained about two hundred words and this proportion of words to a page has remained with me through the fifteen years of my writing life), from the moment I had, in the simplicity of my heart and the amazing ignorance of my mind, written that page the die was cast" (4: 650). Though modernism as a whole might have "begun in the magazines," Conrad's particular brand of it—sampled here in the sentence's serpentine syntax—seems to have commenced less with the churning surge in twentieth-century print culture than with the physical act of "blackening" a manuscript page. The creation of the novelist as a subject is indistinguishable here from the creation of a written object.

At first glance the tale that Conrad is telling comes dangerously close to the modernist fantasy of artistic autonomy that opened his narrative, not to mention the suggestion of permanence and stability that would differentiate his "old" medium from the recursive flow of the digital. When his description of writing his later novel *Nostromo* repeats the emphasis on material pages, however, it expands on the way this phenomenal materiality functions as his work's very entrée into a temporality that once again dramatizes, on a local scale, its inescapable imbrication with the composition's real-world situation and delicately dynamizes its seeming fixity. In a passage that occurs toward the end of the fifth installment of the "Reminiscences," Conrad describes being disturbed at his writing by the daughter of one of his acquaintances. On the one hand, he claims that the woman's interruption causes him to feel as if he had been "uprooted out of one world and flung down into another" since, during his writing, "he had never been aware of the even flow of daily life." But on the other, it's at this moment that he looks about the room and notices how "there were pages of MS. on the table, and under the table, a batch of typed copy on a chair, single leaves had fluttered away into distant corners; *there were there living pages, pages scored and wounded, dead pages that would be burned at the end of the day*—the litter of a cruel battlefield, of a long, long and desperate fray" (5: 66, italics added). By rendering his writing as a protracted struggle between the writer and his materials of composition, the martial metaphors here work to embody the quite real mental efforts and emotional exertion of literary creation.

This figural embodiment finds a more literal incarnation in the material pages scattered about his room, which ultimately serve as the record of the very historical time he has spent laboriously spinning out his visions of Almayer and Nostromo. The redundancy of the "there were there" accentuates the existence of these pages independent of the imaginary world Conrad is creating. The string of adjectives used to describe this "there-ness," which cannot be completely or consistently disregarded in the act of composing the narrative they underwrite, significantly figures it in temporally progressive terms. The ongoing evolution implied by the idea of "living pages"—as well as the mortality suggested by the "dead" and "wounded"—points to the way Conrad imagines these written leaves to have their own kind of dynamism, one that revolves around the ungraspable movement of time itself. Recalling Hägglund's argument, this temporality allows us to nuance, if not wholly reconsider, the "stubborn" stability by which Hayles somewhat too quickly characterizes inscriptive mediums like writing and print. For her, print's persistence across time indicates its constancy and endurance, which is exactly what, for Hägglund, indexes its very dynamism, its fundamental and inescapable succession. In terms that evoke the discussion of Lily Briscoe's painting, he writes, "The material support of the trace is the condition for the synthesis of time, since it enables the past to be retained for the future. The material support of the trace, however, is itself temporal. Without temporalization a trace could not persist across time and relate the past to the future" ("Arche-Materiality" 270).

With this in mind, Conrad's language of "living" pages points to the way a material inscription's durability is the location of its own ungraspable flow, one that complicates the "stability" to which critics of both periodical studies and new media confine more traditional—and seemingly static—formats like the printed book. For instance, Latham emphasizes what he sees as the exceptional features of the magazine in his assertion that, "after all, magazines are not meant to be read a page at a time from cover to cover as one might a novel or a biography." He goes on in terms that sound very much like a new media critic: "Their mixture of textual and visual objects invites and sometimes even requires a more dynamic form of engagement" ("Mess" 412). Even more pointedly, Hayles adds an additional layer of textual dynamism when she distinguishes a printed text from its electronic counterpart by referring to the computational operations that produce it: "Printed lines exist before the book is opened, read, or understood. An electronic text does not have this kind of prior existence. . . . In this sense electronic text is more processual than print; it is performative by its very nature" (*My Mother* 101). What both these discussions elide or minimize in the attention they pay to the more overt motility of their media is the less obviously perceptible temporality to which they are also subject. This is what Conrad's account, like the novels I look at, shows: that texts themselves—electronic or print, magazine or book—are always embodied by and bound to a materiality that *is itself temporal*.

As Conrad recounts, however, his attention to the temporality of his work is emphatically not based in his engagement with the significations of his language (which actually allowed him to think he had shaken off the "flow of daily life") but rather in the otherwise overlooked space and time that he as a subject shares with the material objects of his pages. In contrast the novels in my study draw this temporality out into the open by using their language both to direct readerly attention toward the physical characteristics of their formats and to connect those characteristics more or less explicitly with time's passing. (This is, of course, what the language of Conrad's reminiscences does accomplish—not for him as the writer, it seems, but for us as readers.) In doing so they flesh out the implications of Conrad's additional reference to "dead" pages and show how the temporality on which any kind of vitality is predicated always entails a fundamental relation to mortality. Hägglund describes this situation succinctly: "A temporal being is constantly ceasing to be and can only perpetuate itself by leaving traces of the past for the future. This tracing of time is the movement of survival that transcends a particular moment of finitude and yet is bound to finitude as a general condition" (*Dying* 6). This "general condition of finitude," to which my rhetoric of the book's "death" explicitly appeals, is where my argument about the novels in this study has a final word to say to digital media and the modernist little magazines. It is not that the bookish perspective that these novels allow me to develop places this more traditional format into a continuum with the flux more easily associated with these other, newer or more "mobile" media. Rather—and more important—it's that the dynamism of these media forms in no way exempts them from the mortal temporality disclosed by the book. If, in the end, the book transmits its sense of finitude to us, it is only by embodying the transience by which the material world, with all its subjects and objects, texts and processes, comes to life.

IV

I develop the ephemerality that these novels imagine the book to embody and transmit to its reader most precisely in four chapters on Joyce and Woolf that each treat specific aspects involved in its mediation: the reader's body, the book's print, its pages, and finally its binding. These discussions are preceded by a more general account of the novel's status as an object in Proust, in which I show how the chance appearance of George Sand's *François le Champi* at the end of the novel opens up an unexpectedly material and temporal account of the famously idealist Proustian project. The most peculiar of all the narrator's instances of "involuntary memory," his encounter with this book roots his ambition to "redeem lost time" in an embrace of physical solidity and in a recognition of temporal transience. Triangulating Proust's work with the theoretical insights of Melanie Klein and Maurice Merleau-Ponty, this chapter develops a model of modernist mediation that is deeply engaged with the physical and affective valences of the book object, an engagement that, in Proust, has everything to do with the transmission of a sense of both temporality and mortality. As I offer an overview of reading's temporality that amounts to what I am calling "the death of the book," I outline a critical approach whose emphasis on embodied perception, physical objects, and the finitude implied in time's passing broaches a number of the themes taken up and expanded in my subsequent readings of Joyce's and Woolf's novels.

If, in addition to giving a reading of the *Recherche*, the Proust chapter offers the broad contours of my argument, the chapters on Joyce and Woolf explore more narrowly focused instances of the "death of the book." In doing so, they move away from the explicit reliance on theorists like Klein, Merleau-Ponty, or Hägglund, who, in various configurations, nonetheless remain in the background of the discussion. Rather I look to the particular novel under consideration for the more pointed terms in which it is imagining the role the book plays in its aesthetic project. Moving from an emphasis on the mortal embodiment of the human to the more radically impersonal finitude of the bookish object, these chapters map the continuum between the two in which all of these novels are, finally, invested.

This arc begins with two chapters on the later works of Joyce in which I advance a more detailed "reading of embodiment," a phrase that refers as much to the reader's body as to the book's. Chapter 2,

"The Reader of *Ulysses*," develops one aspect of the Proustian narrator's affective investment in the object of the book by plotting how Joyce's novel progressively draws attention to the mediating agency of the reader's sensory relationship with his reading material. Revolving around the "Sirens" episode, my argument suggests how this central chapter brings together, for the reader, Stephen Dedalus's and Leopold Bloom's respective overemphasis on the operation of the intellectual and physical in the act of reading. "Sirens" illustrates an intersection of these two poles and reveals how Joyce's novel calls out to the perceptual openings of the reader's body that allow for access to its text. More than this, *Ulysses* hints at the way these holes in the body act as figures for its fundamental finitude, a condition of physical fragmentation shared by the form of the novel itself. As we move to the other works in my study, we will see these novels recast such fragmentation in terms that speak more to the format of the book by showing the holes and divisions out of which it is also constituted.

Accordingly chapter 3, "The Dark Print of *Finnegans Wake*," builds on my argument about *Ulysses* and shows how Joyce's later novel trains its focus on the printed body of the book itself and not incidentally figures its printed letters as holes in its pages. Drawing on John Bishop's influential reading of the *Wake* as Joyce's "book of the dark," I argue that the work's multilingual puns and portmanteaux—along with its typographical play—highlight the role of its "dark print" in literary mediation. My reading takes shape around the discovery and exploration of a fragmented letter that acts as one ambiguous center for the swirl of the *Wake*'s obscure narratives. The special attention paid to the historical nature of this letter's material fragments suggests the temporal extension of the work's own printed letters, which the *Wake* develops in lengthy discussions of the readerly acrobatics required by its extreme linguistic performance. As *Finnegans Wake* connects its emphasis on both the letter and its letters with overt and extended meditations on death, the finitude implied in physical embodiment that ends my discussion of *Ulysses* begins to extend to the book itself and, to use a *Wake*an pun, becomes "literally" explicit.

The discussions of embodiment in Joyce set the stage for a broader discussion of the links between human subjects and nonhuman objects in Woolf's *Jacob's Room* and *The Waves*. These novels, in which the object of the book plays a central role, complement and complicate the more obvious interest in subjectivity that has become a hallmark of the Woolfian project. They also provides a renewed understanding of the corpus of her work (and of her works) that deepens the connection between her activity as a printer with the Hogarth Press and her formal literary experimentation. Chapter 4, "The Pages in *Jacob's Room*," considers the novel's unconventional page layout in which empty spaces of varying sizes separate the scenes of the narrative, a printing decision that was significantly tied to the inauguration of the press in 1917. I show how the novel redirects readerly attention toward the pages transmitting its text in a way that echoes the narrative's attempts to situate intersubjective relationships within the larger affiliation we have with the object world external to the subject. As *Jacob's Room* expands my elaboration of Joyce's "reading of embodiment" by using its book to emphasize the readerly subject's own status as an object, I draw out the living reader's place in the nonliving world, a profound belonging to the inanimate implicit in the embodied mortality that my earlier chapters begin to develop.

Chapter 5, "The Binding of *The Waves*," furthers the transformation of the subject's perspective into that of an object by placing the temporal aspects of such a move center stage. It treats the way the novel's meditations on pagination connect with Woolf's stated intention—echoed by one of the novel's six narrators—to represent the very flow of time itself. As *The Waves* imagines how its bound pages might physically index the impersonal passing of narrative time that its curious interludes represent verbally, it underscores the persistence of the object world that undergirds—and exceeds—the reader's subjective experience of the novel. In doing so it shows that what persists is precisely the passing of time itself, a transience that impinges on subject and object alike. As the binding of *The Waves* comes to physically embody this transience without arresting it, it mediates the temporality and finitude of the individual volume and draws together the preceding chapters' arguments as well as the double meaning of "the death of the book."

Drawing attention to the way reading is itself a specific engagement with a time-bound process of mediation, the dynamics of these modernist novels ultimately carve out a space for attending to the adamant historicity embodied in their books. I draw out the ramifications of this timely attention in a brief coda to my argument, entitled "The Afterlives of Reading," that returns to the intersection of modernist and media studies on which this introduction has touched. Ultimately I hope to suggest the relevance that the expansion of readerly awareness detailed by my arguments has for addressing the embodied materiality of so-called virtual media that are themselves also subject to the flow of time. As I trace considerations like this through my chapters with their respective meditations on the reader's body, the book's print, its page, and its binding, I often frame my discussions with short detours into an essayistic mode that might seem to deviate from conventional scholarly protocol. For a book about the way five novels draw attention to their place in the world outside the narratives they're spinning, I momentarily rely on this more introspective method to underscore the temporality of my own reading (as well as my own argumentation), the way these books have intertwined themselves into facets of my experience that go beyond my engagement with their narratives. Situating my arguments within these rather personal reflections should also indicate that my points are not trying to reassert the book's cultural privilege or denigrate the forms of mediation which fly, at various moments in history, under the flag of the new. This is not, let me be clear, an anticinema screed or a Luddite dismissal of digital media. Rather, however nostalgic this might sound, the space this book marks out is meant to reveal a place for reading a so-called old medium in a world that, now no less than in 1900, seems to contain no end of "new" things.

CHAPTER I

The Books of the *Recherche*

The description of the process by which the narrator goes to sleep that opens Proust's seven-volume mediation on art and memory has sometimes seemed to me to be a rather inauspicious launch for the literary odyssey on which the reader is embarking: "For a long time I used to go to bed early. Sometimes, when I had put out my candle, my eyes would close so quickly that I had not even time to say to myself: 'I'm falling asleep.'"[1] What is this fall into unconsciousness doing, I wondered, here at the inauguration of such an insightful—not to mention somewhat interminable—examination of the workings of consciousness? Why begin with something that seems, on the surface, so deliberately mind-numbing, something in which language itself is explicitly disabled? Little did I know, on my first reading, that my trek through the next three thousand pages would involve so many moments of my own readerly ennui, moments in which I would find myself emptily turning pages, bored almost out of my mind. This confession of my wandering attention is not to say that I don't love reading Proust. It is, rather, to say that part of what I love about the experience of reading Proust is precisely the kind of sleepy distraction so assiduously produced (even in translation) by his hypnotic, rhapsodic prose. This paradoxical consciousness of unconsciousness is indeed what the narrator describes in the line that follows his opening statements: "And half an hour later the thought that it was time to sleep would awaken me." When he continues, however, and reports, "I would make as if to put away the book which I imagined was still in my hands" (1: 3), his almost literal gesture to the book significantly connects his readerly unconscious to the physical relationship with this material object in a way that the rest of his novel will elaborate in equally explicit terms.

This chapter is, accordingly, an exploratory account of the connection between reading and the book that the opening of Proust's novel announces. How does the work imagine the reader's engagement with this object, and how do these meditations on the book's agency in the reading experience intersect with the novel's more obvious concerns with time, mortality, and literature? To answer these questions I examine some key moments in Proust together with the thought of Melanie Klein and Maurice Merleau-Ponty, which allows me to elaborate a model of literary experience that is deeply engaged with the physical and affective valences of the book object. In Proust this bookish engagement has everything to do with the passing of time. Indeed there is perhaps no better work to think about this nexus of issues than Proust's, since it is, at bottom, an extended analysis of both sensory phenomena and the creation of a book. I look to the way the novel discusses physical embodiment—of both books and people—which I bring into conversation with the phenomenality of Proust's own literary creation, the fact that his novel is itself made of paper, ink, and glue. The emphasis on the book's phenomenal materiality is perhaps unexpected for a writer like Proust, who is famous for his stringent idealism. Yet in the introduction to his translation of Ruskin's *Sesame and Lilies*, he claims, "Reading is at the threshold of spiritual life; it can introduce us to it; it does not constitute it."[2] The image of the threshold suggests that reading links the spiritual to some other sphere, a sphere that his novel shows to be the finite and temporal world of phenomena in which books—like their readers—take their place.

This focus on objects in Proust links to and extends the recent reassessment of time's place in the project of the *Recherche* by Martin Hägglund. Rather than the standard critical accounts of Proust's work, which emphasize the narrator's discovery of a timeless essence and see the thrust of the novel as an attempt to transcend time through the eternity of art, Hägglund argues that the narrator of the novel does not ultimately seek "to redeem the condition of temporality but, on the contrary, to mobilize it as the source of pathos . . . to intensify the sense of the passage of time" (*Dying* 45). In my argument I show that the object of the book is bound up with precisely this temporal mobilization by exploring two moments in Proust's novel in which the material embodiedness of a book takes on significance for the narrator, namely the night spent reading *François le Champi* with his mother as a young boy and his later discovery of that volume in the Guermantes' library. While Hägglund's argument gestures at this temporality of objects in his discussion of the way "the duration of the past is not spiritual or immaterial but depends on the inscription of the past in a material body . . . whether the body of the self or a work of art" (43), his larger project of developing time's fundamental role in the constitution of desire keeps him focused on what he explicitly calls "the temporality of the self" (27). To draw out what his subjective emphasis minimizes, I use the theoretical vocabulary of Klein's "object relations" to clarify the object's role in the complicated relational dynamics the narrator describes. As Klein's formulation of the paranoid and the depressive positions parses the varied connections that the narrator has with the book, it articulates an implicit emphasis on the narrator's embodied sense perception as the means by which he approaches that object.

My reliance on Klein to focus on the object thus reveals the extent to which the linguistic content of the novel is invested in its own embodiment in the book that mediates and transmits this content to a reader. At the same time, by also offering a way to account for the recognition of temporal finitude that complicates the commitment to eternity in the narrator's concluding literary aspirations, Klein's model allows me to draw a link between this kind of embodied reading and the temporal transience at the heart of the Proustian project. Proust's novel ultimately stages the literary artwork not as an aesthetic transformation or transcendence of the temporal, physical world but as both an intellectual and a sensory engagement with *the very limits of that world*, the transmission of the temporality and finitude that the narrator seems, at times, so determined to deny. This perspective dovetails tellingly with a discussion of Proust's own significantly idiosyncratic and complex compositional habits in his manuscript notebooks, the way his expansion of the novel entails a move away from linguistic signification (discursive directions to his editor on the placement of additional passages) to material manipulation (the creation of his *paperoles* via the pasting of loose sheets onto the edges of his notebook pages).

The last turns of this chapter move the discussion beyond the physical materiality of the book to show my argument's larger ramifications for our relationship to the world external to the readerly subject.

In light of the novel's emphasis on and investigation of multiple forms
of embodiment, I reexamine the narrator's relationship with Albertine's sleeping body in *The Captive*, which has traditionally been figured in terms of his attempt to "read" her. This turn to the literal
body entails a move away from Klein, for whom the body ultimately
plays a very limited role, to the embodied phenomenology of Merleau-Ponty. By triangulating the figures of Proust, Klein, and Merleau-Ponty, this chapter revises our understanding of the role played
by the books of the *Recherche* and offers an overview of a temporality
of reading rooted in those objects that amounts to what I am calling
"the death of the book."

I

I begin toward the end of Proust's work, which is also its own kind of
ambiguous or retroactive beginning, with the series of sensory experiences that instigate the artistic project by which he hopes to redeem
his lost time. Samuel Beckett describes this sequence of events succinctly, if somewhat problematically, thus: "The germ of the Proustian solution is contained in the statement of the problem itself. The
source and point of departure of this 'sacred action,' the elements of
communion, are provided by the physical world, by some immediate and fortuitous act of perception."[3] It is interesting to note that,
in the list of the narrator's "fetishes" that Beckett goes on to assem-
ble and that extends from the taste of the madeleine and the sight of
the steeples of Martinville through the feel of uneven paving stones,
the clink of the spoon on the tray, the brush of a napkin on the narrator's face, the noise of water moving in pipes, and the encounter
with George Sand's *François le Champi*, he includes sensory descriptions in almost all but the instance involving the volume of Sand. This
omission of sensation in relation to the novel stems from the opposition that Beckett's qualification of these perceptual acts as "immediate" sets up with the explicitly mediated nature of books themselves.
In describing "immediate acts of perception," he renders impossible
the application of a sensory verb to an object like a novel: "seeing" a
novel is not part of our habitual understanding of what one does with
such an object. Rather, of course, we *read* novels, an action that is
anything but "immediate."

Beckett thus unintentionally indicates the fact that the narrator's
encounter with the novel is actually quite different from the series of

perceptual acts that precede it. We will begin to see that this moment in Proust's narrative suggests that perception itself is no more immediate than reading, that in fact it is mediated by precisely the conditions of temporality and embodiment on which my discussion focuses. Critical accounts of the encounter with the novel either follow Beckett and elide the strangeness and specificity of sensorially encountering a book by folding it into a general account of the cascading series of events that spark the closing revelations of *Recherche*, or they focus on the significance of the content of Sand's novel.[4] The critical homogenization of these moments takes its cue from the novel itself, which collapses each of the specific experiences into an instance of a more general resurrection of the past; though the moments themselves are different, they all function in the same way. I quote, as is so often necessary with Proust, at length:

> So often, in the course of my life, reality had disappointed me because at the instant when my senses perceived it my imagination, which was the only organ that I possessed for the enjoyment of beauty, could not apply itself to it, in virtue of that ineluctable law which ordains that we can only imagine what is absent. And now, suddenly, the effect of this harsh law had been neutralized, temporarily annulled, by a marvelous expedient of nature which had caused a sensation—the noise made both by the spoon and by the hammer, *even the title of a book*, for instance—to be mirrored at one and the same time in the past, so that my imagination was permitted to savor it, and in the present, where the actual shock to my senses of the noise, the touch of the linen napkin, *or whatever it might be* [etc.], had added to the dreams of the imagination the concept of "existence" which they usually lack, and through this subterfuge had made it possible for my being to secure, to isolate, to immobilize—for a moment brief as a flash of lightning—what normally it never apprehends: a fragment of time in a pure state. The being which had been reborn in me . . . is nourished only by the essence of things, in these alone does it find its sustenance and delight. (3: 905, italics added)[5]

The phrase "whatever it might be" draws out, more explicitly than the "etc." of the French original, the detachment from and indifference to the specificity of the experience that brings about this shock in the narrator. While this affect is due, in part, to the fact that the narrator cannot choose which experiences will elicit a reaction of this kind, his indifference also stems from the way that, in the end, every moment provides him with the same essential experience. As Leo Bersani tersely describes it, "in the later volumes, the phenomenal is more and more absorbed into the universally valid formula, the general law."[6] At the same time, the narrator's emphasis on "securing" and "immobilizing" a "fragment of time in a pure state" suggests that abstracting and universalizing these experiences entails an overcoming—or at least a disregard—of time's insistent flow, a move into the temporally static realm of the eternal that will ultimately be undercut by his encounter with the object of the book. In doing so the book offers a more specific display of Hägglund's unorthodox argument about time's operation in the *Recherche*, the fact that "when the past returns through involuntary memory, it is not because it persists in itself but because it has been inscribed as a trace that remains across time," which, "far from being immaterial or eternal . . . is explicitly material and destructible" (38).

The overtly readerly terms that the narrative uses to explain the "process of decipherment" by which he abstracts the transcendental essence of his sensory experiences cast reading itself as an activity of idealization and abstraction that would seem to offer very little space for the "material and destructible" object on which that reading is based. He writes:

> No doubt the process of decipherment was difficult, but only by accomplishing it could one arrive at whatever truth there was to read. For the truths which the intellect apprehends directly in the world of full and unimpeded light have something less profound, less necessary than those which life communicates to us against our will in an impression which is material [*matèrielle*] because it enters us through the senses but yet has a spiritual meaning [*l'esprit*] which it is possible for us to extract. . . . The task was to interpret the given sensations as signs of so many laws and ideas, by trying to think—that is to say, to draw forth from the shadow—what I had merely felt, by trying to convert it into its spiritual equivalent. And this method, which seemed to me the sole method, what was it but the creation of a work of art? (3: 912)

The unambiguous vocabulary of reading and interpretation, the conception of sensory experiences as "signs," the call to "convert" a "material" sensation to a "spiritual" equivalent all suggest the way the narrator treats his phenomenal experience as something he must ultimately move beyond. He "reads" the world and turns it into a text that communicates, as he puts it in the previous sentence, "something of a quite different kind . . . some thought which [the signs] translated after the fashion of those hieroglyphic characters which at first one might suppose to represent only material objects" (3: 912). Moving from "objects" to "thought" recalls the slide into timeless universalization, what Bersani calls Proust's "redemptive" project that exemplifies precisely a "devaluation of historical experience" (1). In the eyes of the narrator, lived experience is both inherently inferior to and in the service of an experience that has been translated into art. Time-bound presentation is only the handmaiden to an eternal representation.

Yet the repeatedly idealist claims that constitute the narrator's account of a work of art overshadow the less transcendent moments of his description that stem from his "discovery of the destructive action of Time" offered by the aged faces at the Princesse de Guermantes's afternoon party (3: 971). He writes, "The cruel discovery which I had just made could not fail to be of service to me so far as the actual material of my book was concerned. For I had decided that this could not consist uniquely of the full and plenary impressions that were outside time. . . . Time in which, as in some transforming fluid, men and societies and nations are immersed, would play an important part" (3: 974). A closer examination of the narrator's encounter with *François le Champi* in the library of the Prince de Guermantes reveals the extent to which this temporality is embedded in the object of the book, an embedding that draws out the literal valence of the narrator's figurative phrase "the actual material of my book." As the narrator's project of transforming the world into a timeless abstraction becomes considerably more complicated when the object whose sensation he wants to textualize is itself a printed text, the encounter with Sand's novel outlines the singular place that the book has in his cascade of "involuntary memories." If the majority of these memories cause him to attempt to think what he "merely feels," the object of the book transposes this and asks him to *feel* what he usually *thinks*— which, in this case, is precisely the passing of time.

> As I entered the library where I had been pursuing this train of
> thought [regarding the creation of a work of art] I had remembered
> what the Goncourts say about the magnificent first editions which
> it contains and promised myself that I would look at them while I
> was waiting. And all this while, without paying much attention to
> what I was doing, I had been taking first one and then another of the
> precious volumes from the shelves, when suddenly, at the moment
> when I carelessly opened one of them—it was George Sand's *Fran-
> çois le Champi*—I felt myself unpleasantly struck by an impression
> which seemed at first to be utterly out of harmony with the thoughts
> that were passing through my mind, until a moment later, with an
> emotion so strong that tears came to my eyes, I recognized how
> very much in harmony with them it was. Imagine a room in which
> a man has died, a man who rendered great services to his country;

the undertaker's men are getting ready to take the coffin downstairs
and the dead man's son is holding out his hand to the last friends
who are filing past it; suddenly the silence is broken by a flourish of
trumpets beneath the windows and he feels outraged, thinking that
this must be some plot to mock and insult his grief; but presently
this man who until this moment has mastered his emotions dissolves
into tears, for he realizes that what he hears is the band of a regiment
which has come to share in his mourning and to pay honor to his
father's corpse. Like this dead man's son, I had just recognized how
completely in harmony with the thought in my mind was this painful
impression which I had experienced when I had seen this title on the
cover of a book in the library of the Prince de Guermantes, for it was
a title which after a moment's hesitation had given me the idea that
literature did really offer us that world of mystery which I had ceased
to find in it. (3: 918–19)

The "moment's hesitation" to which the narrator refers divides this
event into two parts: the first is the encounter with the book, characterized by the feeling of being "unpleasantly struck by an impression," while the second is the interpretation of that encounter, the
generation of the "idea that literature did really offer us that world of
mystery." The contrast between the sensory and intellectual dimensions suggested, respectively, by the words *impression* and *idea* recalls
the narrator's process of idealistic abstraction; in effect he treats the
book as one more experience from which to extract a transcendental essence. Yet this "impression which first seems to be out of harmony with the thoughts that were passing through [his] mind" is
much closer to an actual "world of mystery" than the "idea" that the
reading of the title offers. The unpleasantness and disharmony of this
"impression" contrast sharply with the joy and happiness that were
hallmarks of his previous thoughts about immortality and the puri-
fied essence of time and map more closely onto the "cruel discovery"
of time's destructive effects. It is thus fitting that the metaphor that
helps to distinguish between the sensory and intellectual dimensions
of his experience revolves around grief, death, and loss. As this metaphor illustrates the way the sensory experience of the trumpets leads
the grieving son to a mournful recognition that overpowers the emotional taming for which social conventions like a wake were designed,
it also suggests the way sensation potentially undercuts the binding
effects of our lexical habits.

We can see this a bit more clearly if we notice that the narrative delay
introduced by the lengthy metaphor mimics the "moment's hesitation"
that precedes the narrator's own cognition and conceptualization of

the title of Sand's novel. As the death-focused metaphor impedes the progress of the narration and lingers in that moment before the narrator comprehends and articulates his preliminary vague physical "impression" into more specific, intellectual terms, it draws out the narrator's sensory experience of the book and connects it to the recognition of time's destructive action. The fact that the son—who seems to exhibit a level of inattention to the coffin that resonates with the narrator's absent-minded survey of the books—is jarred by a "flourish of trumpets" underscores the sensory aspect of the verb *to look* (*at*) (*regarder*), an aspect that might otherwise be eclipsed by its idiomatic usage as a synonym for *examine* in both French and English. Moreover the comparison of the narrator's visual stimulus with the musical metaphor suggests that the intellectual act of reading depends on bringing together multiple sensory registers, both the visual *and* the aural, while the echo of *press* in the word *impression* suggests that the register of touch is also, if only implicitly, in play. This passage thus indicates that, far from being purely mental, reading a book is actually a radically sensory experience, and accordingly the description of being "struck" by an "impression" takes on an insistently physical connotation. Since the experience of the book here leads not to the disembodiment the narrator finds in the earlier moments but rather to an emphasis on the empirical (and hence finite) body, it also brings him face to face with finitude as such, figured here in the son's loss of his father. Functioning less as a mediation of time's eternal essence than as an embodiment of its very passing, *François le Champi* thus seems to transform the "fragment of time in a pure state" that the narrator originally finds into transience itself and offers an explicit example of what I am calling "the death of the book." It is no surprise, then, that narrator finds the initial "impression" "unpleasant" and inharmonious with the rest of his train of thought until he is able to abstract himself from the experience.

Comparing this moment with the narrator's earlier experience as a child going to sleep with *François le Champi* allows us to develop the connection between physical sensation and mortality and also helps to articulate how the experience of the book can lead to a less disavowing attitude toward death. The similarities between the two moments occur most explicitly in the way the son of the dead man in the analogy describing the narrator's initial reaction to seeing Sand's novel loses "mastery of himself," which is also a fitting characterization of the dissolution of self that the narrator experiences going to sleep in the opening of the novel. For him, going to sleep is a precursor of death, a terrifying harbinger of nothingness: "My sleep was so heavy as completely to relax my consciousness . . . and when I awoke in the middle of the night, not knowing where I was, I could not even be sure who I was" (1: 5). He continues, "I had only the most rudimentary sense of existence," which we might rephrase as "I could not even be sure *if* I was."[7] The strange descriptions of liminality in the opening pages of the *Recherche*, of a subject that is trying to recognize its own dissolution into unconsciousness, evokes Klein's hypotheses about the earliest developments of the ego. As she describes the way "the early ego largely lacks cohesion, and a tendency towards integration alternates with a tendency towards disintegration, a falling into bits," she effectively formulates the novel's opening moments into the separate tendencies that, relying on consciousness, the narrator himself cannot fully describe.[8] When she relates this alternation between integration and disintegration to the ego's ability to deal with anxiety, which "arises from the operation of the death instinct within the organism, [and] is felt as fear of annihilation (death) and takes the form of fear of persecution" (179), she gives an implicit account of the way the narrator's "bedroom became the fixed point on which [his] melancholy and anxious thoughts were centered" (*Recherche* 1: 9).

The defense mechanisms of the early ego against this anxiety are numerous and complicated but, according to Klein, involve both a projection outward of the destructive impulse of the death drive and a phantasmatic introjection of both good and bad objects, the former of which offer it resources against its anxiety. This introjection closely describes the narrator's experience of his mother's goodnight kiss, which, at first, is the only reassurance that counters this subjective disintegration into nothingness. He writes of "the calm and serenity she had brought me a moment before, when she had bent her loving face down over my bed, and held it out to me like a host for an act of peace-giving communion in which my lips might imbibe her real presence and with it the power to sleep" (1: 14). The metaphor of communion almost explicitly indicates the way the young narrator wants to take his mother's "real presence" into himself as a guarantee of his existence. In doing so he receives "the *power* to sleep," as if, with his mother's reassurance, he can somehow accept and tolerate the anxiety that accompanies the dissolution of his self.

On that exceptional night when the narrator's mother stays with him in his room, however, *François le Champi* also becomes the object by which the narrator assuages his anxiety.[9] Proust writes, "Mamma went to fetch a parcel of books of which I could not distinguish, through the paper in which they were wrapped, any more than their short, wide format but which, even at first glimpse, brief and obscure as it was, bade fair to eclipse the paintbox of New Year's Day and the silkworms of the year before" (1: 42). He goes on to report, in idealizing language that characterizes what Klein calls the "paranoid position," that for him "a new book was not one of a number of similar objects but, as it were, a unique person, absolutely self-contained" and, in terms that the later encounter in the Guermantes' library reiterates, how the "reddish cover and incomprehensible title [of *François le Champi*] gave it, for me, a distinct personality and a mysterious attraction" (1: 44). As Klein describes it, this moment of abstracting idealization is one in which "the good aspects [of the object] are exaggerated"; it "aim[s] at unlimited gratification and therefore create[s] the picture of an inexhaustible and always bountiful" object (182). As such the book becomes a metonymic stand-in for his mother. The contrast between the books and the gifts like the "paintbox" and the "silkworms" highlights the way the latter, by their nature, expend themselves in their use while the "short, wide format" of the former seems to exhibit a self-sufficient stability. The self-containment with which the narrator idealizes the book suggests that it can quiet his anxiety precisely because, he imagines, it persists through time and beyond the dissolution of his own consciousness. Though the narrative it contains might, like time itself, press ever forward, the object of the book offers, to his mind, a transcendent permanence.

If this reassurance is what the narrator desires from the presence of his mother and the book itself, the mother's reading aloud nuances his idealizations and shows that both her "presence" and the book's reassuring density are actually predicated on an experience of loss and absence bound to its own temporality. This is the case not only because the narrator's mother skips the love scenes of the novel as she reads, a fact Margaret Gray has discussed, but also because of the way she "supplied all the natural tenderness, all the lavish sweetness which they demanded to the sentences which seemed to have been composed for her voice" (*Recherche* 1: 45). Though, at first glance, it seems that the mother's voice takes the lead in imparting affective significance to the sentences of Sand's novel, she does so in response to their "demand"—which is to say, her voice does not communicate its emotion directly but works in tandem with the sentences. Language and the voice here work as mediums for each other; the sentences embody the emotion of the voice to the same extent that the voice expresses the emotion of the sentences. This interpenetration—what Merleau-Ponty calls the chiasm—underscores that the significance of the novel depends on the fact that neither the language of the novel nor the mother's voice is a perfectly transparent medium of transmission. Rather they both have a certain opacity of mediation that not only precludes complete transmission but is also the very condition of communication in the first place.

When he goes on to describe his mother's reading in more detail, the narrator underscores the sensory and temporal elements constituting this opacity and stages the relationship between her voice and the novel's text as a model for considering the book less as an abstracted ideal than as a real sensory object that interpenetrates with the language it transmits: "She smoothed away, as she read, any harshness or discordance in the tenses of the verbs . . . guiding the sentence that was drawing to a close towards the one that was about to begin, now hastening, now slackening the pace of the syllables so as to bring them, despite their differences of quantity, into a uniform rhythm, and breathing into this quite ordinary prose a kind of emotional life and continuity" (1: 46). As the mother voices the sounds that transmit the intellectual ideas of Sand's text, she highlights the sensory experience of the novel in a way that resonates with the encounter in the Guermantes' library. Yet this is significantly not an experience of full plenitude. As she guides the sentences "towards" each other, she maintains and manages—rather than eliding—the gaps between the words to create a sense of continuity *based on discontinuity*, a "uniform rhythm" that underscores the temporal unfolding of Sand's text. The "emotional life" that imbues the prose is thus one intimately related to tolerating this temporal flow, not one that disavows it via timeless idealization.

The narrator's later encounter with *François le Champi* extends this emotional investment and temporal awareness to the object of the book itself. Referring to the theory of memory that explains why, for example, the madeleine evokes Combray so strongly, Proust writes, "And this is true of everything that we see again after a lapse of time, books in this respect behaving just like other things: the way in which the covers of a binding open, the grain of a particular paper, may have preserved in itself as vivid a memory of the fashion in which I once imagined Venice and of the desire that I had to go there as the actual phrases of the book. An even more vivid memory perhaps, for phrases sometimes are an obstruction" (3: 921). In the same way that the narrator's description of his mother's voice takes precedence over the content of Sand's novel, here the narrator effectively dismisses the "actual phrases" as a distraction and focuses on the material aspects of the book—"the way in which the covers of a binding open" and "the grain of a particular paper"—as the site of his memories. Though the qualifier "vivid" suggests a presentness and vitality, as if the past moment returns completely, the specification of the "lapse of time" on which memory itself is predicated indicates that the material aspects of the book actually highlight the passing of time, the "vividly" *non-transcendental* nature of his experience that indicates his awareness of the mutual position he and the book share in the temporal world.

He draws out exactly this sense of temporality when he says that this encounter was "one in which memories of childhood and family were tenderly intermingled and which I had not immediately recognized." He continues, "My first reaction was to ask myself, angrily, who this stranger was who was coming to trouble me. The stranger was none other than myself, the child I had been at that time, brought to life within me by the book, which knowing nothing of me except this child had instantly summoned him to its presence, wanting to be seen only by his eye, to be loved only by his heart, to speak only to him" (3: 919–20). The strange quasi-subjectivity that the narrator imparts to the book here evinces his consideration of the book not as an extension of himself but as an almost independent entity with its own desires and agency, a state rather close to the way Klein describes what she calls the "depressive position." This part of infantile development, which persists in all the experiences of loss and mourning throughout the emotional life of the adult, entails coming to terms with the ego's limits, the fact that the external world is independent of it and does not instantly and entirely satisfy its every desire. Klein explains that the depressive position adds "feelings of sorrow and concern for loved objects, the fears of losing them and the longing to regain them," to the fears and anxieties about the destruction of the ego discussed earlier (151). Accordingly, at the sight of Sand's book, the narrator feels an "emotion so strong that tears came to my eyes" (*Recherche* 1: 918). As the narrator here exemplifies Klein's description of mourning as a simultaneous experience of despair and love, he showcases the different affective orientation toward loss implied by the depressive position. Aware of his own limits without needing to deny their existence or disavow their importance, the narrator effectively embodies the lengthy metaphor involving the son's grief at his father's funeral.

At the same time, however, the narrator also makes explicit claims for the dematerialization of the book: "For things—and among them a book in a red binding—as soon as we have perceived them are transformed within us into something immaterial [*quelque chose d'immatériel*], something of the same nature as all our preoccupations and sensations of that particular time, with which, indissolubly, they blend" (3: 920). The explicit valorization of the immaterial here obscures what, to me, seems more to the point: not the importance of materiality or immateriality as such but the *intersection* of the two. The way the narrator roots his fantasies of immateriality precisely in a physical experience of the material object of the book—which he describes as "not a very extraordinary one"—is what marks it as significant for him. We thus might suppose that a book that *is* "very extraordinary," that *is* written with what he later calls a "magic pen," is perhaps one that draws its reader's attention to its own physical materiality *via its text*. As we will also see in the discussion of the novels of Joyce and Woolf, these extraordinary works will draw a connection between themselves as texts and themselves as books to figure—indeed literally embody—the affective significance and sense of temporality that, due to his childhood experience with it, *François le Champi* has for the Proustian narrator. This need not (and perhaps cannot) be done only through play with the layout of pages, the design of a cover, or the choice of a font, since these would end up as only another kind of "language" to decipher. The example of *François le Champi* emphasizes, on the contrary, the *relation between* a book's physical materiality and the linguistic content that it contains, the fact that one is always implicated in other.

The apparent privileging of "immateriality" here takes part in the insistent idealism that the redemptive assertions put forth in the novel's conclusion. This idealism overshadows the other, less transcendent moments in his closing descriptions (which, accordingly, have received considerably less critical attention). For example, the narrator claims that "once one understands that suffering is the best thing that one can hope to encounter in life, one thinks without terror, and almost as of a deliverance, of death," an almost explicit contradiction of the death-defying assertions he makes elsewhere (3: 947). Likewise, a few pages earlier, he exhorts, "Let us submit to the disintegration of our body,

since each new fragment which breaks away from it returns in a lumi-
nous and significant form to add itself to our work" (3: 944). It seems
to me to be precisely the *vacillation* between descriptions of loss and
finitude and these manically idealistic claims that is in play in the concluding pages of the novel. Klein's term *position* is especially suited to
describe this vacillation, since it is meant to indicate less an established
sequence of affective or developmental states than a more supple mobility between varying affective modes. She thus claims that "when the
depressive position arises, the ego is forced . . . to develop methods of
defense which are essentially directed against the 'pining' for the loved
object" (151); the methods she enumerates are precisely those of idealization and denial that the narrator exhibits in his earlier, more "paranoid" moments. As this more labile idea of the "position" suggests the
close relationship between feelings of omnipotent mania and depres-
sion, it also suggests that the idealistic claims for which the novel is so
famous are themselves potential indicators of a depressive orientation,
which it is the project of the rest of this chapter to elaborate more fully.

II

An examination of Proust's own strategies for composing and
expanding his novel offers a radically concrete demonstration of the
depressive relationship with the book as object for which, I suggest,
his novel calls.[10] The narrative provides a thumbnail sketch of Proust's
idiosyncratic working methods when the narrator describes his plans
for the novel he will write: "I should work beside [Françoise] and in
a way almost as she worked herself . . . in pinning here and there an
extra page, I should construct [*bâtirais*] my book, I dare not say ambi-
tiously like a cathedral, but quite simply like a dress" (3: 1090). In
her reading of the novel, Mary Lydon focuses on Proust's knowledge
and use of the figure of Fortuny and argues that the designer offered
Proust a model and taught him a "professional secret . . . a *tour de
main* that defies analysis, and hence imitation."[11] For her the development of the *Recherche*, "proceeding, as it does, by the pinning on
of supplementary pages, might be viewed as the history of Proust's
laborious pursuit and ultimate acquisition of such a *tour de main*,
his apprenticeship to a profession (writing) whose manual aspect, the
word 'manuscript' notwithstanding, is all too often ignored" (175–
76). My argument follows Lydon's but takes a more precise look at
the "manual aspect" of Proust's compositional process.

The notebooks in which Proust composed his novel are rightly famous for their complexity, and they are especially fascinating for the way they illustrate the importance of the material page for his compositional process. Jean-Yves Tadié, one of Proust's major biographers, describes this process as one in which Proust used a series of sequential notebooks to develop his narrative while, at the same time, he elaborated other ideas in fragmentary form in separate notebooks. These latter were then often dismantled into a number of loose pages, which Proust pasted into other notebooks to create what he came to call his *paperoles*. This pasting technique became especially prevalent toward the late phases of the novel's composition, when Proust was expanding the figure of Albertine and adding the narrative that involves her.[12] Here Proust abandoned the discursive directions he had used in earlier drafts to instruct his editor on how to collate additional passages in favor of this kind of pasting, as if material manipulation had come to supplant linguistic signification.

An examination of a particularly complex notebook in which we can see Proust experimenting with this new strategy of pasting passages toward the end of the composition of *Cities of the Plain* sheds light on the consequences of the material awareness that the unconventional cutting and pasting evinces. In the notebooks from later stages of the novel's composition, when Proust adds a piece of paper to the edge of a page (usually the top or the bottom), he does so almost invariably without comment; the pasting of the additional material speaks for itself, as it were. In this notebook, however, Proust includes directions on the pasted addition. For example, we find an extension pasted to the top of the page with the direction "not to place on the facing recto, but on the following recto."[13] Though Proust does not completely eschew the discursivity of his earlier directions, the fact that he refers to pages and spatial locations rather than citing the language of his text suggests that this strategy of pasting requires a heightened awareness of his composition's status as a physical object, something that has spatiotemporal coordinates in the world.

The operation of this heightened material awareness becomes clearer when considered in light of a particularly heavily revised page that displays the close relationship among sense perception, affect, and temporality on which my reading of the novel in the previous section centered. On this page Proust includes the standard reference direction "See the page" but follows it not with a page number but with the word "AMOUR" drawn in large letters with a heavy red pencil. Additionally, in the margin of the

Figure 2.   Marcel Proust, autograph manuscript, Bibliothèque nationale de France, Département des manuscrits, NAF 16686, pp. 52v-52A–53r.

following page there is a discursive direction that reads "this page and that which should come after the part that begins 22 pages farther on at the sign AMOUR," a reference to a passage appropriately found twenty-two pages later in this same notebook whose cross-reference is signaled by the twin sign of another heavy, red-penciled AMOUR (61v). Here the word's ostentatious color and size call attention to its visual aspects, the features of writing that, far from being strictly verbal, appeal instead to the senses. In doing so it exposes the integral part that the senses play in reading, the fact that to read we must also see. At the same time, however, the lexical associations that spring up around the word *love* suggest that these sensory features of writing, which the intellectual act of reading necessarily looks past, become conspicuous through an affective approach to the work. To put it crudely, it is perhaps a kind of love that can recognize the sensory relationship we have with the physical materiality of a literary work. In making the otherwise invisible commerce between the sensible and the intelligible aspects of writing conspicuous, the example of the word AMOUR offers a way to understand the heightened material awareness that Proust's use of *paperoles* demand. That is, the cut-and-paste work by which he revises and expands his novel involves him in his own affective, even amorous relationship to the materials of his novel's composition, not unlike the narrator's relation to *François le Champi*.[14]

The affective investment on which I'm focusing productively overlaps with one of the conclusions that Hägglund draws from his account of temporality, what he calls "the attachment to temporal life that is the source of all care" (*Dying* 9). As he elucidates that "it is *because* of temporal finitude that one cares about life in the first place" (8), the account of desire Hägglund is ultimately interested in advancing suggests that the "love" I'm discussing tacitly involves temporality as such. At the same time, recall the way Klein describes the working through of the depressive position: at the height of grief, "love for the object wells up," and the ego begins to "pine" for the object (163). If Hägglund's discussion points to the implicit workings of temporality in the depressive position, Klein's elaboration on this kind of love formulates Hägglund's abstract notion of "care" and desire in the specific terms of the material object. When the ego realizes the effect of its own paranoid aggression on its loved object, she writes, it responds "with anxiety for it (of its disintegration), with guilt and remorse, with a sense of responsibility for preserving it intact against persecutors and the id, and with sadness relating to expectation of impending loss of it. These emotions, whether conscious or unconscious, are in my view among the essential and fundamental elements of the feelings we call love" (125). These feelings of love, remorse, and guilt awaken in the ego a desire to repair the loved object, to make it whole again; this desire is what Klein calls reparation. As Proust's cutting and pasting functions as a concrete, embodied example of this "reparation" (which, in Klein's model, is wholly phantasmatic), it speaks to the important role played by the body and its temporality in the affective stance toward the book that I have been developing.

In fact his narrator points to how we might further investigate the role of the body when he uses the language of love to draw a connection

Figure 3.   Marcel Proust, autograph manuscript, Bibliothèque nationale de France, Département des manuscrits, NAF 16686, pp. 61v–62r.

between his feelings for books and women. Recalling the image of a dress, he states, "The first edition of a work would have been more precious in my eyes than any other, but by this term I should have understood the edition in which I read it for the first time. . . . I should collect old-fashioned bindings, those of the period when I read my first novels, those that so often heard Papa say to me: 'Sit up straight.' Like the dress which a woman was wearing when we saw her for the first time, they would help me to rediscover the love that I then had" (3: 923). It is the narrator's preeminent amorous affair with Albertine, who comes to drape herself in the gowns of Fortuny, that will help me to round off—or flesh out—the embodied account I have been developing of literary experience. I thus turn now to the narrator's relationship with Albertine and Merleau-Ponty's phenomenology of "the flesh" to further explore the operation of the physical body in reading.

III

Constellating the narrative of Albertine's imprisonment with Proust's extratextual strategies of composition and his encounters with *François le Champi* is no arbitrary decision. Not only are there significant thematic resonances among them, but Proust's introduction of

the character of Albertine in 1914 (when the war halted publication
of his work and further extended its composition in time) also had
a profound effect on the structure of the novel and, in fact, precipi-
tated many of the idiosyncratic revisionary practices I've just been
examining. As Proust developed the plot lines involving Albertine, he
expanded what essentially would have been the three-volume novel
that *Swann's Way* promised on its contents page (with *The Guermantes' Way* and *Time Regained* as the two volumes to come) into the
quite time-consuming seven-volume structure that it has today. The
character of Albertine thus allowed the first trip to Balbec to grow
into a full volume that became *Within a Budding Grove*; her potential
lesbianism provided additional subject matter for *Cities of the Plain*;
and, most interesting, the experience and aftermath of the narrator's
love affair with her in Paris composed the whole of *The Captive* and
The Fugitive.

Tadié describes how, at this moment, Proust added parts involving Albertine to chapters and sections that had already been written
to form the volume *Cities of the Plain*, while, with *The Captive* and
The Fugitive, "everything is reversed: the sections that are already
written are inserted into Albertine's story" (608). The introduction of
Albertine thus becomes the place in the novel's composition where the
material aspect of the work takes on the most agency for Proust himself. This finds a significant analogue in the reception history of the
novel: Christine Cano has detailed how contemporary reviewers saw
the *roman d'Albertine* as a "disharmonious and dysfunctional excres-
cence" that remained heterogeneous to the rest of the novel—in much
the same way that critics had condemned the "Swann in Love" section
of the 1913 *Swann's Way*.[15] These critiques of "disharmony" seem to
echo the narrator's own reaction to his encounter with *François le
Champi*, as if to suggest an alliance between the *roman d'Albertine*
and the material and temporal awareness that later disturbs him in
the Guermantes' library. The correlation of Proust's extreme revisions
with the sense of "disharmony" claimed by the novel's critics ultimately casts the strange relationship between the narrator and Albertine as an implicit investigation of material awareness as Albertine's
body itself strikes the narrator as similarly "disharmonious."

Paying attention to the role played by Albertine's body extends
my discussion of the book's physical materiality to a consideration of
the subject's relationship to the rest of the external world, a relationship between the inanimate and the animate that Hägglund describes

in broader terms as "the continuity between the non-living and the living" ("Arche-Materiality" 274). At the same time, my argument also expands on the "readerly" terms that critics have used in their extensive discussion of the narrator's paranoiacally jealous relationship with her. Perhaps the most explicit of these arguments is David Ellison's claim in his book *The Reading of Proust* that "the entirety of *La Prisonnière* tells the story of a reader's vacillations: it is the figural narration of the interpretive process as such. Marcel's relationship to Albertine is that of a jealous decipherer to a dark code, and his judgements alternate between . . . the poles of delusion and critical penetration, which like vice and virtue in the *Recherche*, cannot exist independently of one another."[16] The polarized view of the narrator's relationship with Albertine forecloses any middle ground between delusion and penetration and limits him to the role that, in her extension of Klein's model to "critical practices," Eve Kosofsky Sedgwick describes as the "paranoid reader," one who adopts an "anticipatory mimetic strategy whereby a certain, stylized violence . . . must always be *presumed* or *self-assumed*."[17] As Sedgwick's language of anticipation suggests, the narrator's paranoid maneuvers—in which he imagines all the ways Albertine not only could betray him but already has betrayed him—involve an attempt to get outside time itself, an attempt to survey all possibilities and contingencies that would allow him to have stable and final knowledge of Albertine. This approach to the narrator's relationship with Albertine seems to disregard—or take for granted—the limits of this endeavor, that fact that, time-bound as his "reading" is, total comprehension of her is an impossibility. The narrator is implicitly aware of this impossibility and comes, at moments, to give up the readerly tactics on which the critical conversation has focused and to tolerate the opacity that usually incites his paranoia. Without discounting these paranoid tactics, I more closely interrogate the moments when he gives up penetrating her to sketch out the way he unknowingly inhabits a depressive relationship to her and her body. In doing so I show how this relationship involves the narrator's implicit awareness of his own body in a way that deepens the important and intertwined roles played by embodiment and temporality on which I have focused in the affective encounters with the book.

We begin to see the agency of the spatiotemporal body when, for all of the narrator's hermeneutical acumen, he exhibits a certain skepticism toward the possibility of getting hold of Albertine. He observes

that, after her imprisonment, "it was no longer the same Albertine, because she was not, as at Balbec, incessantly in flight upon
her bicycle . . . because, shut up in my house, docile and alone, she
was no longer what at Balbec, even when I had succeeded in finding
her, she used to be upon the beach, that fugitive, cautious, deceitful
creature . . . [and] because, above all, I had clipped her wings, and
she had ceased to be a winged Victory [*une Victoire*] and become
a burdensome slave [*pesante esclave*] of whom I would have liked
to rid myself" (3: 378). As happens so often in the novel, the narrator's perspicacity anticipates that of the reader. The terms in which he
explicitly formulates the paradox of Proustian desire—how his grasp
of Albertine destroys exactly the mobility that made him desire her
in the first place—illuminate this paradox in telling ways. The alle-
gorical image of the *Victoire* points to an interdependence between
her dynamism and his tendency to treat Albertine as a sign that he
might interpret. In other words, Albertine can function as exactly the
"fugitive creature" he desires insofar as she represents *something else*,
namely the eternity of art that, in his more paranoid moments, he
also wants to capture. When the narrator sets up a contrast between
the image of flight and movement and the description of Albertine
as a "burdensome slave," however, he points to the way this readerly
idealization disregards—to the same extent that it is refuted by—her
physical embodiment. As Lydon puts it, "the more successfully she
functions as a metaphor, the more her literal body poses itself as an
obstacle" (173). Recognizing the impossibility of his attempt to seize
her, the narrator thus begins to hint at the way his desire to grasp her
mobility and dynamism as such entails a denial of her very temporality, a disavowal of her ongoing existence as a temporal being indexed
by the physical body he tries to look beyond.

Yet when *The Captive* offers a different attitude toward Albertine's body in the scenes in which the narrator surveys her while she
is asleep, it paints a more complicated picture of "grasping" Albertine
and her dynamism at the same time as it replays the bedroom scene
in which he first experiences *François le Champi*. As these moments
nuance the model of "reading" that dominates critical understanding
of the volume, they indicate the extent to which the narrator's body—
rather than his mind—becomes his medium for accessing Albertine
(as well as, by comparison, that of the book itself): "Her personality
was not constantly escaping, as when we talked, by the outlets of her
unacknowledged thoughts and of her eyes. She had called back into

herself everything that lay outside, had withdrawn, enclosed, reabsorbed herself into her body. In keeping her in front of my eyes, in my hands, I had an impression of possessing her entirely [*En la tenant sous mon regard, dans mes mains, j'avais cette impression de la posséder tout entière*] which I never had when she was awake" (3: 64).[18] Here, rather than disregarding her body's physicality, the narrator seems to find new value in it: as her flesh "reabsorbs" the mobility of her "constantly escaping" personality and becomes the literal incarnation of her dynamism, it takes on a numinous quality. Paradoxically the body contains that dynamism by unleashing or uncovering the temporality with which the vagaries of her personality are bound up. Interestingly the narrator transforms his approach to her: instead of trying to penetrate her intellectually, he "keep[s] her in front of [his] eyes, in [his] hands"—in other words, not penetrated but sensed. The use of prepositional phrases here—those grammatical structures that describe the relation of one object to another—undercuts his claim to "possess her entirely" since they refer only to his physical relationship with her body and do not necessarily extend beyond that. With this perspective it is significant to notice how prominent a role the preposition plays in what is perhaps the most rigorous attempt to theorize an embodied mode of sense perception, namely Merleau-Ponty's reconsideration of phenomenology in *The Visible and the Invisible*. Using terms of possession that echo the narrator, Merleau-Ponty writes, "He who sees cannot possess the visible unless he is possessed by it, unless he *is of it*."[19] The "of" here becomes the index of a shared space and time, a fundamental phenomenological affiliation (what Merleau-Ponty calls the "flesh") and a common belongingness to the same temporal world. Because the preposition describes—if only implicitly—a two-way relationship, one in which the objects necessarily come into contact with *each other*, the narrator's description of "keeping her *in front of* my eyes, *in* my hands" underscores that Albertine's body is in contact with Marcel's hands to the same extent that his hands are in contact with it.

Bringing Merleau-Ponty's thinking to bear on this moment in Proust's novel is somewhat counterintuitive, especially in light of the description of the narrator's sexual enjoyment of Albertine while she is asleep. Marcel's physical molestation and "possession" of Albertine seems to suggest exactly the opposite of the reciprocal relationship entailed in Merleau-Ponty's model.[20] The latter's perspective, however, makes conceptual space to highlight the temporal limitations that undergird—and undercut—the narrator's claims for omnipotent possession and total comprehension at these moments. He reports, "So long as [her sleep] lasted, I was free to dream about her and yet at the same time to look at her, and, when that sleep grew deeper, to touch, to kiss her," and, a few pages later, "I felt at such moments that I had possessed her more completely, like an unconscious and unresisting object of dumb nature" (3: 64, 67). While most discussions of these descriptions understandably focus on his exploitation of Albertine, they elide the explicitly fleeting and ephemeral nature of these opportunities. Keeping this temporal framing in mind suggests that Albertine's unconscious state does not necessarily imply the total passivity the narrator asserts but rather recalls the dynamism by which we have seen him characterize her sleeping body. It is not only that he cannot entirely possess her because the opportunities for possession are themselves situated in and delimited by temporal progression. Rather this temporality is itself at the heart of a fundamentally impenetrable dynamism; it is precisely what he cannot (and does not) grasp.

The narrator provides his own implicit account of this axiomatic incapacity when he describes how, though Albertine is the one who is asleep, it is he who is "free to dream." As Leo Bersani puts it, he "can love her most gently now [that she is asleep] because it is really he who is at rest,"[21] as if to suggest that the narrator becomes his own kind of "unresisting object of dumb nature." As the sensory approach to her sleeping body allows him to share in her unconsciousness (a rather significant transformation given his earlier anxiety over going to sleep), he effectively exhibits—indeed literally embraces—his affiliation with all the other objects of the temporal world. This is, in effect, the continuity of the animate and the inanimate to which Hägglund's argument about temporality leads.[22] Moreover when the narrator connects this shared condition of embodiment with a disregard of language, he ultimately offers resources that relate these scenes to the role played by the temporal (but inanimate) materiality of the book and the sensory nature of (animated) reading with which my discussion began: "I was not troubled by the words that she murmured from time to time in her sleep; their meaning was closed to me, and besides, whoever the unknown person to whom they referred, it was upon my hand, upon my cheek that her hand, stirred by an occasional faint tremor, stiffened for an instant" (3: 67). There is a clear privileging of the sensual over the linguistic here. The "closed" meaning of her words mimics the "closed" or bounded state of her unconscious body and paves the way for the mutuality of sense perception suggested by the preposition *upon*. His insistent receptivity to his own body ("upon my hand, upon my cheek") entails a comparable sensitivity to time's passage—the "instant" he is sharing with her—rather than a search for the more permanent or stable intellectual knowledge that he imagines deciphering her words would provide him.

Indeed the narrator forgoes discursive knowledge altogether when, a paragraph later, he comments on the fact that "all her letters were in the inner pocket of [her] kimono, into which she always thrust them." Though he observes that "a signature, an assignation, would have sufficed to prove a lie or to dispel a suspicion," he admits, "Never once did I touch the kimono, put my hand in the pocket, examine the letters . . . realizing that I would never make up my mind, I would creep back to my bedside and begin again to watch the sleeping Albertine, who would tell me nothing, whereas I could see lying across the arm of the chair that kimono which would perhaps have told me much" (3: 67, 68). In his recent work on Proust, Joshua Landy proposes that the narrator dispenses with a perusal of the letters out of a fear of finding his suspicions confirmed. For Landy the narrator seeks not the truth but a "convincing lie" with the power to "send all his doubts to sleep."[23] Given the paranoia so persistently displayed by the narrator, the idea of a "convincing lie" in the Proustian universe seems to be a logical impossibility: the condition of his epistemological relationship with Albertine is that *no lie is ever convincing enough*. It is only when he sidesteps the truth-lie framework—when, we might say, he stops looking for enduring and unchanging truths as such—that he escapes from his doubts. Accordingly, in focusing instead on his sense perception ("I began to watch the sleeping Albertine"), he takes on his own sensory body and ultimately puts to sleep his penetrating intellect and its imperative for eternal verities.

Not only does this instance of going to sleep recall the early scene in his bedroom with *François le Champi*, but it also bears an important resonance with the descriptions of artistic creation with which Proust ends the novel. In doing so it reveals the work of literature to include a similar kind of intellectually soporific process and makes space for the sensory receptivity and the destructive progression of time thereby entailed that we have seen the narrator progressively come to admit: "This work of the artist, this struggle to discern beneath matter, beneath experience, beneath words, something that is different from them, is a process exactly the reverse of that which, in those everyday lives which we live with our gaze averted from ourself, is at every moment being accomplished by vanity and passion and the intellect, and habit too, when they smother our true impressions, so as entirely to conceal them from us, beneath a whole heap of verbal concepts and practical goals which we falsely call life" (3: 932). The way "vanity and passion and the intellect, and habit too" get in the way of our "true impressions" by covering them with "a whole heap of verbal concepts" speaks to the timeless, linguistically formulated abstractions that he ultimately eschews in his experience with Albertine's letters. Indeed in looking for something "beneath" (*sous*) the intellectual understanding of experience, the artist effectively treats all of experience, language, and matter like a sleeping Albertine, whose embodied dynamism was literally "beneath" the hands of the narrator. Accordingly the hazy imprecision of the description of the artist's search for "something that is different" suggests that, just as the narrator does not ultimately penetrate the sleeping Albertine, neither can the artist seize any kind of transcendent meaning from these other experiences. Rather the artistic work he is describing is meant to approach or to recognize an ultimately impenetrable mystery, an impenetrability that the scenes with Albertine (no less than the very title of the work we are reading) link with the dynamism of temporality itself.

This distinction the narrator draws between "reality" and "realist art" clarifies what is entailed in approaching temporality without immobilizing it. Contrasting the kind of art he wants to make with "the kind of literature which contents itself with 'describing things,' with giving of them merely a miserable abstract of lines and surfaces," the narrator denigrates a strictly representationalist conception of literature, one exclusively concerned with description and information (3: 920–21). As his language suggests, this kind of literature would be motionless and skeletal, without any flesh or depth that might suggest a sense of ongoing vitality. The narrator also describes "the falseness of so-called realist art, which would not be so untruthful if we had not in life acquired the habit of giving to what we feel a form of expression which differs so much from, and which we nevertheless after a little time take to be, reality itself" (3: 915). Representation, or "giving to what we feel a form of expression," falls short of "reality" to the extent that we confuse the static "form" for the mobility of experience itself. It is not necessary to reject representation completely (which would be impossible); rather the narrator's statement suggests that the sphere of representation needs to be more precisely defined and situated.

By allying representation with habit and "expression," the narrator makes space for "reality," which he significantly describes via an appeal to the object of the book: "This book, more laborious to decipher than any other, is also the only one that has been dictated to us by reality, the only one of which the 'impression' has been printed in us by reality itself" (3: 914). As reality makes a book out of the self by "printing" with "impressions," it recalls a nonmetaphorical book, namely the volume of *François le Champi*, to suggest that "reality" includes all the physical, sensory experiences that the object of the book ("among other things") provides but that an exclusive focus on descriptive reportage discounts. The connection the narrator's metaphor draws between the inner self and the literal object of the book suggests that artistic creation, even for a literary artist, does not exclusively consist of verbal representation but also of a more capacious act of mediation. The book thus comes to function as a metaphor for our experience and also as *part of* our sensory experience of a dynamic "reality." Proust makes this practically explicit when he writes, "If I tried to understand what actually happens at the moment when a thing makes some particular impression on me . . . I realized that the words in each case were a long way removed from the impressions that I or Bloch had received. So that the essential, the only true book, though in the ordinary sense of the word it did not have to be 'invented' by a great writer—for it already exists in each one of us—has to be translated by him. The function and task of a writer are those of a translator" (3: 925–26). In light of the role the literal book *François le Champi* plays in the narrator's experience and the metaphorical book plays in his conception of "reality," his comments suggests that part of what he must "translate"—or communicate—is the sensory experience of the book itself.

The agency of the book here calls us back to the mystery inherent in artistic creation. Proust writes of the "inner book of unknown symbols" and describes the "symbols carved in relief they might have been, which my attention, as it explored my unconscious, groped for and stumbled again and followed the contours of, like a diver exploring the ocean-bed" (3: 913). These phrases depict the recognition of impenetrability that we saw earlier and, not coincidentally, could also apply to the narrator's "exploration" of Albertine's sleeping body. Significantly he is not shining a light onto these symbols but fumbling blindly in the dark; the symbols remain "unknown." The temporal experience of the book that it is part of the narrator's task to communicate is thus not one that can be understood via the illumination (or grasping) of the intellect. Rather time must be explored in the dark, indeed *as* a kind of darkness. This darkness takes center stage, in fact, in the narrator's plans for composing his novel: "By day, the most I could hope for was to try to sleep. If I worked, it would be only at night" (3: 1101). Though he provides no explanation for the necessity of inverting day and night, the other passages I have examined suggest that, by this inversion, he can complicate, if not totally avert, the work of the mind by mixing it with the intellectual unconsciousness entailed by the night—in much the same way that Proust's compositional methods combine the discursive and the material in his *paperoles*.

Darkness, in fact, is a major, if mostly overlooked, thematic of the *Recherche*, since images of the dark begin and end the novel. It opens with the image of the narrator going to bed, while many of the closing sequences take place in a wartime Paris that is cloaked in darkness to avoid German bombs. The effect of the darkened Paris extends—indeed "translates"—the mode of reading that the narrator uses for his "inner book of unknown symbols" from the internal, psychic register to the outside world and offers a final elaboration of the temporalized, sensory reading that my argument puts forth. In a passage that details people seeking shelter in underground Metro stations during a bombing, Proust writes, "And darkness, which envelops all things like a new element, has the effect, irresistibly tempting for some people, of suppressing the first halt on the road to pleasure—it permits us to enter without impediment into a region of caresses to which normally we gain access only after a certain delay" (3: 864). He explains, "In the darkness this time-honoured ritual [of courtship] is instantly abolished—hands, lips, bodies may go into action at once" (3: 864). As the Parisians in the Metro station leave off the various social conventions or "habits" that precede a romantic encounter, they jump into temporality—no "halting," just action. In so doing they become all body, much like the sleeping Albertine or even the narrator in his moments of involuntary memory when he is "struck by an impression." In the same way darkness might reveal the agency of the temporal body in reading and break, for a moment, the eternalizing habits of the intellect that the narrator wants to supplement.

This is the image that begins the novel, namely the narration of the narrator going to sleep. To quote again those lines of Marcel going to be early, "Sometimes, when I had put out my candle, my eyes would close so quickly that I had not even time to say to myself: 'I'm falling asleep.' And half an hour later the thought that it was time to go to sleep would awaken me; I would make as if to put away the book which I imagined was still in my hands" (1: 3). As sleep disables language, it exposes—if only for a moment—the way the act of reading involves a physical relationship with a material object. "At the same time," he continues a few lines later, "my sight would return and I would be astonished to find myself in a state of darkness, pleasant and restful enough for my eyes, but even more, perhaps, for my mind, to which it appeared incomprehensible, without a cause, something dark indeed" (1: 3). The explicit play with the literal and figurative valences of "darkness" suggests that the reawakening of sense perception leads not to a greater but to a *lesser* level of comprehension, a less "penetrating" stance that might open itself to the rhythmic murmurs of the word *time* in these lines. To awaken a sense of time, to awaken the senses to time is, in this case, to put the intellect to sleep. This is not a wholly privative phenomenon, however; the narrator describes how, throughout the night, he "would reawaken for short snatches only, just long enough . . . to open my eyes to stare at the shifting kaleidoscope of the darkness, to savour, in a momentary glimmer of consciousness, the sleep which lay heavy upon the furniture, the room, the whole of which I formed but an insignificant part" (1: 4). For brief moments the narrator experiences sensation stripped of a determinate content, what we might think of as sensation itself, not yet mixed with the operation of the intellect. To overstate my point: the narrator is, momentarily, a body without a mind—a dead piece of furniture or a dumb object like the book he is holding.

The opening sequences thus imagine the way reading entails moments in which, quite unexpectedly, the operation of the mind is *not yet* in play, a mindless, objectifying reading that it is the task of the narrator to "translate" for us. In response we must envision reading as a thoroughly liminal activity, one in which, as the books of the *Recherche* show us, the narrative world in our imagination is rooted in the book's material status in *our* world. This is precisely what the next four chapters attempt as I examine how the works of Joyce and Woolf stage specific aspects of the book—its pages, its print, its binding—to give us a sense of our own bodies' places in the temporal world. As these ask us, in effect, to open our eyes *to the dark*, to the way the strange squiggles printed on their pages themselves function as a "kaleidoscope of darkness," we will see how these books effectively awaken us to our own sleepy, even deathlike reading. In the end (or is it at the beginning?) we will see the physical materiality of the book, the insistence of our own body, and, most of all, the time they share, a temporality that is, finally, "incomprehensible, without a cause, something dark indeed."

CHAPTER 2

The Reader of *Ulysses*

The first time I read *Ulysses* was in an undergraduate course on the twentieth-century novel. The professor had ordered what has become known as the "Gabler edition," published by Vintage Books, and for the month that we spent reading it I carried around the large gray book with a cover design reminiscent of the primary colors and rectangular patterns of a Mondrian painting. By the time I reached Molly's final "Yes," the pages had come unglued from the paperback spine and fell out in large chunks every time I opened the book. Proclaiming the well-nigh physical effort I'd expended plodding through this initial encounter with the novel, the disintegrated book stood on my shelf as an embodied record of the weeks I'd spent on my reading. Given this material fragility, however, it was thus fortunate that, when I returned to Joyce's novel in my first year of graduate school, it was in the smaller format edition (published by Vintage International) that contains Judge Woolsey's famous legal decision, a less stately but more plump volume that stayed together even after I had broken the spine. Notably the cover design of this edition is almost completely monochrome, with the title reading vertically from the bottom (see figure 4). Superimposed over the last *S* is a pair of green spectacles that transforms the horizontal serpentine shape into a vague approximation of a mustache, above which is the drawing of a hat that transforms the type composing the novel's title into a body. The mustache, glasses, and hat recall Joyce's own bespectacled appearance as well as standard depictions of the modern-day Odysseus, Leopold Bloom. As the cover design thus takes up the parallel between the body of the

Figure 4. James Joyce, Ulysses (New York: Vintage
International, 1990), cover.

book and the physical body that I introduced in chapter 1, it gestures
at the way this chapter will be examining this parallel—and the common temporality implied in it—more deliberately.

And, of course, Joyce himself famously commented that his novel
was "more an epic of the body than of the human spirit."[1] While the
schema he provided for *Ulysses* assigns an organ of the body to each
episode (with the exception of the first three of the Telemachiad, a fact
that is not insignificant for my argument), *Ulysses* imagines extending
this bodily emphasis to that of the reader. By treating the role of the

readerly body and its relationship to the object of the book, my argument refines the previous chapter's general account of how the novel's status as an object takes on significance for its reader. The odyssey of *Ulysses* involves a progressive awareness of the readerly body as it insists on the role played by the reader's perceptual organs in the act of reading. As these organs are those sites of the body where it is in contact with—because open to—the object of the book, they point to the way *Ulysses* stages the act of reading as an implicit investigation of the body's limits. In doing so Joyce's novel allows me to develop my discussion of bookish temporality and readerly finitude in explicitly embodied terms.

The resources *Ulysses* offers to hone my argument announce the way each of the coming chapters approaches these issues less through the theoretical terms provided by Hägglund, Klein, or Merleau-Ponty than through the textual, narrative, and material dynamics of Joyce's and Woolf's novels themselves. This is by no means to suggest that I abandon the theoretical lines of inquiry that these thinkers have helped me to develop. Rather I gesture toward the places where the works of Joyce and Woolf intersect with and nuance these more theoretical arguments while placing my main focus on the way these novels add their own texture to my discussion of temporality, embodiment, and materiality. In this chapter specifically, I map the nexus of these issues in the way *Ulysses* imagines the readerly body by taking the Sirens episode as the center of my discussion. This is not least because of the way it stands out among the important middle chapters of *Ulysses* that both Michael Groden and Franco Moretti characterize as a kind of experimental, transitional space in which Joyce develops the polyphonic style of the later episodes.[2] As the first chapter of the novel to twist and bend language *itself* as part of its experimentation (rather than playing with either narrative structure, as in the interpolations of Wandering Rocks, or generic conventions, as in the headlines of Aeolus), it mediates between the more stylistically homogeneous beginning of the novel and its varied second half by meditating on the mediums they all share. More than just the novel's midpoint—Michael Stanier observes that "this chapter takes place in the very center of Bloom's day, four p.m. (eight hours after he 'ate with relish'; eight hours before 'He rests. He has travelled')"—we might instead call it the novel's "medium point," a pun that alludes to the way this "musical" episode also calls particular attention to the worldly medium of print on which the communication of its linguistic

sounds depends.[3] In doing so Sirens investigates the multiple registers
of sense perception on which the reader's access to that communication relies, the physical openness to the external world that, *Ulysses*
ultimately shows, necessarily exposes sensory experience to temporality itself.

The myth of the Sirens on which the episode is based provides an
entrée into a discussion of this kind of readerly openness if we imagine the divergent, though related, experiences of Odysseus tied to the
mast of his ship and his sailors with their wax-plugged ears: as Odysseus loses himself in the sounds of the Sirens' melodies and harmo-
nies, his crew deafly spies on the three bird-like women as they are
singing. This unpacking of the myth frames an account of the episode
that is notably more complex than the critical treatments that focus
on either its "musical" form or its rhetoric and "silence" and gestures at a reading of Sirens that actually combines Odysseus's aural
encounter with his crew's visual experiences.[4] The Sirens episode is
ultimately concerned with the *relation between* the visual and the
aural, the strange way visual signs relate to the sounds that reverberate—however fantastically—in the minds of the episode's readers.

In revealing the connection between the sensory acts of the body
and the kind of mental activity by which reading is normally (and
almost exclusively) characterized, Sirens brings together Stephen's
and Bloom's respective overemphases on the operation of the intellectual and physical in the act of reading. This allows me to pick up standard claims about their contrary natures and refine them in terms of
their readerly orientations. Recalling the lability of the Kleinian term
position that I examined in chapter 1, Sirens illustrates a vacillation
between or even an intersection of these two poles as it asks readers to
treat their reading material as both a text to be read and an object to
be perceived. It thus unveils a *reading of embodiment*, a double-edged
genitive that refers as much to the agency of the reader's physical body
as to the object of the book on which my discussion of *Finnegans
Wake* in the next chapter will focus more pointedly. The significant
role played by the sensory organs of the eyes and ears in the Sirens
myth, however, should indicate that, in this chapter, my argument
will revolve around the bodily orifices with which our perception of
the book is intimately connected, the "holes" in the body that open
us to the world outside our selves. In a way that combines the corporeal emphasis on the body in Merleau-Ponty with Klein's account of
the psyche, this approach uses explicitly physical terms to reformulate

the ego's "depressive" acceptance of its limits. As *Ulysses* grounds our reading within the limits of the material, phenomenal world, it also meditates on the points at which our body ends and the rest of the material world begins, as well as—and perhaps more important—the mortal limits that the physical body places on the intellectual experience of reading.

I

As the Sirens episode opens, it offers readers of *Ulysses* what is arguably the most jarring beginning they have yet encountered.[5] Here are the first few lines (paragraph breaks preserved):

> Bronze by Gold heard the hoofirons, steelyringing imperthnthn, thnthnthn.
> Chips, picking chips off rocky thumbnail, chips. Horrid! And gold flushed more.
> A husky fifenote blew.
> Blew. Blue Bloom is on the
> Gold pinnacled hair.[6]

Immediately the reader notices the lack of standard syntax, conventional spelling, and seemingly normal narrative. Customary accounts of the first sixty-seven lines of the episode think of them as a kind of "overture" that employs a number of phrases to allude to moments in the narrative to come. While critical debates swirl around the suitability of this term,[7] I am more interested in the way the list-like string of the chapter's words and syllables that composes this overture recalls Joyce's own compositional practices as described by Derek Attridge and Roy Gottfried. As Attridge details, Joyce composed much of *Ulysses* by transferring his notes from a "heterogeneous collection written on scraps of paper" to a notebook and then to his drafts, while Gottfried's account of how Joyce's iritis forced him to use a magnifying glass to enlarge words suggests that his well-known eye maladies had the effect of "separating [words] out of context and even making prominent the individual letters in them."[8] In a sense we might think of the beginning of Sirens as a kind of cut-and-paste collage made of the chapter's linguistic material, as if Joyce almost literally arrayed his "scraps of paper" into a patchwork that recalls the kind of material awareness we saw in Proust's manuscript notebooks.

As the idea of the collage might just as easily be described by the cinematic term *montage* as the musical term *overture*, it bridges the work of the eye and the ear that I located in the episode's Homeric parallel.[9] Examining the first, seemingly incomprehensible line indicates further that Sirens announces the sensory combination implied in the embodied perception of the material book: "Bronze by Gold heard the hoofirons, steelyringing imperthnthn, thnthnthn." Beginning with the colors bronze and gold, visual synecdoches for the barmaids at the Ormond Hotel with their red and blonde hair, the episode emphasizes its interest in the visual. Almost immediately, however, the verb "heard" points to the explicitly aural dimension of the episode, the fact that hearing will be a major—if not wholly exclusive—thematic to the chapter.

It is with the line's last words, "imperthnthn thnthnthn," that the two sensory registers of the visual and the aural come together at the same time as the words introduce a third category of sense perception, one that often (especially in the phenomenology of Merleau-Ponty) functions as the hallmark of embodiedness, namely the tactile. While Attridge considers this moment an example of "non-lexical onomatopoeia" and argues that the letters on the page "remain resolutely visual, rendering any attempt to convert them into sound arbitrary and inadequate," the combination of a tongue thrust with a dental closure required by any attempt to pronounce the combinations of *t*, *h*, and *n* aloud involves precisely this third category.[10] That is, the scrape of his tongue on the bottom of his teeth by which the reader voices what, by the next page, he will realize is a barkeep's lisping mockery of the words "impertinent insolence" highlights the usually overlooked intertwining of the visual, the aural, and the tactile in this act of reading. This moment emphasizes the complex way the Sirens episode calls out to the sensory organs of our bodies as much as it does to our minds. As my analysis recalls the confluence of sensory registers indexed by the word *impression* in my discussion of Proust's narrator's experience in the Guermantes' library, we might say that the lines that open the chapter also open our body to the act of reading itself. The play on *open* here is deliberate, since it is exactly with the *openings* of our body (eyes, ears, mouth, as well as other bodily orifices) that we approach the book.

Indeed the opening for which Sirens calls is in direct opposition to an earlier elaboration of sense perception vis-à-vis reading in the Proteus episode, encapsulated by Stephen's instruction to himself, "Shut your eyes and see" (37). Stephen's impulse to close himself off from the external world finds confirmation in his elaboration of the

obscure "ineluctable modality of the visible" that begins his monologue. Reflecting "at least that if no more, thought through my eyes,"
he indicates the extent to which he conceives of vision as primarily
an intellectual rather than a physical act. This closing off of the body
goes hand in hand with a certain kind of intellectual will to power
in Stephen, one that treats the material world as a kind of immaterial
idea and disavows any continuity with or connection to the objects
of his perception. For instance, he immediately slides into a discourse
of signification and language that seeks to grasp or possess the seascape he is observing: "Signatures of all the things I am here to read,
seaspawn and seawrack, the nearing tide, that rusty boot. Snotgreen,
bluesilver, rust: coloured signs" (37). As Stephen conceives of the visible—however "ineluctable"—as a kind of text to be cognized and
deciphered, he implies that the intellectualization of his own senses
also effects a kind of textualization of the world (as would only be
appropriate for an episode whose "art," according to Joyce's schema,
is "philology").[11]

Stephen affirms this textualization a few pages later when he looks
at the sand piled up on both a dog's carcass and the gunwale of a
boat and thinks, "These heavy sands are language tide and wind have
silted here" (44). Walking with his eyes closed and listening to "his
boots crush crackling wrack and shells," he sings a snatch of song
to himself and thinks, "Rhythm begins, you see. I hear. A catalectic
tetrameter of iambs marching" (37). Here Stephen relates the verse he
sings to the sounds his boots make and parses the latter in terms of
poetic meter, as if the sounds of the world are nothing more than a
text to be analyzed in the abstracted language of literary criticism. It is
thus telling that he follows the observation "Sounds solid," by which
he responds to the sound of his ashplant tapping the beach, with the
thought that the earth was "made by the mallet of *Los Demiurgos*," a
reference to one of the mythical figures created by William Blake. As
he imagines the world being created by the mind of the creator (Los)
organizing itself,[12] he recalls the idealizing tactics of Klein's paranoid
position and suggests that his linguistic abstractions cast the world as
a purely mental phenomenon without the limitations of the physical
or the temporal. Stephen goes on to make this decidedly transcendental orientation explicit, in the following sentence, when he asks himself, "Am I walking into eternity along Sandymount strand?" (37).

These appeals to language become even more significant in light of
the abstracted, transcendental relationship he has to his own written

compositions. Taking up his pen to compose a poem on a slip of paper torn from Deasy's letter, he asks himself, "Who ever anywhere will read these written words? Signs on a white field. . . . The good bishop of Cloyne took the veil of the temple out of his shovel hat: veil of space with coloured emblems hatched on its field. Hold hard. Coloured yes on a flat: yes, that's right. Flat I see, then think distance, near, far, flat I see, east back" (48). While the "signs on a white field" function in apposition with the "written words" of the poem, the phrase also recalls the "signature of all the things I am here to read" by which he closed himself off from the phenomenal world at the episode's beginning. The phrase not only confirms the interchangeable relationship that signs and objects have for Stephen, but it also characterizes writing itself as something without material substance. Moreover the appeal to Berkeley ("the good bishop of Cloyne"), whose theory of vision quite significantly places visual agency in the mind rather than in the eye,[13] effectively forestalls any kind of awareness that Stephen might have of his physical relationship with his composition. For Stephen, then, the actions of reading a text and perceiving the world are not only synonymous but also imply a kind of abstracted, disembodied position that refuses any spatiotemporal relation between the perceiving-reading subject and the perceived-read object.

This focus on a disembodied mind finds its intellectual seeds in the aesthetic theory Stephen proposes in *A Portrait of the Artist as a Young Man*, in which he draws on the thought of Thomas Aquinas and claims that "beauty expressed by the artist cannot awaken in us an emotion which is kinetic or a sensation which is purely physical" but rather must raise the mind above the body.[14] At the same time, the disavowal of his physical limits possibly finds an affective motivation in the recent death of his mother (the figure, incidentally, at the center of both Proust's narrator's experience of the book and Kleinian psychoanalysis). Earlier in *Ulysses* Stephen has recalled a dream of her corpse: "her wasted body within its loose graveclothes giving off an odour of wax and rosewood, her breath bent over him with mute secret words, a faint odour of wetted ashes" (10). The focus on her physical remains and the scents that accost him imply the close alliance, in his mind, of death and embodiment. He even calls out in defiance, "No, mother. Let me be and let me live" (a specific reprise, perhaps, of *Portrait*'s more general "*Non serviam*"), as if to suggest his own refusal to acknowledge the mortal traits he shares with her (10).[15] In this sense Stephen acts in much the same way as the

Proustian narrator in his paranoid moments, but without the alternation with a depressive relationship with the maternal body (or the material book) that allows the narrator to countenance and momentarily tolerate his own mortality.

The content of Stephen's poem expands on the denial of mortality that seems to be at play in such an exclusively intellectual conception of both perception and language: "He comes, pale vampire, through storm his eyes, his bat sails bloodying the sea, mouth to her mouth's kiss" (48). As the mouth of the vampire and that of the woman come together (Stephen muses "Glue 'em well" in the following line), the kiss, usually a sign of affection and often a synecdoche for (procreative) sexual relations, transforms into a signal of death and decay, as if to suggest that the body is itself never anything more than the animated corpse so clearly instanced by the figure of the vampire. This focus on a sordid, disgusting mortality surfaces again toward the end of the episode, when Stephen imagines not only the discovery of the drowned man he has heard about but also the way his own body forces him into constant close contact with death. In words that recall the sensory experience of his dead mother, he thinks, "Bag of corpsegas sopping in foul brine. . . . Dead breaths I living breathe, tread dead dust, devour a urinous offal from all dead" (50). It thus seems particularly appropriate that, as Stephen composes the poem and deliberates over his choice of words, he seems to fantasize a paradoxically bodiless body: "His lips lipped and mouthed fleshless lips of air. . . . His mouth molded issuing breath, unspeeched: ooeeehah: roar of cataractic planets, globed, blazing, roaring wayawayaway-awayawayaway" (48). The focus on "fleshless lips" and the molding of "breath, unspeeched" intimate a certain fetishization of air as something both imperceptible and immaterial, while the mention of "planets," along with the repetitive emphasis of the word "away," suggest his desire to exist in some kind of nonearthly, otherworldly environment.

As a result of these fantasies of disembodiment and transcendence—in fact precisely because he cannot actually escape from either the world or his body—Stephen develops a relationship with the material world based on antagonism and hostility (not unlike the way Klein describes the infant's "bad objects"). In an example of Hugh Kenner's "Uncle Charles principle,"[16] in which the narrative voice takes on features of the character whose experiences it is narrating, the episode offers another example of this antagonism: "Unwholesome sandflats

waited to suck his treading soles, breathing upward sewage breath.
He coasted them, walking warily" (41). While, as Don Gifford points
out, the "upward sewage breath" refers to the fact that Dublin's sew-
ers emptied into the River Liffey and Dublin Bay where Stephen is
walking (51), the "breathing" suggests the way the shore shares characteristics with Stephen's image of the drowned man's corpse: both, in
a sense, take on a life of their own that menaces Stephen's own existence. As his anxiety transforms the landscape of the earth itself into
a voracious mouth that threatens—almost vampirically—to "suck"
him in, it turns the inescapable act of touching it into an ever-present
hazard. A few pages later, as he reaches "the edge of the sea," his
feet begin "to sink slowly in the quaking soil," since, at this point in
the day, the tide is rising (44). Stephen comments on his own body to
articulate this threat. The narrative states that "he watched through
peacocktwittering lashes the southing sun" and suggests the extent to
which the sight of his eyelashes is an unavoidable part of his vision, an
inescapability that he expresses in terms of restriction and imprisonment when he thinks "I am caught in this burning scene" (49).

Ultimately Stephen's antagonistic conception of his embodied place
in the world comes to color the way he views humanity in general.
At the sight of two cocklepickers, one of whom "swung lourdily her
midwife's bag" (37), Stephen meditates on human birth: "One of her
sisterhood lugged me squealing into life" (37), and on the next page,
"Wombed in sin darkness I was too, made not begotten. By them,
the man with my voice and my eyes and a ghostwoman with ashes
on her breath. They clasped and sundered, did the coupler's will"
(38). His diction here suggests his disdain for being born of bone-
and-flesh parents and his disappointment at being "made" by such a
common and unexceptional act as "the coupler's will" rather than the
more autonomous "begotten." Significantly his model for the latter is
Adam and his "spouse and helpmate," Eve, who "had no navel. Gaze.
Belly without blemish, bulging big, a buckler of taut vellum" (38). As
the lack of a navel indicates that Eve was not born of woman, it also
hints at Stephen's own fantasy of having no need for connections outside himself. Moreover the description of her stomach as a "buckler of
taut vellum" suggests the way that, in Stephen's mind, paper and writing surfaces ("vellum") act as a kind of shield ("buckler") against any
kind of external dependency or embodied connection. His gaze here,
far from describing an act of vision that would take place in the world
outside himself, actually refers to navel gazing, which the episode first

mentions a few lines earlier with an allusion to the telephone, another
means of connection: "Will you be as gods? Gaze in your omphalos. Hello. Kinch here. Put me on to Edenville. Aleph, alpha: nought,
nought, one" (38). While the tongue-in-cheek parody of telephoning
Eden may make the reader chuckle, it should not mask that Stephen
is attempting to establish his own radical self-sufficiency by turning
a means of reaching out to someone else into a technique for walling
himself in and separating himself from the material world as such.
Imagining the descent into his navel by appealing to the very building
blocks of text in the letters and number of the telephone exchange A A
001, Stephen finally extends the textualization of the world resulting
from the intellectualization of his sense perceptions to the object of
his own body as well and places it into the timeless, eternal world of
the abstracting idealizations I have been tracing. Stephen thus resists,
in more ways than one, being "in touch" with the world.

II

In light of Stephen's extreme rejection of both his body and the material world, it is curious that the Proteus episode is set on the beach.
As the location in which the land meets the water, the beach is precisely where the solidity of the ground, which we normally can ignore
and take for granted, begins to dissolve into the fluidity of the water.
In its in-between state we are brought into a much greater awareness of the function of the ground; we *feel* it differently (as Stephen
is so quick to disavow), the way it supports us and touches us, how it
shapes itself or resists being shaped.[17] In a subtle moment of intratex-
tuality, the Sirens episode recalls Stephen's stroll on the beach when
it refers to Bellini's 1831 opera *La sonnambula* (The Sleepwalker),
since Stephen's sensory experiments leave him, for the beginning of
Proteus, walking in his own kind of unconscious slumber. On hearing Richie Goulding begin to sing the aria "All Is Lost Now" from
that opera, Bloom thinks, "Yes, I remember. Lovely air. In sleep she
went to him. Innocence in the moon. Still hold her back. Brave, don't
know their danger. Call name. Touch water" (273). As Bloom muses
on the content of the aria and the traditional ways to safely wake
sleepwalkers (by calling their name or having them touch water), he
effectively describes how Stephen's contact with water in the narrative
of Proteus works to wake him up or, in other words, to forestall the
elision of the body and the material world. In a somewhat analogous

way, as *Ulysses* progresses it begins to mix what we might think of as the solidities of a grammatical language and a standard narrative with experimental fluidity—which reaches an extreme in Sirens—and wakes the reader from the kind of somnambulistic reading that would ignore its dependence on the body's sensory organs. That is, as language bends and twists itself in the Sirens episode in ways that reveal the sense modalities by which the reader always approaches writing—most obviously vision and (imagined) hearing—the reader becomes aware of the way in which his body is a necessarily open vessel or echo chamber for the language of the text.

Accordingly Sirens includes two characters—Pat the deaf waiter and the blind stripling who tunes the piano—whose sensory impairments present a kind of "sleepwalking" that, unlike Stephen's, actually underscores the relationship between language and the body. The description of the sounds made by the blind tuner's tuning fork illustrates this rather palpably: "From the saloon a call came, long in dying. That was a tuningfork the tuner had that he forgot that he now struck. A call again. That he now pointed that it now throbbed. You hear? It throbbed, pure, purer, softly and softlier, its buzzing prongs" (264). The repetition of "that" throughout the passage imparts a rhythm that recalls a physical pulse, as if the syntax of the sentences begins to "throb" like a tuning fork. The choice of the word "throbbed" in fact suggests the way sound is produced by mimicking the functioning of the heart (another bodily organ that "opens" and "closes," if only figuratively). Later, when Bloom sees Pat the deaf waiter, his comment to himself extends this relationship between sound and the body to language explicitly: he thinks, "He seehears lipspeech" (283). The verbal combinations in this statement describe the inextricability of the sensory registers ("seehears") that Stephen tries to comprehend separately and, more specifically, the way speech itself is not merely an aural phenomenon but arises from and is closely connected to our physical lips, which we can both feel and see. Pat the deaf waiter thus recalls Ulysses's sailors with their wax-plugged ears, and, even more interesting, he stands as a figure for the reader, who shares with him a kind of deafness for which his other senses—in this case vision—must compensate.

Before we submerge ourselves completely into the stream of Sirens, however, an examination of the way Bloom opens himself to the physical world, including the materiality of written words, offers resources to further flesh out (the idiom is, of course, quite appropriate) the way the sense perceptions emphasized by Sirens relate to the act of reading more specifically. As the reference to the flesh should suggest, Bloom offers us the opportunity to consider the way *Ulysses* introduces the more Merleau-Pontean terms of embodiment. At the same time, while he provides a well-known counterpoint to Stephen—which it will be the work of Sirens to harmonize—he also seems at moments to over-emphasize the body at the expense of the mind. The beginning of the Calypso chapter is a particularly clear example of how Bloom's atti-tude toward the world differs from Stephen's: "Mr. Leopold Bloom ate with relish the inner organs of beasts and fowls. He liked thick giblet soup, nutty gizzards, a stuffed roast heart, liver slices fried with crustcrumbs, fried hencod's roes. Most of all he liked grilled mut-ton kidneys which gave to his palate a fine tang of faintly scented urine" (55). The immediate association of Bloom and "inner organs" obviously points to his embrace of an embodied physicality, which Stephen, with his "lack" of organs, ignores. What is more, the fact that the "inner organs" he so relishes are also parts of the body that metabolize and filter toxins suggests that Bloom's interest in and rela-tion to the body extends beyond any kind of idealized notion of purity or perfection; they indicate a wholesale embrace of the cycles and processes by which life constantly renews and sustains itself in a way that hints at Bloom's openness to the movement of time. Though this temporality remains mostly in the background of the novel's first half, eventually *Ulysses* picks up and develops this idea by aligning the various physical openings that Bloom exhibits with the very mortality that Stephen is so quick to deny.

Not only is the reader's first picture of Bloom one in which, signifi-cantly, he is opening his mouth rather than shutting himself off, but the interjection "O" that is his first word in the novel also reinforces that image, as the book's type offers the reader an icon that depicts the shape his mouth must make to speak aloud (as well as to "eat with relish"). The visual echo of the typography here gestures at the way Joyce's novel stages reading itself in sensory terms that has every-thing to do with the temporal progress from which neither reader nor book is exempt. At the same time, the difficulty in pronouncing the virtually unsayable "Mkgnao!" of the cat that immediately precedes Bloom's "O" primes the reader to voice the words on the page, a situ-ation that allows us to imagine the reader's mouth taking the same shape as Bloom's so that an opening of *his* body subtly mirrors the signifier on the page. Additionally the cat's "Mkgnao!" and Bloom's phatic "O" function as moments of textual opacity that resist the kind of straightforward comprehension usually at play in reading and draw attention to the material page on which they are printed. Taking both into account, we see that the specular relationship between the reader and the book depends, in a way that recalls the Proustian narrator's interaction with Albertine, on the kind of *mutual* embodiedness that Merleau-Ponty emphasizes so insistently.[18] The experience of reading this episode's opening thus incites an awareness both of reading as an embodied act and of the book as a substantial object that takes its place in the world in a way that Stephen's intellectualizing textualization is unable to consider.

In fact Bloom's first scene of reading continues this physical emphasis and displays a similar awareness of the embodiedness of reading, which the narration of Bloom reading an advertisement for a farm in Israel while he is waiting in Dlugacz's butcher shop effectively transmits to the reader:

> He took up a page from the pile of cut sheets. *The model farm at Kinnereth on the lakeshore of Tiberias. Can become ideal winter sanatorium.* Moses Montefiore. I thought he was. Farmhouse, wall round it, blurred cattle cropping. **He held the page from him: interesting: read it nearer, the blurred cropping cattle, the page rustling.** A young white heifer. Those mornings in the cattlemarket the beasts lowing in their pens, branded sheep, flop and fall of dung, the breeders in hobnailed boots trudging through the litter, slapping a palm on a ripemeated hindquarter, there's a prime one, unpeeled switches in their hands. **He held the page aslant patiently, bending his senses and his will, his soft subject gaze at rest.** (59, italics and bold added)

The passage is an illuminating mix of intellection, sense perception, and fancy that portrays the inextricability of the three in the act of reading. While the fantasies of the cattle market that the advertisement incites in Bloom recall the kind of physical awareness suggested by the opening lines of the chapter, the narrative interweaves snippets of the text Bloom is reading (in italics) to effectively put the reader at a double remove from the text, a move that forces us to read—literally—through Bloom's eyes. While the specifications of the distance and angle at which Bloom holds the page (in bold) describe his attempts to find the position in which his eyesight can bring the advertisement into focus, the narrative also asks the reader to take on the kind of momentarily blurred vision that confronts Bloom by imaginatively "bending his senses." As Gottfried puts it in the extended analogy comparing the vision difficulties produced by Joyce's iritis and the confusion experienced by the reader, at moments like this "the reader literally confronts the book, face to face, holding it in hand, as a book has its own first order reality as a material object" (52).

When Calypso expands on this bodily relationship with textual objects in the scenes aligning reading with the physical processes that most obviously involve bodily openings other than the eyes and the ears—namely eating and excretion—it returns to Bloom's interest in the body's cycles and allows me to go beyond the overemphasis Gottfried's argument places on the cognitive aspects of reading. Having saved the kidney from burning, Bloom sits down to breakfast with a letter from his daughter, Milly: "He shore away the burnt flesh and flung it to the cat. Then he put a forkful into his mouth, chewing with discernment the toothsome pliant meat. . . . He creased out the letter at his side, reading it slowly as he chewed, sopping another die of bread in the gravy and raising it to his mouth" (65). The rhyming between the actions of cutting away the burned part of the kidney and smoothing out the creases of the letter, which prepare for eating and reading, respectively, draws a connection between the two and casts reading in terms of a kind of bodily consumption. (This rhyming occurs again a page later, when Bloom "ate piece after piece of kidney" and "read the letter again: twice" [66].) Interestingly the novel immediately follows this alliance of reading and eating with a transcription of Milly's letter. In her wide-ranging treatment of letters in *Ulysses*, Shari Benstock points out that Milly's letter—as well as the letter from Martha with which Bloom has such an erotic relationship—displays "a greater degree of textual 'facticity'" than other letters in the novel (like Deasy's letter to the newspaper, for instance) "simply because [both Milly's and Martha's letters] appear as separate texts, set aside from the narration."[19] Though Benstock's argument about facticity is in the service of an analysis of the "verisimilitude" and "reliability" of the novel's narrative voices, the close proximity between the heightened facticity of Milly's letter and the connection the narrative draws between Bloom's readerly and physical consumption draws attention to the dependence of this facticity on the sensorium of the reader, the fact that the reader's senses must—like Bloom's mouth—be open to the embodiment of the text in an object.

Bloom ends this episode with a radical example of this kind of openness. Indeed whereas he begins the Calypso chapter with an open mouth, he ends it, appropriately, with an open anus: as the narrative points out, Bloom "liked to read at stool" (67). It goes on to give the details of Bloom's doings in the outhouse: "Quietly he read, restraining himself, the first column and, yielding but resisting, began the second. Midway, his last resistance yielding, he allowed his bowels to ease themselves quietly as he read, reading still patiently, that slight constipation of yesterday quite gone" (69). The syntactical construction of the sentences explicitly interweaves the actions of reading and moving one's bowels. The "restraining" and "yielding" in the first sentence initially seem to refer to reading itself before the second sentence clarifies the object of those actions, as if the controlled and steady pace at which Bloom encounters the words of the newspaper is commensurate with the rhythms of his bowel movement. Additionally the way the participial phrases break into the description also causes the reader to share in the kind of rhythmic peristalsis by which Bloom defecates, a rhythm of contraction and relaxation that will become, according to Joyce's schema, the "technique" of the entire Lestrygonians episode. When the narrative goes on to observe, with typical referential ambiguity, "It did not move or touch him but it was something quick and neat" (69), it sets up a telling contrast between the product of his colonic efforts and his reading material. That is, the fact that Bloom "tore away half the prize story sharply and wiped himself with it" (70) indicates the extent to which the page he is reading *does* touch him (quite intimately) and, once he is finished with it, is anything but "quick and neat." The resonance between the images that open and close an episode whose content is so full of reading demarcates the limits of the body itself and emphasizes the way bodily openings function as the quite literal interface between the reader and the book.

III

As the chapters detailing the beginning of Bloom's day progress, they offer further examples of the attention he pays to the material aspects of the texts with which he is confronted. In doing so they indicate that what we might think of as Bloom's overly physical relationship to texts often forestalls the intellection necessary to comprehend them. (For all its physical "openness," his use of the newspaper as toilet paper certainly does not help him decipher the "prize story.") Similarly when Bloom transforms his newspaper into a kind of ersatz walking stick in the Lotos-Eaters episode, he indicates that his awareness of the materiality of texts can keep him from reading them: "As he walked he took the folded *Freeman* from his sidepocket, unfolded it, rolled it lengthwise in a baton and tapped it at each sauntering step against his trouser leg" (72). Here, as Bloom recognizes and leverages the materiality of paper—its fine but by no means nonexistent thickness—to create a "baton," a musical term that brings with it echoes of the "tapping" of both Stephen's ashplant and the walking stick of the blind stripling, he effectively disables himself from reading the paper. At the same time, the subtle similarity between Bloom's actions and his masochistic fantasies of being beaten that surface throughout the day (most explicitly in the Circe episode) suggest the erotic valence that a physical relationship with a written text entails. Additionally we see the transfer of the amorous nature of Bloom's epistolary exchange with Martha to the physical object of the letter itself in the colorfully descriptive language that details the masturbatory actions of opening the envelope: "He strolled out of the postoffice and turned to the right. . . . His hand went into his pocket and a forefinger felt its way under the flap of the envelope, ripping it open in jerks" (73).[20]

I defer further discussion of the erotics of an embodied reading to the end of this chapter and make a final foray into the Sirens episode to show that this central episode stages a rapprochement between Stephen's overly intellectualized, disembodied approach to reading and the world at large with Bloom's insistently embodied orientation. This chapter at the center of the novel, what I have cited as its navel, ultimately explores the profound connection between the two that my discussion thus far has treated as separate or opposed. At the same time as it posits reading as an action of *both* mind *and* body, Sirens ultimately draws out the temporality that has so far remained in the background of my argument. As I have suggested, this central episode is particularly suited for this task. In his claims for a transition from the stream-of-consciousness technique in the early chapters to "polyphonic devices of various kinds" that dominate the style of each of the later chapters (183), Franco Moretti notes that much of Bloom's stream of consciousness consists of "undigested" fragments of other people's speech (and, given Stephen's penchant for intellectual citation, the same would be true for him). He proposes that the novel itself acts similarly: "*it is precisely from this undigested language that the polyphony of* Ulysses *develops*," and, indeed, we have already seen examples of the way Sirens employs details and motifs from earlier in the novel (188). As he points out, however, the novel picks up and reworks this "undigested" language "without any longer passing

through Bloom's mind" (188). As Moretti opens up the potential
for the novel itself to partake in a kind of authorial (or narrational)
agency, his metaphor of digestion imparts a kind of body *to the novel*
and suggests the way it exercises this agency by opening itself up to a
process of alteration and transformation.

Sirens offers an allegory of this agency in the scene where the bar-
maid Lydia Douce holds a seashell up to George Lidwell's and Mina
Kennedy's ears. The episode thus picks up and, in Moretti's terms,
"digests" Stephen's promenade on the beach at the same time as it
also gives an almost explicit example of the way the production of
bodily sensation and intellectual meaning depends on the contact
between the body and an external object: "To the end of the bar to
him she bore lightly the spiked and winding seahorn that he, George
Lidwell, solicitor, might hear" (281). The female figure holding a seashell recalls the cocklepickers in "Proteus," as if Lydia Douce is a kind
of "metempsychosis" of the woman collecting shells that morning on
Sandymount strand, and George Lidwell responds with an answer
reminiscent of Stephen's "discursive" treatment of sense perception
when he asks a few lines later, "What are the wild waves saying?"
Moreover the repeated instance of "Tap" in this moment signifies
the sound of the blind stripling's walking cane and recalls Stephen's
experiment in blindness along with his observation "My ash sword
hangs at my side. Tap with it: they do" (37).

Yet these parallels serve only to emphasize the important differences between this moment and the earlier one in Proteus. In fact the
episode's description of the act of listening to the shell indicates the
influence of the kind of embodiedness at work in my treatment of
Bloom: "Ah, now he heard, she holding it to his ear. Hear! He heard.
Wonderful. She held it to her own ear and through the sifted light pale
gold in contrast glided. To hear" (281). Most obviously the rhyme
between "hear" and "ear" binds auditory sense perception to the
physical organ on which it depends, while the homophony between
the verb "hear" and the deictic "here" suggests that the act of listening entails an awareness of the surrounding environment.[21] Indeed
the imperative form of "hear" turns that suggestion into a kind of
demand, as if the musical nature of Sirens compels a consciousness of
the spatiotemporal situation in which the sensory experience is taking
place. Relatedly the combination of this homophony with the structure of the infinitive in "to hear" also recalls a prepositional phrase
that would describe the movement of Mina Kennedy ("pale gold") to a

specific position. Thus, far from taking listeners away from the world or out of their body, listening in Sirens is as earthbound as reading in Calypso. Part of this situation is the physical openness Lydia and Lidwell share with the shell, the fact that they allow it to come into contact with their ears (which, Joyce was later to observe, can never be "closed").[22] We might push this point and draw a parallel between the shell in Sirens and the book itself since they both function, to a certain extent, by coming into a relationship with our bodies.

In combining Stephen's and Bloom's orientations toward sense perception in this scene, Sirens points to the way that reading is neither purely mental nor purely physical but involves both registers. My reading of this moment necessarily separates this coincidence, as I take the raw sound of a word like *hear* and subject it to an act of interpretation that points back to the sensory experience on which it is predicated. (As such it is only the most recent example of my more general critical strategies.) Bloom articulates this combination explicitly when he emphasizes the connection between the workings of the body and the sound effects of the shell. He thinks to himself, "The sea they think they hear. Singing. A roar. The blood is it. Souse in the ear sometimes. Well, it's a sea. Corpuscle islands" (281). The use of the verb "think" in the phrase "the sea they think they hear" indicates, on the one hand, that Lydia and Lidwell "believe" or "suppose" that they hear the sea, while, on the other, it suggests that this belief stems from a cognitive act of deliberation, that, not unlike Stephen in Proteus, their auditory sense perception has been the subject of an act of interpretation. At the same time, however, as Bloom's customary role as amateur scientist leads him to observe (mistakenly, as it turns out) that the sounds Lydia and Lidwell are interpreting as the sea are actually caused by the echo of the pumping of their own blood, he also indicates that sense perception is itself an embodied activity. Even more significant, the emphasis on this kind of embodied sense perception suggests that the intellectual act of interpretation is *itself* also embodied. The cognitive actions that lead us to an understanding of meaning and that Stephen's example makes so explicit depend on the kind of sensory perception on which Bloom's earlier example places such emphasis and themselves take place within and coincide with the functioning of a physical body.

As if to underscore this idea, the narrative points out that Bloom's pseudoscientific insight into the shell's production of sounds depends, much as the imagined sounds that result from reading do, on an act of visual perception: "Bloom through the bar door saw a shell held at their ears. He heard more faintly that that they heard, each for herself alone, then each for other, hearing the plash of waves, loudly, a silent roar" (281). As Bloom's vision of the shell at their ears allows him to posit the embodiedness of hearing at the same time as it incites him to imagine the sounds reaching Lydia and Lidwell, it casts our Odysseus in the position that the sailors, with their wax-plugged ears, inhabit in the Sirens myth. It also draws the connection between physical perception and mental acts that I am developing in my treatment of the body and reading in *Ulysses* as a whole and in Sirens in particular. The contradiction within the oxymoron "silent roar" is a particularly apt description of reading this musically influenced chapter, since the letters that comprise the chapter are not so much instruments—they make no sounds themselves—as they are representatives of sounds for us to activate and hear in our minds. As we have seen, however, the musical emphasis of the chapter makes especially lurid solicitations to our inner ear via our eye's perception of the silent letters on the page. We might say that the sounds of the chapter are especially "loud" (hence the "roar"), an imagined sonic amplitude that finds its visual analogue in what Attridge describes as "sequences of letters which go beyond the normal configurations of written English" (*Peculiar* 142). Yet the tie between the imagined sounds and their visual basis should not only indicate the extent to which this "silent," mental reading is itself an embodied act that, like hearing and sight, takes place within the perceptual world. It also suggests the way reading functions as *a link between* the body and the mind.

Reading also puts the body and mind into a relationship with an external object, a relationship that calls for the body to be open—or to open itself—to the world outside itself. The moment in the episode when Bloom composes a response to Martha's letter offers an explicit example of this bodily openness to a material text. As this moment in the narrative reformulates and literalizes the metaphorical significance of the shell, it also shows how the bodily interaction with a text *also* (indeed necessarily) relates to the acts of intellection by which we normally conceive of reading and which were the hallmark of Stephen's orientation to sense perception: "He held unfurled his *Freeman*. Can't see now. Remember write Greek ees. Bloom dipped, Bloo mur: dear sir. Dear Henry wrote: dear Mady. Got your lett and flow. Hell did I put? Some pock or oth. It is utterl imposs. Underline *imposs*. To write today" (279). In his anxiety over being seen composing his letter to Martha, Bloom swings here between sense perception and intellection when he treats language as both a transparent medium of communication and as an opaque object. In an action that recalls the moment in the Lotos-Eaters episode when he "opened the letter [he received from Martha] within the newspaper" (77), Bloom hides his note by placing it under the *Freeman* newspaper. By concealing the writing of his note under more writing (creating a literal "subtext"), Bloom illustrates the dual capacity of writing's materiality to communicate and conceal. Writing, that is, not only creates a communicative text that can be deciphered (a process itself by no means fully transparent), but it also yields an opaque object to be sensed. My analysis should not suggest, however, that there is ever a pure moment of either sensation or intellection. Rather the close proximity of the letter and the newspaper dramatizes the fact that the two are always intertwined. This intertwining extends beyond writing, however, when he speaks the words "dear sir" to cover the "dear Mady" he is writing and suggests that spoken language also participates in the double role of transparency and opacity.

The complex narrative structure of this moment contributes to the embodiment of the intellectual act of reading by weaving together three separate discourses. The descriptions of Bloom's actions alternate with his own inner monologue and his voiced recitation of the language composing his letter. Benstock suggests that the result of this narrative weaving is to produce the letter as "a text which cannot be easily teased out of its narrative environment" (419). Bloom's letter thus becomes as much a linguistic text to be read or deciphered as it is *also* an object in the world of the novel that, as with any other object, it is the job of the narrative voice to present and describe. The letter cannot be "teased out" of the world of the novel precisely because it is an integral part of the scene the narrative is describing. Indeed the truncated words that the narrative uses to report the language of the letter underscore this doubleness. At the same time as they function to transmit an intellectual meaning we process cognitively, the words also effectively function as part of the narrative depiction of Bloom writing by dramatizing the speed with which he moves from one thought to the next. In so doing the language of the novel itself, like that of both the *Freeman* and Bloom's letter, draws attention to itself as part of an (opaque) material object by way of its very function as a transparent communication medium.

When Bloom reminds himself to "write Greek ees" and signals that his eyes are open to the appearance of his letters on the page, he

also indicates that this visual appearance has a communicative meaning; Gifford notes that "handwriting with Greek e's (ε) was thought
to indicate artistic temperament" (304). As Bloom's letters thus take
on a kind of body that both transmits and departs from the meaning
they signify, they call out to *both* the eye and the mind. Accordingly
the phonetic spelling of the letter *E* in the text incites a visual awareness in the reader similar to Bloom's, but, rather than being based, as
elsewhere in the text, on a phonetically unpronounceable or intellectually incomprehensible set of letters, the emphasis on the visual here
takes place via phonetics itself. In other words, the reader becomes
aware of his readerly eye by way of the cognitive act of processing
the meaning of the letters he sees and brings together the orientations
toward reading and sense perception that Stephen and Bloom typify
earlier in the novel.

Maud Ellmann comments on the "Greek e" by drawing on Plutar-
ch's report that "the letter *E* was carved into the navel of the world,
the stone of the Delphic oracle." She characterizes Bloom's writing
here as opening up a similar kind of cavity: "When he countersigns
his pseudo-signature with two 'Greek ees,' Bloom commemorates this
ancient graffito, and hollows out an omphalos within his name."[23]
And it is with this "literal" hole—a pun *Finnegans Wake* exploits
more fully—that my argument returns to the physical limits Stephen
so stridently denies. For the closing lines of the Sirens episode weave
together the narration of Bloom's fart with his inner monologue
and his reading of Robert Emmet's epitaph to reassert the connection between reading and bodily openings in a way that involves an
explicit consideration of death and finitude:

> Seabloom, greasabloom viewed last words. Softly. *When my country*
> *takes her place among.*
>   Prrprr.
>   Must be the bur.
>   Fff. Oo. Rrpr.
>   *Nations of the earth.* No-one behind. She's passed. *Then and*
> *not till then.* Tram. Kran, kran, kran. Good oppor. Coming.
> Krandlkrankran. I'm sure it's the burgundy. Yes. One, two. *Let my*
> *epitaph be.* Karaaaaaaa. *Written. I have.*
>   Pprrpffrrppffff.
>   *Done.* (291)

In the same way that the unpronounceableness of the episode's opening lines emphasizes the visual nature of the aural signifiers, so too
does this closing narration of Bloom's flatulence open the reader's eyes

to the work of the visual in reading. Not only this, but the episode also ends with the reader's own "lipspeech," as an attempt to pronounce the series of plosive *p*'s and fricative *f*'s draw attention to the agency of his lips. In this case, however, he alternates between incomprehensible sequences of letters and more easily cognizable words. In so doing he vacillates between an awareness of his bodily organs in the sensory aspects of his reading and the more general awareness of his own internal readerly ego, between sensation and intellection.

Ellmann writes, "As writing, [Bloom's] fart cajoles the eye: as voice, it saturates the ear. But there is a third organ which can detect the fart when it is neither audible nor visible." She goes on to finish her point with the appropriately Joycean pun, "What the ear hears, and the eye sees, give way to what the nose knows" (68, 69). She appeals to what I might use my own pun to call the "knowledge of scents." As a phrase that names exactly the interpenetration of the sensual and the intellectual that the episode is demonstrating, it describes the awareness of and familiarity with the modalities of sense perception on which reading depends, a knowledge that *Ulysses* does not let its reader forget. Rather, as we have seen, the reader must maintain a global awareness that takes in the novel as a whole—as both a book to be perceived and as a text to be read. Yet far from leading to the domination and intellectual will to power we saw in Stephen, this global relationship with the novel speaks to the other meaning of the phrase *knowledge of sense*: the idea that there is a knowledge *contained in* sense perception. The emphasis on ending in the narration of Robert Emmet's last words at the very close of the episode allies this sensory knowledge with mortality and death. More specifically the last word of the episode, itself the very last of Emmet's last words—"Done"— suggests that to be aware of having a physical body is to be aware of one's own finitude, the way the body ages and moves, inexorably, toward being *done*. We should also note that the songs that make up the music of this chapter—"All Is Lost Now" and "The Croppy Boy" in particular—themselves focus on loss and death.

Yet "Done" is not just the last word of the episode but also the last word of the overture that opens it. Immediately following, however, is the imperative "Begin!," which many critics read as a conductor's direction to start the musical "performance" of the chapter. For me, this "Done. Begin!" dyad presages in its meaning the cyclic circularity that *Finnegans Wake* later takes (and complicates) as its structuring principle. The rhythmic punctuality of its form also mimics the movement of the rest of *Ulysses*. Moretti explains that the "last seven" chapters (that is, those following Sirens) are "dominated by polyphony" rather than by stream of consciousness and observes that "when polyphony *within* individual chapters diminishes, heterogeneity *between* one chapter and another, by contrast, intensifies" (183). As the stylistic pluralism that crescendos after Sirens works to underscore the ending and the subsequent new beginnings of each episode, what Moretti calls the "second *Ulysses*" makes its progress in fits and starts. Unlike the circular macrostructure of the *Wake*, each of the later episodes in *Ulysses* becomes a closed system that separates itself from what precedes and follows it. We might say that the text of *Ulysses* itself falls into pieces as it progresses.

Such a tendency toward disintegration is, recall, the condition of the infantile ego that sparks the object relations Klein describes through the paranoid and depressive positions. It should thus come as no surprise that, at the moment *Ulysses* begins to ask readers to tolerate its own formal disintegration, it offers an example of a Kleinian "depressive" relationship, one that is occurring between Bloom and his own body. For Bloom's fart is a moment that, in a sense, "decomposes" his body as he opens the other of his bodily orifices for the second time in the novel. Momentarily relaxing his sphincter to open his rectum, Bloom effectively offers an extreme version of the opening of the reader's sensory organs that an encounter with this novel demands. Indeed the instance of the fart indicates an even more radical openness than the earlier scene in the outhouse. While solid waste effectively fills the opening of the anus on which the act of defecation depends, the relaxation of the sphincter for the passing of gas creates a hole in the body, if only for an instant. As it discloses—or better, uncloses—an actual space within Bloom's body, the fart suggests the way that sensory experiences are themselves predicated on the "disintegrated" nature of the body. That is, the body itself is not wholly solid or self-sufficient but encases a hollow openness that is the condition of its interaction with the surrounding environment. Based, as it is, on the bodily openings to which the novel has drawn attention (eyes, mouth, ears, nose, anus), sensation is, it seems, a phenomenon that is always concerned with the limits (physical and temporal) of our bodies.

This point may, in the end, address the question Molly Bloom poses to herself as she muses over her afternoon tryst with Boylan: "Whats the idea of making us like that with a big hole in the middle of us" (742). At the same time, her own meditation on holes offers a rather exuberantly Joycean answer that ultimately draws out the implication of my argument in terms of erotic pleasure. For it is not only Bloom's anus that plays a central role in *Ulysses* but Molly's does as well in a way that ultimately links this eroticism to the finitude contained in the so-called knowledge of sense. Indeed the orgasm with which the novel ends is—at least according to the French—its own "little death." Molly's comment on Bloom's enjoyment of "kissing her bottom" implicitly points to the important way sensation functions differently than intellection: "Hed kiss anything unnatural where we havent 1 atom of any kind of expression in us all of us the same 2 lumps of lard" (777). Bloom's taste for Molly's hole indicates his literal embrace of the physical openness that allows for sense perception in the first place, and Molly's characterization of her anus as definitively without "expression" also suggests the extent to which this bodily interaction has very little to do with meaning as such. Rather this insistent lack of expression reveals the "2 lumps of lard" and speaks to the physical valence of reading that this chapter has been developing, as if paying attention to our bodily relationship with the novel's expressionless format is to provide a readerly version of Bloom's pleasure.

The significant malapropism that Molly commits in the following description of her visit to a doctor draws out this kind of pleasure in terms that relate it precisely to the physical holes on which I have been focusing: "How much is that doctor one guinea please and asking me had I frequent omissions where do those old fellows get all the words they have omissions with his shortsighted eyes on me cocked sideways" (770). Here, at the same time as "omission" signifies a lack or absence, the replacement of the *e* in "emissions" with an *o* visually performs the way Molly's verbal mistake transfers emphasis from the content of her body to the gap from which it discharges. The *o* of Molly's "omission" returns to the "O" that introduced Bloom to the reader and becomes, if only more obviously than the unreadable characters that signify the sound of his fart, a quasi-hole vaguely mimetic of the lower bodily orifices that she is discussing. (We might also notice how the displaced *e* reappears in the description of her own fart, offering an image of the rectal compression by which she tries to muffle her flatulence: "piano quietly sweeeee theres that train far away pianissimo eeeeeeee one more song" [763]). At this moment, however, the way the doctor's eyes are "cocked" at her obviously allies them with the penis and suggests the figurative intercourse entailed in the act of looking. Molly's earlier description of the penis as having a "kind of eye in it," emphasizes that the penis—like the body itself—has its own hollowness and suggests that this cock-eyed look at her omission is actually a sort of meeting or, in an even more graphic phrase, a coming together of holes.

This coming together is ultimately the result of the embodiment of reading and the emphasis on the sensory organs by which the reader approaches the book. It is not only Bloom's and Molly's physical bodies that dis-integrate but the reader's own, as *Ulysses* calls out to those holes in his body—his eyes and ears, his mouth and, perhaps more imaginatively, his anus. It opens up and de-composes its text as well as the body of the book itself by subtly playing with its print and its pages in ways that the next two chapters on *Finnegans Wake* and *Jacob's Room*, respectively, will develop. In this instance, however, "opening up the body of the book" also takes on a literal connotation. I began this chapter by relating how the Gabler edition of *Ulysses* that I first read fell to pieces as I progressed through it; now I must confess that, during the composition of this chapter, as I flipped back and forth between Proteus, Calypso, and Sirens in the volume published by Viking International, it too began to fall apart. The matte surface of the cover separated along the spine from the rest of the paper stock on which it had been affixed, and the remaining material was not strong enough to support the broken spine that resulted from my sometimes overvigorous reading. The novel thus split down the middle—in the first pages of the Cyclops chapter, right after the end of Sirens—and I resorted to placing a large strip of silver duct tape on the inside of the split to bring the two stacks of pages together; a piece of clear packing tape on the outside cover allows the tattered spine to remain visible but protected. Even as this splitting works, once again, as a record of my physical effort, my actions in response all too literally illustrate the reparation in play in Proust's pasting of his *paperoles* (and that Klein describes as part of the response to the depressive position). We might use the vocabulary of this chapter, however, to say this reconstruction was a reckoning with a different kind of "little death," indeed a little death of the book to which the aging of both my editions of *Ulysses* speaks. My own body also participates, if in a different way, in this aging for which *Ulysses* offers me not exactly consolation but rather a comforting solidarity. *Solidarity* is both a perfectly appropriate and a slightly ironic term, a productive ambivalence to which I will return later in this book, since, like the human body, my preferred copy of *Ulysses* now has a hole—a physical gap—right in its middle.

CHAPTER 3

The Dark Print of *Finnegans Wake*

Opening Joyce's last work one will immediately notice that *Finnegans Wake* does not reward our well-practiced lexical habits; almost every word offers a new and unexpected challenge. Derek Attridge offers the best general description of the work's language in his discussion of the pun and the portmanteau word, the latter of which he calls "a monster, a word that is not a word" (*Peculiar* 196). As a word that, like the suitcase from which it takes its name, packs in two or more meanings, "the portmanteau will contain as much as the verbal context permits it to contain" (202). When it comes to the *Wake*, however, "the context *itself* is made up of puns and portmanteaux," which causes a "spiraling increase in potential meaning [that] is one of the grounds on which the *Wake* is left unread" (202–3). An implicit pun in Attridge's own language gestures at the central claim of this chapter: the "ground" on which the *Wake* is left baldly "unread" is the work's embodiment in the object of the book. My reading of *Ulysses* traced a developing emphasis on the body of the reader; the *Wake* builds on this emphasis by focusing more explicitly on the book's body—and, more specifically, on the printed letters it contains. As its meditations ultimately stage print in terms of holes and fragmentation that offer a more objective complement to the openly personal comments that ended chapter 2, they imagine the way print gives "literal" spatial form to time's essential negativity in a way that obscurely illustrates the finite temporality with which reading is always bound up.

I approach the *Wake*'s reflections on its own print and the fundamental finitude with which it is aligned through the lens provided by

John Bishop's well-known exploration of Joyce's "book of the dark." In doing so I locate my argument within what has become a standard approach to Joyce's last work, one of its few full-scale treatments that offers something close to a comprehensive reading without reducing its complexity and "obscurity." However, I recast the figurative nature of Bishop's claim, based in Joyce's stated intentions to write a book about the night, that "only a little reflection, I think, will demonstrate that the systematic darkening of every term in *Finnegans Wake* was an absolute necessity, dictated by Joyce's subject."[1] As I show that the reader comes to an inescapable awareness of the fact that the work is made up of dark print on white pages, I rely on and reorient Bishop's foundational reading to reveal the *Wake* as quite a tangible "book of the dark" and examine the way its material support rather plainly underwrites its complex linguistic play.

The *Wake* itself specifies something close to my point: "For that (the rapt one warns) is what papyr is meed of, made of, hides and hints and misses in prints. Till ye finally (though not yet endlike) meet with the acquaintances of Mister Typus, Mistress Tope and all the little typtopies."[2] By considering the "acquaintances" facilitated with the typographical figures described here in a way that takes seriously the explicit connection that the lines are drawing between the black characters on its pages and the murky "characters" that populate its narrative world, my argument addresses the role the *Wake* imagines print to play in textual reception and complements accounts that focus on the work's self-conscious treatment of its own textual production. While Jed Rasula discusses the *Wake*'s ongoing publication in Eugene Jolas's magazine *transition* in order to place it in the context of other experimental work seeking to activate the agency of alphabetic characters, the emphasis on finality in this line leads me beyond the contemporary sociocultural setting on which he focuses to draw out the implications of the fact that, as he puts it, "letters are actually the initial point of immersion in the *Wake*."[3] The Egyptian references to papyrus ("papyr") and mummies (the "rapt" or wrapped one) casts this "book of the dark" as also a "Book of the Dead" to indicate that my discussion of the work's print will be a more explicit exploration of our relation to finitude and mortality gestured at in my titular phrase the "death of the book."[4]

When the *Wake* rather noticeably exercises—indeed "capitalizes" on—its own material typography in an early passage, some four pages in, that expands on the allusion that makes up the title, it explicitly posits an introductory connection between death and the work's print that it will doggedly develop. Refashioning the well-known Irish folk song "Finnegan's Wake," which serves as one explanatory subtext for the book, the description typographically performs the way Finnegan—transformed into HCE—is laid out for his wake: "Him a being so on the flounder of his bulk like an overgrown babeling, let wee peep, see, at Hom, well, see peegee ought he ought, platterplate. ш" (6.30–32). As the print itself offers readers their own vision of a man laid out on his back, flat like a "flounder," in the literal analogue of the overturned *E*, the narrative content of this moment bleeds into the typography that transmits it. The *E* thus functions as a character in the *Wake* in both senses of the word: as a building block of written signification and as an actor in its narrative. Additionally, in a way that recalls the attention to readerly sense perception in my discussion of *Ulysses*, the descriptions of peeping and seeing underscore the visual activity entailed both by a wake (also called, significantly, a "view[ing]" [6.30]) and the process of reading itself. As the phrase "overgrown babeling" characterizes HCE as a large infant, it also aligns the manipulated letter with the prelinguistic realm of the newborn which I've approached through Melanie Klein, as if to suggest that the sensory perception of print (and, by extension, the less than straightforward sounds it signifies) precedes the linguistic ordering by which we make meaning out of these signs.

This moment opens an understanding of print as a medium that complicates the account that Marshall McLuhan develops out of his engagement with the *Wake*. Detailing the process by which the phonetic alphabet abstracts meaning from sound and translates that sound into the visual signifiers of letters, McLuhan sees print as the apotheosis of a process that "makes a break between eye and ear, between semantic meaning and visual code."[5] He appeals to the technological advances of the electronic age to ameliorate these kinds of sensory partitions in a way that treats print simply as a phase overcome in the advance toward digitization and the computer. Leaving little room to consider the book and print *as such*, it is in this tradition that some of the most well-known media-centric treatments of the *Wake* proceed. The almost utopian faith in the electronic that conditions both Derrida's characterization of the *Wake* as a "1000th generation computer" and Donald Theall's claim in *Beyond the Word* that Joyce's last work anticipates the multimedia production of contemporary cyberculture and promises to do away with media altogether

bulldozes over the very finitude of print their arguments assume.[6]
Indeed when the description of the knocked-out HCE proceeds a few
lines later to ask "Whase on the joint of a desh?" (7.9), or "Who is on
the point of death?," it conflates print—here in the form of the dash—
with death and mortality itself. At the same time, the implications
of connection in the word "joint" and the figure of the dash indicate
that, in the *Wake*, death is not an isolated phenomenon but is in play
at the heart of things, that it functions as the fulcrum around which
Joyce's last work relentlessly revolves. As the description continues,
the sense of finitude becomes even more explicit and ties directly to
the action of looking by which the previous lines described our access
to printed letters: "Behold of him as behemoth for he is nowwhemoe.
Finiche! Only a fadograph of a yestern scene" (7.14–15). As this con-
frontation with being finished is exactly what our attention to the
medium of print—figured as a faded photograph, a metaphor that we
will encounter again—will open for us, it materializes the temporal
finitude on which the dark print of the *Wake* incessantly insists.

I

Despite my preliminary claims for the *Wake*'s literal visuality, it is
also, with its multilingual puns, an inescapably rich auditory text.
One of the more accurate self-referential descriptions of reading the
Wake itself states, "You is feeling like you was lost in the bush, boy?
You says: It is a puling sample jungle of woods" (112.3–4). Here the
feeling of being lost to which the first sentence refers is a direct result
of the puns in the second sentence. That is, if we read "puling sample jungle of woods" aloud, then (with the help of the *Annotations*,
perhaps) we might also hear the echo of "pure and simple jumble of
words." The phonetic sounds of the words here—and throughout the
Wake—exhibit a fluidity and an openness to multiple meanings that
indicate the radically polysemic potential of the pun. Arguing that it
is sound that dissolves the strict duality of and significant power differential between the subject as observer and the object as observed
installed by a visual relationship, Steven Connor puts the *Wake* in
conversation with the multimedium of cinema and suggests that, in
the *Wake*, sound and visualization are at odds: "The force of sound
is made so pervasive as to interfere with the processes of visualization that are otherwise to the fore in reading."[7] When Bishop points
out the relationship in "Wakean 'adamelegy' [etymology]" among

"phonetics," "phenomenon," and "phantasm," he describes the exact opposite of Connor's claim: words in the *Wake* "share a common 'sound sense'" and also "stand in spectral relationship to one another" (291). Accordingly the insistent attention paid to letters in the reading experience of the *Wake* quietly reverberates with Merleau-Ponty's more reciprocal account of vision and creates exactly the kind of "listening eye" that Connor finds in cinema, a type of viewing (indeed a viewing of type) that complicates the unilateral agency of the perceiving subject assumed by conventional accounts of vision.

The *Wake* provides its most forceful articulation of the materiality of written documents—and the sense of vision necessary to access them—in the chapter in book 1 that details the discovery and exploration of a letter. Considered something of a commentary on reading the *Wake* itself, the letter opens, after a lengthy litany of titles, with an account of the difficulty of deciphering its meaning and origin, which it rather quickly disavows for "another cant to the questy," or "another side to the question" (109.1). As it goes on to ask "Has any ornery josser . . . ever looked sufficiently longly at a quite everyday looking stamped addressed envelope?" (109.3–8), the chapter suggests that the other side of this questions is precisely that of the material envelope that transmits the content of the letter. The phrase "everyday looking" describes the extent to which a reader is always seeing the format of a written text at the same time as it suggests the unremarkable quality that so easily allows it to go unnoticed. In fact the material format of the *Wake*'s print itself is, with only a few exceptions, such as the overturned E, for the most part quite ordinary. Nonetheless in the case of the letter—as of the *Wake*—"its face in all its featureful perfection of imperfection is its fortune" (109.8–9). The "face" on which this description trains its focus moves the discourse of the letter beyond a discussion of its function in the process of signification (as in the structuralist and poststructuralist focus on the signifier-signified divide that informs most treatments of this moment) to a phenomenon worthy of consideration in its own right.[8] As Samuel Beckett famously puts it, Joyce's writing "is not *about* something; *it is that something itself.*"[9] This is not to claim that Joyce's writing is a perfect manifestation of what it is signifying (indeed if it manifests anything perfectly it is, as this line from the *Wake* points out, *imperfection* and lack) but to explore the operation of its material embodiment as it calls out to the readerly sensorium that I developed in my reading of *Ulysses*.

Thus when the *Wake* turns to a photographic analogy to describe the letter's material distortion and deformation, it begins to flesh out that "something itself" and uncovers (which is not necessarily to illuminate) the literal darkness that makes up its print: "If a negative of a horse happens to melt enough while drying, well, what do you get is, well, a positively grotesquely distorted macromass of all sorts of horsehappy values and masses of meltwhile horse. Tip. Well, this freely is what must have occurred to our missive" (111.27–31). As the negative melts and loses its referential qualities to become "a positively grotesquely distorted macromass," the qualifier "positively" has two obvious functions: on the one hand, it modifies "grotesquely" and means "absolutely" or "completely," while, on the other, it modifies "distorted" and functions as the opposite of "negative." From the latter perspective, a "positively distorted macromass" suggests that the effect of the melting is to grant an insistent, corporeal presence to the piece of film. In other words, when the filmic negative stops clearly pointing to a referent beyond itself, it evinces its own presence and shows itself to be a "macromass." Yet this macromass is nonetheless still a negative; in this description what takes on a positive value is negativity itself, or, in a *Wake*an twist on Merleau-Ponty, darkness visible.

In the same way that the photographic negative melts to obscure its representational quality, "macromass" is a linguistic melting in which words themselves have coalesced and lost their referential powers. Accordingly when Bishop draws a close relation between the "general referential opacity" of the *Wake* and the fact that "so much of the *Wake* is hard to visualize," he also describes the condition in which the language of the *Wake* itself might assume a body and become visible (216). That is, as "macromass" does not necessarily refer to anything beyond itself, it takes on, like the photographic negative, a textual corporeality. The resistance it raises against being read in any kind of straightforward, effortless way unveils the request it makes simply to be looked at (a task that is by no means simple). This "visible darkness" allows print's own visual nature as a medium to come to the fore. The *Wake* includes a sentence to this effect a few pages later: "[We] may have our irremovable doubts as to the whole sense of the lot . . . but one who deeper thinks will always bear in the baccbuccus of his mind that this downright there you are and there it is is only all in his eye" (117.35–36, 118.15–17).

With this in mind, the well-known phrase describing the reading of the *Wake*—"that ideal reader suffering from an ideal insomnia"

(120.13–14)—takes on a curious and important implication for *Finnegans Wake* as a literal book of the dark. While "ideal insomnia" implies a perfect sleeplessness and evokes a reader who is constantly and perpetually awake, it might also suggest that the "ideal" itself is never ultimately put to sleep—that, to use Stephen's words in *Ulysses*, the visual is an "ineluctable modality." If, as Roland McHugh points out, *ideal* comes from the Greek *eidô*, meaning literally "to see," "ideal insomnia" might also indicate that the oblivion accompanying sleep does not elide the visual. Though somewhat of a paradox since one's eyes close in sleep, the fact that the covering of the eyelid nonetheless remains technically "visible" suggests that, in a book about sleep and the night, darkness is the one thing to which we are not blind; it is exactly what is there *to be seen*. Picking up on the same etymology, an "ideal reader" would then be one who reads in an ideal way, that is, one who sees, and more specifically one who is able to open his eyes to obscurity itself.

Attending to the darknesses on the *Wake*'s pages presents a much more radical revision (or perhaps re-visioning) of reading than the critical strategy through which Bishop constructs his argument. Although he writes that, in approaching the *Wake*'s nighttime language, which functions in a way diametrically opposed to the daytime, rational language to which we are accustomed, one "must abandon the monied and privileged reflex of literacy in order to attain the 'dummyship' and become as good an illiterate as HCE" (304), his work certainly cannot be characterized as especially "illiterate" (for which at least a generation of *Wake* readers, myself included, are no doubt thankful). When he makes the claim, which he revised in a conversation with me some twenty years later, that "the printed letters and words in *Finnegans Wake* are mere 'vehicles' leading to hidden meanings that are nowhere explicitly evident to a reader's literate consciousness," he indicates his commitment to intellectual comprehension that is perhaps inescapable for a literary critic (310). At the same time, however, he overlooks the fact that the "printed letters and words" might be "explicitly evident" to the reader's "illiterate" consciousness; in other words, they may be "only all in his eye."

Perhaps this is putting it a bit too strongly. But surely it is not *only* that "the printed letters and words in *Finnegans Wake* are mere 'vehicles' leading to hidden meanings." (Is phonetic writing not *always* a vehicle leading to an unknown meaning?) Rather, as I have begun to suggest, the printed letters and words in *Finnegans Wake also* function as a nonreferential medium. In so doing they approximate the experience of illiteracy itself, the way a child may view words on a page as a set of strange squiggles with no more meaning than its own playful scrawl. Along these lines the description of the letter specifies that "the stain, and that a teastain . . . marked it off on the spout of the moment as a genuine relique of ancient Irish pleasant pottery of that lydialike languishing class known as hurry-me-o'er-the-hazy" (III.20–24). The homophony between the prefix of the specification "*tea*stain" and the letter *T* links stains with letters, themselves the building blocks of writing, as if writing is indeed no more than a specific kind of stain that is as much seen as read. Of course the stain *is* read, or decoded, as a signifier of the letter's authenticity, its genuine belonging to the class of objects "known as hurry-me-o'er-the-hazy." Interestingly, however, the metaphorics of obscurity in which "hazy" here participates seem to be spurned by the insistence on "hurrying over," as if to imply that letters contain an injunction to rush beyond any kind of obscurity or darkness and reach the light of understanding—an injunction, I might add, to which it is very difficult not to respond. I want in fact to claim the notion of "hurrying over the hazy" as an explicit definition for the amorphous term *reading* that I have been mobilizing.

The disregard of the visual code of letters entailed in reading is precisely what the "suffering of an ideal insomnia" opposes and precisely what an "ideal reader" resists in what we might call an "ideal *illiteracy*." Yet the illiteracy I'm positing is less about uncovering the meanings of the text that are hidden from the reader's literate consciousness than it is about the much more radical task of accessing (without dispelling) hiddenness *as such*—of, as I have suggested, looking at the *Wake*'s dark print itself. Yet attending to the visual register on which print functions is not a panacea for avoiding the "reflex of literacy" or for accessing this hiddenness, since it all too easily leads to its own kind of abstractions and intellectualizations. Indeed when the *Wake* describes a "visual" reading based on attention to the visible signs of the letter (figured in terms of an illuminated manuscript), it gives an implicit, if caricatured, account of the associative method on which Bishop bases his explications: "the curious warning sign before our protoparents *ipsissima verba* (a very pure nondescript, by the way, sometimes a palmtailed otter, more often the arbutus fruitflowerleaf of the cainapple) which paleographers call *a leak in the thatch* or *the Aranman ingperwhis through the hole of his hat*, indicating that the words which follow may be taken in any order desired, hole of Aran man the hat through the whispering ho (here keen again and begin again to make soundsense and sensesound kin again)" (121.8–16). The kind of reading sketched out here, the idea that "the words which follow may be taken in any order desired," with its explicit freedom from any sense of prescribed succession, describes, on the one hand, the way an eye might rove freely over an image and, on the other, the way Bishop abandons the sequentiality of linguistic syntax in favor of, as he puts it, "cultivat[ing] sense by a broad-ranging and digressive association whose only limits have been the covers of the book and the terms contained in it" (305).

Unlike the way the eye deciphers a printed text, following the fixed order of the words and pages, the eye takes in an image in a much less constricted way: it is free to move forward and backward, upward, downward, and diagonally. Analogously Bishop's method of bringing together far-flung phrases as a way of making sense of the *Wake* transforms its text into a spatialized object across which he can rove with abandon.[10] Yet as the nonsense phrase "hole of Aran man the hat through the whispering ho" mixes up the order of the italicized words from the previous line while the word "ing-per-whis" (hyphenated here for clarity) does the same on the level of syllables, the passage not only signals the potential absurdity inherent in this spatialized comprehension of the text, but it also suggests the importance—indeed inevitability—of the sequential unfolding of language. The passage thus hints at the way the act of reading the *Wake*'s dark print should open up a vision performed by a listening eye and by a temporalizing one as well.

With this in mind, exploring Shaun's alliance with space and an abstracting form of vision offers an opportunity to more explicitly consider the assumptions behind a critical strategy like Bishop's. It will also stake out the borders of a temporalized readerly deportment for which I'm suggesting the *Wake* is calling, one that is ultimately engaged with the very spatiality of its print in a way that contributes to the repeated rapprochements of the work's various conflicting polarities (Shaun vs. Shem, eye vs. ear, and, most explicitly, space vs. time). When, in answering the climactic question of the riddle chapter (1.6) from the "blinkpoint of so eminent a spatialist" (149.18–19), Shaun discusses the work of "Professor Loewy-Brueller" (150.15), he alludes to the effects of the spatialized thinking on which Bishop's critical readings—if only more obviously than those of the rest

of us professors—depends. In terms that expand on Bishop's own
appeal to the "covers of the book" that constitute the boundaries of
his investigation, Shaun describes the Professor working "to make us
see how though, as he says: 'by Allswill' the inception and the descent
and the endswell of Man is *temporarily* wrapped in obscenity, looking through at these accidents with the faroscope of television . . . I
can easily believe *h*eartily in my own most spacious immensity as my
ownhouse and microbemost cosm" (150.29–151.1). The general substance of the passage tracks a shift from a bewildering temporality to
a spatialization whose totalizing tendency offers a sense of certainty
and clarity to the life of the man (assumedly from the emphasized
acrostic HCE) that it is considering. More specifically, by taking on
the distant viewpoint indicated by the echoes of faraway seeing in the
phrase "faroscope of television," the Professor also finds a kind of
fire escape from the demands of time itself. From this vantage point,
the unfolding of the myriad moments that would constitute the life of
man—what the passage calls "these accidents"—assumes a timeless
immortality as they become a "spacious immensity" that he can survey all at once.

Attridge makes a resonant point in what is perhaps the most
explicit criticism of the wholesale embrace of the night/dream framework in *Wake* studies in general and Bishop's book in particular. He
describes Bishop's extreme critical method as indicative of a "dream
that we will be able to find in a text a structure of pure meanings that
has its own separate being, and that can be contemplated apart from
the letters through which we reach it."[11] The otherworldly nature of
the "separate being" in which he locates these (illusory) "pure meanings" speaks to the abstract spatialization that I'm discussing. Moreover the way he characterizes the reliance on the dream metaphor as
a means of "reduc[ing] the book's dizzying multiplicity" (134) finds
its own revealing correlation in the statement that immediately follows the lines I just quoted: "I am reassured by ratio that the cube
of my volumes is to the surfaces of their subject as the, sphericity of
these globes . . . is to the feracity of Fairynelly's vacuum" (151.1–7).
The metaphor of the "cube of my volumes" (which resonates with
the "cubehouse" [5.14] that obliquely refers to the *Wake* itself early
in this volume) allows us to see that this spatializing thinking has an
effect on the format of the book itself. That is, the link between "volume" and "surface" in the first "ratio" that the Professor mentions
points to a *flattening*, as if to suggest that bringing together moments

from disparate parts of the *text* is tied to overlooking the very volume of the *book* that transmits them.

While this total and totalizing spatial view of the *Wake* is what Bishop provides in his comprehensive reading of the *Wake* as a book of the dark, it also describes virtually any critical discussion, including the one on which I am presently embarked, since treatments of wide-ranging passages are a staple of our critical methods. However, reframing Bishop's argument in literal terms allows us to come down from the "faroscope of television" and consider the insistently temporal aspect of the volume of dark print that we are reading.

II

The *Wake* calls for precisely the temporally and materially sensitive approach I am developing when, near the beginning of the letter chapter, the narrator asserts that "to concentrate solely on the literal sense or even the psychological content of any document to the sore neglect of the enveloping facts themselves circumstantiating it is just as hurtful to sound sense" (109.12–15), a line that explicitly locates the signified content of the document within a "circumstantiating" container literally standing around it. Suggesting the extent to which the material format physically encloses the radically mobile linguistic fireworks that make the *Wake* such a lively read, the narrator gestures at a strange coincidence of movement and stasis that its other descriptions of these various "enveloping facts" develop. Using terms that speak to the inextricable link between living and dying inherent in temporal progress, the most expansive of the *Wake*'s metaphors for this envelope is the "fatal midden or chip factory or comicalbottomed copsjute (dump for short)" where the letter is discovered (110.25–26). Embedding the letter in a trash mound's collection of decomposing materials, the *Wake* casts the object of the book as a literal container of dead letters. Even as it pulls back from the tight focus that I trained on the ⊔ to take a "proudseye view . . . of our mounding's mass," or a bird's-eye view on a mountain's mass (7.36–8.1), such a high-altitude consolidation does not abstract away the emphasis on finitude I located earlier in the overturned *E*. Rather the reference to the mound in the word "mounding" transforms the stately mountain into nothing more than a heap of discarded trash.

The description of the mound that Mutt gives to Jute early in the *Wake* supports the connection I'm drawing between it and the object of the book by characterizing the mound's waste products in terms of tattered pages: "Countlessness of livestories have netherfallen by this plage, flick as flowflakes, litters from aloft, like a waast wizard all of whirlworlds. Now are all tombed to the mound, isges to isges, erde from erde" (17.26–30). The "litters from aloft" that are buried in the mound transform "livestories" into dead letters that are also waste products buried in the "plage," a beach that itself resembles a "page." The mound thus becomes a "tomb" as the echo of "ashes to ashes, dust to dust" in the final phrases indicates the funereal landscape in which these pages take their place. Indeed what is whirling around in the vast blizzard here is precisely "waast." We thus might say that the pages of the *Wake* are nothing more than the swirling contents in the literal dustbin of history. This is not to dismiss them, however, but rather to reveal the importance of the *Wake*'s attempt to commemorate the very deadness of these dead letters, or, in even more paradoxical phrasing, to animate them *as dead*.

Returning to a more detailed description of the letter itself illustrates this point in arguably clearer terms as it expands on the embrace of mortality implied here. The narrator identifies "this radiooscillating epiepistle to which, cotton, silk or samite, kohol, gall or brickdust, we must ceaselessly return" (108.23–25). The sense of "radiooscillating" speaks to the polysemy of sound always at play in the *Wake*, as the aurality evoked by "radio" bounces endlessly back and forth between and among the multiple words to which the sounds simultaneously refer. As an overtly nonprogressive movement that would tellingly characterize the sonic action inside a tomblike echo chamber, oscillation also describes a combination of both movement and immobility that might offer a figure for the animation of death at which the *Wake* seems to be pointing. The subsequent list of writing materials that constitute the object of the letter adds some substance to this figure, as our "ceaseless return" to these materials repeats the oscillatory movement of sound in terms of readerly action. More specifically the *Annotations* point out that the ancient Chinese wrote on silk with a mixture of brick dust and water, while samite was a rich silk fabric worn in the Middle Ages; kohol is a black coloring agent, and "gall" refers to ink made from outgrowths on trees called nutgall. As these references to historical materials of written discourse point to the letter's age, they suggest that part of the "ceaseless return" of its material distraction is the repeated reminder to the reader of the passage of historical time.

The idea of a "ceaseless return" also recalls the *Wake*'s cyclical structure in a way that might revise the traditional understanding of the work as a never-ending circle, since the emphasis on material format hints that our repeated returns are only ever to an inhuman object that functions here as the index of the very force of time with which our human mortality is bound up. Indeed as the ostensibly revitalizing "riverrun" that announces the ongoing flow of time and life at the beginning of the work leads only "by a commodious vicus of recirculation back to Howth Castle and Environs" (3.1–3), it seems to indicate less the resurrection of HCE than his transformation into a physical structure planted in a landscape (which, not incidentally, is very close to how Joyce describes the overturned *E* in a letter to his patron Harriet Shaw Weaver).[12] This is not to deny that awakening and resurrection are major themes of the *Wake* but rather to suggest that what we wake up to is precisely finitude itself, the impossibility of moving out of and the necessity of persisting with the materially finite confines embodied by the book's print.

One of the most obvious tropes in the *Wake* for this material persistence is the letter's repeatedly botched delivery, the difficulty that Shaun has separating himself from it. Unlike the lengthy account in book 3 that emphasizes Shaun's process of (failed) delivery, the early instance of this trope in book 1 focuses on the letter itself and Shaun's rather physical connection to it. The narrator asks, "Will it ever be next morning the post unionist's (officially called carrier's, Letters Scotch, Limited) strange fate . . . to hand in a *h*uge *c*hain *e*nvelope"? (66.10–14). The ambiguity in the phrase "hand in a huge chain envelope" questions the possibility of ever delivering the letter by conflating the action of "hand[ing] in" the envelope with the condition of having one's "hand in [it]." Picking up on the other images in the line, it is Shaun's "strange fate" to be "chained" to the envelope, which the acrostic aligns with HCE himself. As the questions that continue later on the page pick up on the implicit reference to the night in the plea for the coming of morning, they build on the emphasis on this physical chain at the same time as they use the rhetoric of darkness to transform the relationship between writing and enlightenment into exactly its opposite. In doing so they begin to refocus the discussion from the multiple ways that the *Wake* treats the letter's (temporal) materiality to the more specific consideration of print with which I am ultimately concerned.

Referring to the letter's writing, the narrator asks, "Will whatever will be written in lappish language with inbursts of Maggyer always seem semposed, black looking white and white guarding black, in that

siamixed twoatalk used twixt stern swift and jolly roger?" (66.18–21).
If HCE was present in the previous line, the rest of the *Wake*'s characters appear here with the "*lap*pish" language of ALP and the faintly
Hungarian "Maggyer" dialect of Issy and the Maggies "semposed"—
or superimposed by Shem—into the Siamese twintalk that mixes up
the clear distinction between black and white. We get a viewpoint on
this mix-up in the crisscrossing chiasmus of the phrase "black looking white and white guarding black," whose present participles are
also ambiguous modifiers suggesting both that white appears black
(black-looking white) and, more straightforwardly, that black appears
white. The question that immediately follows—"Will it bright upon
us, nightle, and we plunging to our plight? Well, it might now, mircle,
so it light" (66.21–23)—takes up and draws out the implications of
this confusion. In a way that recalls the "darkness visible" that I discussed in the previous section, what "brights upon us," which might
be another way of saying what dawns upon or occurs to us, is "nightle," or a little bit of the night, whose obscurity obliterates any sense
of distinction. This puts us into quite a plight, the acknowledgment of
which is something of a corrupted miracle.

When the chapter goes on to figure the letter as a "coffin" (66.27), it
suggests that the plight into which this dark distinctionlessness plunges
us is precisely that of the mortal limits that I have been investigating. We
read, "What else in this mortal world, now ours, when meet there night,
mid their nackt, me there naket, made their nought the hour strikes
would bring them rightcame back in the flesh, thumbs down, to their
orses and their hashes" (67.2–6). The general thrust of these lines seems
to be the power of the dark, sepulchral letter to remind its viewers of
their mortality and to return them to the finite material world. The per-
mutations of the word *Mitternacht*, German for "midnight," produce
twelve words that correspond with the twelve strokes of the clock and
describe the multiple ways in which the letter accomplishes its effect.
That is, a face-to-face encounter with the darkness of the night—"meet
there night"—also becomes an experience of nothingness since it "made
their nought" and reveals precisely the naked vulnerability—"mid their
nackt, me there naket"—of the flesh they cannot ignore.

III

The introduction of nakedness recalls the commentary on clothing
and nudity from the letter chapter, which asks, "Who in his heart

doubts either that the facts of feminine clothiering are there all the time or that the feminine fiction, stranger than facts, is there also at the same time, only a little to the rere?" (109.30–33). At the same time, it also speaks to the moment when Shem and Shaun witness ALP's nakedness, which is precisely an experience of dark nothingness. Moreover the experimental page layout of the "Night Lessons" chapter in which this occurs—and which constitutes the section of the *Wake* that many, including Joyce himself, consider to be the most obscure part of the work—provides the reader with a lexical experience that puts into practice many of the points I have been examining in the discursive descriptions of the dark, deathly reading for which the *Wake* so literally calls. One of the last pieces that Joyce composed, this chapter recounts the education of Shem, Shaun, and Issy, what Shem describes at the end of the chapter thus: "We've had our day at triv and quad and writ our bit as intermidgets" (306.11–12). "Triv and quad" refers to the medieval division of the seven liberal arts into the trivium (grammar, rhetoric, and logic) and the quadrivium (arithmetic, geometry, astronomy, and music). "Intermidgets" functions as a telling portmanteau that suggests that the writing of these small children ("midgets") works to "intermediate" the various arts in a way that recalls the emphasis I have been developing on the confluence of the visual and the verbal. In his discussion of this chapter's treatment of the trivium and quadrivium, Christopher Eagle describes Joyce's "method of representing traditional domains of knowledge so as to reveal a fundamental interconnection between their abstract and concrete aspects," an interconnection that also characterizes the embodiment of reading I am developing.[13]

The format of the chapter, which Joyce described in a letter as "a reproduction of a schoolboy's (and schoolgirl's) old classbook complete with marginalia by the twins, who change sides at halftime, footnotes by the girl (who doesn't), a Euclid diagram, funny drawings, etc." (*Letters* 1: 405–6), performs this intermediation from the get-go. Eagle places the schoolbook format in the tradition of the medieval illuminated manuscript and notes that Joyce "commissioned his daughter Lucia to draw one of her lettrines of the opening letter 'A' in red" for the first published version of the section in a 1937 issue of *transition* (118). In the full volume of the *Wake*, however, this emphasis on the text's visuality is achieved only by the experiment in page layout: two wide margins that comment, in italicized print on the left-hand side and smalls caps on the right, on a central column of justified text, all of which hover over the footnotes mentioned by Joyce, replace the standard lines of uniform type that fill the work's other pages. And this layout is not even completely consistent, as a lengthy parenthetical interrupts the layout toward the middle of the chapter and the "Euclid diagram" and "funny drawings" add other graphic ornament (see figure 5).

In his reconstruction of the chapter's composition, Luca Crispi observes that this layout "immediately attracts the reader's attention" and makes reading the chapter "a disorienting experience" even for those accustomed to the difficulties of the *Wake*.[14] Part of this disorientation is the demand the layout makes on the eye: it must break out of the uniformly delimited left-right movement involved in conventional reading and roam beyond the normal parameters of standard page design. This necessarily entails leaving off the main text in the central column and venturing to the far right, left, or bottom of the page. In a way that materializes Bishop's spatialized reading practices, the page thus begins to function as an image with a deliberate spatial arrangement in addition to being a set of signifiers to be deciphered. As this mobility of the eye forestalls any attempt at linear comprehension, it transforms the intellectual effort of simultaneously considering the multiple meanings of the *Wake*'s portmanteaux vocabulary into the physical—or, more specifically, the perceptual—effort of remaining aware of the multiple components that constitute these pages. The layout of the page in the "Night Lessons" chapter thus becomes a graphic performance of the implicit reading lessons that the *Wake* offers in its emphasis on the agency of the reader's senses and the perception of the materiality of the letter and of letters themselves. As such, though Crispi affirms the dominant critical view that the main "lesson" of the chapter is actually "a caricature of instruction and learning" (214), we might try to take its explicit scenes of instruction—however parodic—a little more seriously. Indeed the geometry lesson, which, as Crispi points out, was the first part of the chapter Joyce composed and which remains "the chapter's dramatic centerpiece," offers an embedded reading lesson that speaks to the close and careful attention we must pay to the dark print on the page as well as the mortal ramifications of doing so.

The first thing to notice about the geometry lesson is that Shem provides the instruction rather than the more rationally minded and intellectual Shaun, a fitting switch since Shem is more closely allied to darkness and the body. The lesson begins with a permutation of

Coss? Cossist? Your parn! You, you make   WHY MY AS
what name? (and in truth, as a poor soul is   LIKEWISE
between shift and shift ere the death he has   WHIS HIS.
lived through becomes the life he is to die
into, he or he had albut — he was rickets as to
reasons but the balance of his minds was
stables — lost himself or himself some som-
nione sciupiones, soswhitchoverswetch had
he or he gazet, murphy come, murphy go,
murphy plant, murphy grow, a maryamyria-
meliamurphies, in the lazily eye of his lapis,

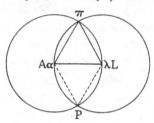

Uteralterance or   Vieus Von DVbLIn, 'twas one of dozedeams
the Interplay of   a darkies ding in dewood) the Turnpike under
Bones in the   the Great Ulm with Mearingstone in Fore
Womb.   ground).[1] Given now ann linch you take enn
all. Allow me. And, heaving alljawbreakical
expressions out of old Sare Isaac's[2] universal
The Vortex.   of specious aristmystic unsaid, A is for Anna
Spring of Sprung   like L is for liv. Aha hahah, Ante Ann you're
Verse. The Ver-   apt to ape aunty annalive! Dawn gives rise.
tex.   Lo, lo, lives love! Eve takes fall. La, la, laugh
leaves alass! Aiaiaiai, Antiann, we're last to
the lost, Loulou! Tis perfect. Now (lens

[1] Draumcondra's Dreamcountry where the betterlies blow.
[2] O, Laughing Sally, are we going to be toadhauntered by that old Pantifox
Sir Somebody Something, Burtt, for the rest of our secret stripture.

293

Figure 5. James Joyce, Finnegans Wake (New York: Penguin
Books, 1976), 293.

the first problem in Euclid's *Elements of Geometry*, the construction
of an equilateral triangle: "Problem ye ferst, construct ann aquilittoral dryankle Probe loom! . . . Concoct an equoangular trillitter"
(286.17–20). The reference to "ann" and the acrostic "a . . . Pl"
announce ALP's presence here, a fact that has dominated discussions
of this passage since, as it develops, we learn that the triangle the

twins construct overlaps with ALP's "delta," or the triangular shape
between her legs. Less considered, however, are the echoes of the
word *letter* in "aquilittoral" and "trillitter." As the puns here align
the figure's sides ("lateral") and angles with letters, they explicitly
recall the delta sign (Δ) and, more generally, point to the way letters
are themselves made up of a combination of line segments that meet
at various (if not strictly equal) angles.

Following Euclid's proof, the twins begin to construct this triangle
by making two overlapping circles: "To find a locus for an alp get a
howlth on her bayrings as a prisme O and for a second O unbox your
compasses" (287.8–10). The general sense of this complicated instruction is that to find a spot for a triangle (an alp, in addition to referring
to ALP, is also a mountain with its vaguely triangular shape), "get a
hold of your bearings" by taking the topography of Dublin—namely
Howth Hill, which completes the "ring" of Dublin Bay—as the first
circle ("prisme O"), and then construct a second one using a compass.
As the puns here draw out the literal meaning of *geometry* as "earth
measuring," the reference to compasses suggests the exploration of
the space occupied by the letter O. While the multiple circles that the
twins are drawing recall the cyclical nature of the *Wake* itself, the
survey of this O's shape takes on important shades of meaning at the
end of the proof that resignify this circularity in a way similar to the
alignment with finitude that I discussed in the previous section.

This resignification begins when the two triangles that Shem helps
Shaun to draw within the space of the circles' overlap allow him to
"make you to see figuratleavely the whome of your eternal geomater"
(296.31–297.1). The focus on the maternal recalls the central place
the mother has in Kleinian psychoanalysis and the move it traces to a
depressive psychic position more tolerant of anxiety and finitude. As
the puns in "whome" underscore that ALP's womb is both a home
and a whole, the word play in "figuratleavely" turns the fig leaf of
figuration on its head to reveal this integral whole as also a fractured
hole. Shem thus describes how he lifts "the maidsapron of our A.L.P.,
fearfully! Till its nether nadir is vortically where (allow me aright to
two cute winkles) its naval's napex will have to beandbe" (297.11–
14). Eagle explains that, at this moment, "the children gaze up at
the lowest point possible, the 'nether nadir' standing both for the
origo mundi of female genitalia and that point in the celestial spheres
directly opposed to the zenith" (333); the references to aligning "winkles" (German for "angle") combined with moving the fabric of the

"maidsapron" imply that this revelation is occurring through a kind of page-turning.

A corresponding statement from earlier in the chapter confirms this reading as it also draws out exactly what makes witnessing this whole so fearful. Claiming that the paradise of "Wonderlawn's lost to us for ever" (270.20), the textbook instructs, "You may spin on youthlit's bike and multiplease your Mike and Nike with your kickshoes on your algebrars but, volve the virgil page and view, the O of woman is long when burly those two muters sequent her so from Nebob see you never stray who'll nimm you nice and nehm the day" (270.22–28). Hardly a straightforward statement, this line suggests that, for all the abstract, mathematical tricks youthfully played with Euclid's bike and its algebraic handlebars, turning the page reveals a concrete materiality embodied in a female O. This O is as much the origin of the world as it is the very index of nothingness, a zero affirmed by the distorted mnemonic for remembering the declension of the Latin *nemo* or "no one" ("For *nemo* let me never say *neminis* or *nemine*"). With this in mind, we might build off of Eagle's description of the way that "Joyce has taken . . . what is traditionally seen as the most abstract, least worldly knowledge, the *Elements of Geometry*, and rematerialized it" to suggest the way that a materialization of abstraction is itself an embodiment of nothingness (333).

Shem gestures at this embodiment of nothingness when he comments to Shaun, "You must proach near mear for at is dark. Lob. And light your mech. Jeldy! And this is what you'll say.[2] Waaaaaa. Tch! Sluice! Pla!" (297.14–17). The beginning of the line declares that looking into this hole confronts the twins with a darkness that disrupts the grammar of Shem's statement by replacing the definite spatial designation of *it* with an "at" whose lack of an object suggests that the exact contours of this hole are unknown if not ultimately unknowable. The transformation of *see* into "say" later in the line hints at the effort to grasp this experience of "watching" nothingness by articulating it into language, an effort that only breaks down into a vision of the "Waaaaaa"'s typographical obscurity. Finally, however, his choice of words at the end of this line characterizes the O more fully: it is both a "sluice," the term for a water channel that is used as a slang for a vagina, and a kind of ending, from the German *Schluss*, meaning "end" or "conclusion." The place of birth is, simultaneously, an entrance into dying. Shem expands on this coincidence in a way that speaks to the *Wake*'s own cycle of finitude when, a few lines later, he describes "the living spit of dead waters" (297.19). What circulates through the stream suggested by ALP's association with the River Liffey is actually death itself—death, that is, as a never-ending cycle. This is, in effect, quite close to the first response Shem gives when Shaun asks in pidgin English "You make what name?" ("What are you making?") at the beginning of the construction of the triangle: "as a poor soul is between shift and shift ere the death he has lived through becomes the life he is to die into" (293.2–5).

IV

The instance of the geometrical construction in "Night Lessons" is one of the few moments in the *Wake* where Shem and Shaun, themselves allied respectively with time and space, work together rather than, as in almost every other chapter, fighting with each other; it thus gestures at the way the darkness they mutually witness works to defuse the very distinction on which their conflict depends. As Shaun himself puts it, "We shared the twin chamber and we winked on the wench and what Sim sobs todie I'll reeve tomorry, for 'twill be, I have hopes of, Sam Dizzier's feedst" (408.20–23). The "twin chamber" that they occupied, their mother's dark womb on which they spy or "wink" and which the *Wake* aligns with the very darkness of printed letters, maps out a space of mutuality. Appropriately this space is one in which what Shem's "sobs" rather tearfully sow in the explicitly mortal present of today ("todie") becomes exactly the content of Shaun's dreamlike reading (from the French *rêver*). At the same time, this readerly reverie also celebrates St. Dizier, the town where *transition*, the magazine in which Joyce's Work in Progress originally appeared, was printed. This line thus draws together in miniature many of the terms that have been in play in my discussion and that this final section reexamines in a concluding comparison of Shaun and Shem. Restaging the dynamic I drew out between Stephen and Bloom in *Ulysses*, this section functions as a Viconian "ricorso" that will, in an unsurprisingly literal way, bring us by "commodious vicus of recirculation back to Howth Castle and Environs" (3.2–3).

If Shem is the writer at this moment, Shaun's description a few pages later of how much better he could accomplish such a task gives an image of exactly the kind of immaterial, idealist work that the *Wake* refuses to become: "My trifolium librotto, the authordux Book of Lief, would, if given to daylight, (I hold a most incredible faith about it) far exceed what that bogus bolshy of a shame, my soamheis brother, Gaoy Fecks, is conversant with in audible black and prink" (425.20–24). The imagery here is insistently Christian, with the vaguely Trinitarian shape of the "trifolium," or shamrock clover, offering an authorial orthodoxy that creates the immortality promised in an all-redemptive Book of Life. The transposition of characters in "Lief" transforms the leaves, as in pages, that the *Wake* codes as nothing more than waste in a midden heap into the very vehicle of this salvation in a way that recalls Christ's own overcoming of his earthly body in the Resurrection. A "daylight" rather than nighttime book, it also goes beyond the "black and prink," a layering of *ink* on *print* that draws attention to the resulting blackness that Shaun (rightly, we will see) attributes to Shem. Apostrophizing "Outragedy of poetscalds! Acomedy of letters!" in the line that follows, Shaun overlooks the death that would end a tragedy in his move to comedy, which ends in marriage with the promise of children, a transition enabled by his assertion, regarding these postcards and letters, that "I have them all, tame, deep and harried, in my mine's I" (425.24–25). Any outrage that might result from the unsettling consideration of mortality is tamed via an embrace of a disembodied imagination (the mind's eye, not the body's) that, with the mind's/mine's and eye/I puns, also aligns with a perfectly self-possessed ego.

It should thus come as no surprise that this disembodiment extends to the letter itself, as we can see from Shaun's response to the request of his followers to read it. They ask, "Could you, of course, decent Lettrechaun, we knew (to change your name of not your nation) while still in the barrel, read the strangewrote anaglyptics of those shemletters patent for His Christian's Em?," to which Shaun, after proclaiming his lexical ability and denigrating the content of the letter, replies, "Flummery is what I would call it if you were to ask me to put it on a single dimension what pronounced opinion I might possibly orally have" (419.17–20, 420.1–3). While the "single dimension" of Shaun's exclusive focus on orality leads him to characterize the letter as nonsense or "flummery," the terms in which his followers' request is articulated indicate the other dimensions of the letter to which he is blind. Not only does the allusion to the printer's measure of the "Em" emphasize the medium of print, but the image of the "strangewrote anaglyptics," a reference to a white, embossed wall-covering originally made of cotton and paper pulp, once again underscores the material composition of the "shemletter." Indeed the description of the "shemletters patent for His Christian's Em" conflates Shem's name with the letter in a way that his well-known practice of writing "over every square inch of the only foolscap available, his own body," literally personifies (185.35–36). It also refers to the legal instrument of the letters patent that here grants agency and authority to the very printed materiality Shaun disregards.

The sketch that Joyce offers of Shem's reading practices formulates this agency in terms that connect with print's literal opacity. He writes of "the shuddersome spectacle of this semidemented zany amid the inspissated grime of his glaucous den making believe to read his usylessly unreadable Blue Book of Eccles, *édition de ténèbres*" (179.24–27). As *Ulysses* (the original edition of which was bound in blue paper) becomes an "unreadable" book, these lines highlight its visual aspects instead, as if to suggest that not only the image of Shem reading but the book itself is a "shuddersome spectacle." The French "édition de ténèbres," or "edition of shadows," nuances the idea of the book's unreadability by transforming its opacity from figurative to literal: the print of the book itself is as dark as the "inspissated grime of [Shem's] glaucous den." This association between opaque letters and Shem's dark den is not by chance, since we find out a few pages later that "the house of O'Shea or O'Shame" was "known as the Haunted Inkbottle" (182.30–31). The description continues, detailing that, as he reads, Shem is "turning over three sheets at a wind, telling himself delightedly, no espellor mor so, that every splurge on the vellum he blundered over was an aisling vision more gorgeous than the one before," thus expanding on the underlying forces at play in his reading (179.29–32). While the word "aisling" is Irish for a dream or vision and refers to a poetic genre in which the poet dreams of Ireland, the redundancy of the phrase "aisling vision" suggests that Shem might be experiencing a double spectacle. The fact that part of this double vision is "every splurge on the vellum," a colorful description of the marks on the book's pages, suggests that Shem is attentive to both the scenes he is imagining and his perception of the letters on which the transmission of those scenes depend. We thus might consider reading as itself a literal waking dream, not just in the sense that the reader dreamily produces mental images by deciphering linguistic signifiers, but also, and more radically, in the sense that the letters *themselves* are a magic dreamlike vision.[15]

As Shem, that "poor acheseyeld from Ailing" (148.33), or an exile with aching eyes, thus reveals the process of reading as a highly sensory action, he also illustrates that reading is always accomplished within the limits of the physical world. Indeed as the Portuguese word *espelho* or "mirror" transforms from an image-reflecting surface to a characterization of Shem as he pieces words together out of their letters in the phrase "no espellor mor so," it links the visual and the lexical and also suggests the progressive, timebound nature of spelling out words. One of the limitations the physical places on reading is that of the temporal—exactly what Shaun's "authordux Book of Lief" denies in its redemptive ambitions. Thus we also see Shem's "turning over three sheets at a wind" and his attention to the parade of his visions, which—much like the letters of his spelling—are each "more gorgeous than the one before."

The connection I am positing between the attention to individual letters and the temporal unfolding of the reading process finds an explicit—and rather pointed—articulation in the presentation of the letter's own historicity, namely the analogical relationship set up between it and the Irish *Book of Kells*. With the parody of Sir Edward Sullivan's exegesis of the origin of punctuation, however, this timeliness goes beyond a general suggestion of the antique implied in either the historical writing materials on which I focused in the previous section or in the *Wake*'s claim that the letter preceded and was itself the inspiration for the *Book of Kells*. For all the silliness in the lampoon's hilarious speculation on the four different punctuation marks used in the *Book of Kells*, it also has the very serious effects of revising the mechanism of written signification and allowing us to attend to the functioning of time at play across the spatial display of writing:

> These paper wounds, four in type, were gradually and correctly understood to mean stop, please stop, do please stop, and O do please stop respectively, and following up their one true clue, the circumflexuous wall of a singleminded men's asylum, accentuated by bi tso fb rok engl a ssan dspl itch ina,—Yard inquiries pointed out → that they ad bîn "provoked" ay fork , of à grave Brofèsor; àth é's Bréak—fast—table; ; acutely profèššionally *piquéd*, to=introduce a notion of time [upon à plane (?) sù ' ' fàç'e'] by pùnct! ingh oles (sic) in iSpace?! (124.3–12)

The rhythm that the catalogue of increasingly imploring indications to "stop" imparts to the beginning of the passage offers a sonic performance of the very temporal starting and stopping that punctuation—or "paper wounds"—is meant to produce. As the passage proceeds, however, this sonic performance of rhythm becomes a visual performance of typography whose effect is also, as the passage states, to introduce a notion of time upon a plane surface. Casting the typographical punctuation as a "hole," the lines (literally) portray the way these holes break up a homogeneous expanse of space into discrete parts that draws the sequential out of the simultaneous, the *nacheinander* out of the *nebeneinander*. In doing so they create a visual rhythm that temporalizes the spatial as the eyes follow it.[16]

When Lydia Liu makes a similar point in her discussion of the way Joyce anticipates Claude Shannon's treatment of printed language as a statistical structure in his mathematical theory of communication, she separates "the statistical properties of letter sequences and spaces" from the "'linguistic facts'" of "phonemes, semes and mythemes" that readers find in *Finnegans Wake*.[17] For her, "reading" splits into "the movement of a reading head *avant la lettre* or our eyes doing the visual scanning" and the subsequent construal of these linguistic facts (524). The appeal to the machinic "reading head" points to the way Liu's argument, like those of Theall and McLuhan mentioned earlier, moves into the abstract world of computing and cybernetics, while the ideographic potential that she locates in the phonetic alphabet through her examination of the "dancing of printed '*words of silent power*' on the page of the *Wake*" also suggests the much more temporally and spatially situated actions of sense perception that I have been showing the *Wake* itself both thematizes and performs.[18]

The literal performance in this case resonates importantly with the starting point of my argument, which, in true *Wake*an fashion, will also be its end point, namely HCE laid out on his back. For here, as Liu intimates the way our eyes track the lines of type across the space of the page, we can see that, no less than the surfeit of punctuating diacritical marks, the letters themselves also have the potential to impart a sense of the temporally sequential to the spatially simultaneous, as if, like "the stabs and foliated gashes made by the pronged instrument" with which the *Wake* describes the "paper wounds" in the lines that precede this passage (124.2–3), they too are a type of hole in the page. While the punning phrase "type of hole" at the end of the previous sentence should suggest that this idea is not so far removed from what occurs when metal shapes press into paper to form letters, we will have occasion to more closely consider the printing process in the next chapter's account of Virginia Woolf's Hogarth Press and her novel *Jacob's Room*. Here, however, as these literal holes unearth the darkness with which they punctuate this plane surface, the reader of the *Wake* faces the ultimate result of his situation in time, namely the return to a dumb materiality that temporal progress always and inescapably implies.

To close this chapter, however, the *Wake*'s material letters function as a visual index of both the space and the time of their reading and also become the site at which Shaun and Shem meet in accord. Indeed the emphasis on the sense perception of the eye and the ear in the close reading of the letter works to give access to that site in a way that revises the split between the two in their roles as the Mookse and Gripes. In that fable the narrator describes how, as night mounts, "Metamnisia was allsoonome colorform brune; citherior spane an eulande, innemorous and unnumerose. The Mookse had a sound eyes right but he could not all hear. The Gripes had light ears left yet he could but ill see. He ceased. And he ceased, tung and trit, and it was neversoever so dusk of both of them" (158.10–15). As "Metamnisia" refers, according to McHugh, to "land beyond the river," it describes an otherworldly, imaginative space that evokes the dream world produced in reading. The coming of darkness quickly turns everything into a uniform brown that obliterates all distinctions, including those between the Mookse and the Gripes, who find themselves "ceased," a rather death-like dissipation into the dusk that could, significantly, characterize the conclusion of almost every chapter in the *Wake*'s repetitive narrative cycle.

The resolving uniformity of the growing dark finds its literal manifestation in the letter, whose directions for reading echo the description of the Mookse's and Gripes's ambiguously divided sensory faculties—with one important difference. Following an injunction to "talk straight turkey meet to mate" that might describe the conditions of an act of reconciliation between the warring twins, the narrator explains that "while the ears, be we mikealls or nicholists, may sometimes be inclined to believe others the eyes, whether browned or nolensed, find it devilish hard now and again even to believe itself. *Habes aures et num videbus? Habes oculos ac mannepalpabuat?*" (113.26–30). Though, like the description of the Mookse and Gripes, these lines begin by explicitly dividing up the function of the ears and the eyes, the Latin sentences, which roughly read "Do you have ears and now you will see? And do you have eyes and might you feel?," trouble this division by introducing the third sensory faculty of touch. In doing so they map out a tactile register in which both the ear and the eye are ineffective, in which they abut the limits of their power and share a common inoperability. Formulating these lines in Latin, an ossified and so-called *dead* language that, if only more palpably than the rest of the language in the *Wake*, offers minimal association with standard auditory codes or even potential for straightforward visual recognition, suggests that reaching these ocular and auditory limits is a form of finitude tantamount to a kind of death.

These limits are exactly what the *Wake*'s letter (and, in my argument, its letters too) explores *not* in order to transcend them but in order, paradoxically and with difficulty, to remain within them. The text continues, "Drawing nearer to take our slant at [the letter] (since after all it has met with misfortune while underground), let us see all there may remain to be seen" (113.30–33). Unwittingly participating in a rhetoric of close reading, the directions describe a kind of attention that, far from eliding the physical materiality of the letter for the sense that it signifies, focuses on the ruined, hole-y nature of this materiality. These holes—what I have repeatedly tried to figure as a literal darkness—are precisely what subsumes the distinctions between the Mookse and Gripes, Shaun and Shem, eye and ear, space and time. Not only do these poles dissipate into the undifferentiation of the night, but we too might also forget about them as we train our eyes on the dark print of the *Wake*. At the same time, the fragmentariness suggested here resists an assumption that the letter (in both senses) is or could ever be fully present and, as such, also touches on the finitude and limits of the senses. In considering *Jacob's Room* in the next chapter, we will see Woolf's novel figure this finitude in terms that meditate on the page rather than print to more explicitly explore the reader's fundamental connection to and situation within the world of objects. For now, though, we can see that to touch on the dark print of *Finnegans Wake* is to depend not on the imagination or the intellect but ultimately on the body, what remains when the mind goes to sleep, exactly what we share with the inanimate matter of HCE, laid out on his back, dead to the world.

CHAPTER 4

The Pages in *Jacob's Room*

Abide with me:
Fast falls the eventide;
The shadows deepen;
     Lord, with me abide.

English hymn, popular at funerals,
quoted in *Jacob's Room*

With a nod to the embodied and even erotic mode of reading on which I have been focusing, I have to confess that, after reading Virginia Woolf's first experimental novel, I have a crush on its main character, Jacob Flanders. He is just my type. The oft-noted combination of charming awkwardness and unexplainable distinction in his appearance casts him, for me, in the mold of a young Kennedy, with the chiseled features and straight, sandy-blond hair that falls, without any effort on his part, into just the right kind of tussled foppishness. I might even go so far as to say that my protracted rereadings of Woolf's novel have been motivated by a desire to enter Jacob's room. At the same time, the repeated frustrations of my imaginative attempts to possess Jacob have revealed the way the novel works to cultivate an appreciation of what, to use the temporal vocabulary of this chapter's epigraph, merely "abiding" outside it can provide.

While this description of what I am deliberately and no doubt excessively referring to as my crush on Jacob might serve to introduce an investigation of the impossibilities of same-sex attraction or the tension between the desire to have and the desire to be, this is not, as they say, "that kind" of project. Rather my comment offers a more graphic, if personal, version of an observation made by A. S. McDowall in a 1922 review of Woolf's novel in the *Times Literary Supplement*. He writes, "We do not know Jacob as an individual, though we promptly seize his type."[1] On the one hand, McDowall's statement proclaims that the issue of knowing and relating to someone (or something) else is at the heart of Woolf's novel. On the other, its language of "seizure"—like mine of the "crush"—points to the possible violence inherent in these attempts at external knowledge, a violence that entails an immobilization of dynamic qualities. Both McDowall's and my colloquial appeal to "types" of people portray this violence as a pigeonholing, a restriction of Jacob's character to a set of static, preestablished criteria. At the same time, the language of "typing" inadvertently calls out to the printed letters that serve as the basis for my "crush" on the novel's main character. Given Woolf's almost contemporaneous inauguration of her work as a printer at the Hogarth Press, the pun is particularly apt and picks up the focus on print's mediation from the previous two chapters. As the blanks of *Jacob's Room*'s experimental page layout widen my focus from the sensory holes shared by the reader and the printed book to include the mediating function of the paper on which that print appears, they offer a way to nuance the immobilization implied in the idea of types.

It has become something of a critical commonplace to connect the experimental developments in Woolf's literary style exhibited by *Jacob's Room* to her and her husband Leonard's founding of the Hogarth Press in 1917. Most critics, however, approach the connection from an exclusively textual perspective that minimizes the operation of the book in favor of focusing on the narrative it transmits.[2] I will instead show that Woolf's experimentation with page layout often explores the novel's more general interest in subject-object relations through more specific meditations on the relationship between the reader and the page she is facing. Together with the metaphorics of pages and printing that establish and explore the continuity between subjects and objects, *Jacob's Room* also draws out the implicit role played by time in this continuity. Ultimately the novel works to map the fundamental mortality entailed in the temporality that the animate subject shares with the inanimate world. Though the issue of time's passing remains mostly tacit, mortality is a central issue running throughout the novel, from Jacob's seaside discovery of a cow's skull that opens the novel to his death in the Great War that concludes it.

As I intimated in my opening sketch, part of this consideration of the relationship between temporality and reading the novel's printed pages entails a more complicated understanding of typing or printing, which an examination of Woolf's concurrent work with the Hogarth Press will help to elaborate. More than just the production of an impression or the standardization of written form, printing in this case functions as a rather more extended and dynamic process, one

that underscores the reciprocal contact between two materials necessary to make a printed impression. It is through this extended and
reciprocal notion of printing that the novel envisions the relationship between the reader and the page. Woolf makes a preliminary
gesture—which it will be the work of this chapter to develop more
fully—at the print-based terms of this reader-page connection in "Mr.
Bennett and Mrs. Brown," the theoretical descriptions of the modernist novel's purpose and function that she pens in response to Arnold
Bennett's critical review of *Jacob's Room*. She claims that all novels
"deal with character, and that it is to *express character* . . . that the
form of the novels, so clumsy, verbose, and undramatic, so rich, elas-
tic, and alive, has been evolved. To express character, I have said;
but you will at once reflect that *the very widest interpretation* can
be put upon those words."[3] On the face of it, her comments indicate the centrality of character for the novel as well as the capacious-
ness of that category. Bringing Woolf's use of words like *express* and
character into the light cast by the historical coincidence of the inauguration of the Hogarth Press and the beginning of her literary experiments, however, suggests that her point about the novel here has at
least an implicit relationship to the occupation of printing. For the
"great novelist with composing stick in hand, Virginia Woolf inky
and determined," as J. H. Willis Jr. describes her, the words *express*
and *character* also bear the traces of the pressing of characters that
creates a printed page.[4]

As printing seems to condition (however unconsciously) Woolf's
thinking about the proper *function* of the novel, it also suggests that
the printed status of a novel is integral to its *functioning*. Not only is
the novel designed to express character in the sense of communicating
the personalities and attributes of the figures that populate its plot,
but the expression of characters is also the means by which the novel
accomplishes its aim. Moreover the language Woolf uses to describe
the effect of Mrs. Brown's character—"The impression she made was
overwhelming" (1: 323)—underscores the way a reader might experience pressure from the characters of a novel. The puns and double
entendres that I'm tracing here are meant to gesture at the way we
might consider the printed pages of *Jacob's Room* to press onto the
mind of the reader. This metaphorical pressure is not, of course, iden-
tical to the functioning of Woolf's hand press but rather functions
temporally. Building on the way our own embodiment corresponds
to the material objects in the world, the novel uses examples of both

materially sensitive and materially indifferent reading to cultivate a practice of lingering over the blank spaces on its pages, an abiding that does not disregard those pages in a rush to grasp the language they transmit.

As the lingering over pages to which *Jacob's Room* enjoins its reader is one part of the novel's larger attentiveness to the object world, it participates in the sensitivity to the material features of objects that was a major facet of the artistic and intellectual milieu in which Woolf composed her novel. Roger Fry's Omega Workshop (1913–19), for example, which functioned as a model for the Hogarth Press, offers an investment in objects that resonates with Woolf's own interest in the book. Ann Banfield has masterfully shown that Woolf's later works, particularly *To the Lighthouse* and *The Waves*, were greatly influenced by the abstractions of the postimpressionist aesthetics that Fry developed with the help of the analytic philosophy of Cambridge, yet there is another, radically concrete strain in Woolf's work that focuses on the role the object plays in mediating and constituting subjective experience.[5] The connection I develop among the Omega Workshops, the Hogarth Press, and Woolf's early experimentalism excavates this interest in the mediation of the object—and of the book-object in particular—that has been overshadowed by linking the logical abstractions in Fry's thinking of the later 1920s to Woolf's novels. I thus trace the way her literary experiments also develop out of a commitment to the physicality of objects exhibited by the Omega Workshop, a commitment that has everything to do with revealing the common temporality on the basis of which the subject is literally incorporated into the lifeless world of objects.

I

The influence of books on an understanding of relationality in *Jacob's Room* is not a chance critical charge. Books—and reading in general—function as major metaphors throughout the novel, and the narrator appeals to these tropes in a number of instances to describe interactions between people. Woolf's description of Jacob's room at Cambridge, in fact, focuses almost exclusively on the books that fill it:

> There were books enough; very few French books; but then any one who's worth anything reads just what he likes, as the mood takes him, with extravagant enthusiasm. Lives of the Duke of Wellington, for example; Spinoza; the works of Dickens; the *Faery Queen*; a

Greek dictionary with the petals of poppies pressed to silk between
the pages; all the Elizabethans. His slippers were incredibly shabby,
likes boats burnt to the water's rim. Then there were photographs
from the Greeks, and a mezzotint from Sir Joshua—all very English. The works of Jane Austen, too, in deference, perhaps, to someone else's standard. Carlyle was a prize. There were books upon the
Italian painters of the Renaissance, a *Manual of the Diseases of the
Horse*, and all the usual text-books.[6]

The narrator's claim that "any one who's worth anything reads just
what he likes" suggests that a list of Jacob's reading preferences offers
a window into the type of person he is. As such, however, she essentially looks past Jacob and any particularity of character that he might
have in her drive to "read" him. Her commentary on his possession
of the works of Austen, for instance, is meant to explain what might
seem an anomalous choice for a young man otherwise interested in
titles of a more "masculine" bent, though it also indicates that the
narrator approaches Jacob's books with some preconceived notions,
a set of expectations she is looking to the books to fulfill. Indeed the
narrator's observation that Jacob has "all the usual textbooks" points
explicitly to a predetermined standard by which she is judging him.
She limits him, that is, to a manifestation of a general, established
type, what we might call the "Cambridge gentleman." By developing her judgment of Jacob through a consideration of the books in
his room, however, she also discounts their status as objects in favor
of focusing exclusively on the intersubjective knowledge she is trying
to glean. As she transforms the books into signifiers of the type by
which she believes she comprehends Jacob, she abstracts their content
from their format and effectively flattens them in a way not unlike
her stereotyping of Jacob himself. Not only this, but she does not at
all distinguish between the books and the other media forms in the
room—the photographs and the mezzotint, for example—but indis-
criminately treats them as part of a larger text she is reading in her
effort to seize Jacob's character.

An earlier moment in the novel offers a resonant situation that
allows me to interrogate this epistemological approach more specifically and to show that such an indifference to material objects is also
bound up with readerly impatience, an insistence on minimizing the
time spent reaching a conclusion. In a scene that recalls the description of Mrs. Brown in "Mr. Bennett and Mrs. Brown," Jacob is trav-
eling to Cambridge in a railway car with an elderly lady. Nervous
about being shut up alone with a young man ("It is a fact that men are

dangerous," she thinks), the elderly woman eyes Jacob to gauge the situation: "She read half a column of her newspaper; then stealthily looked over the edge to decide the question of safety by the infallible test of appearance. . . . She would like to offer him her paper. But do young men read the *Morning Post*? She looked to see what he was reading—the *Daily Telegraph*" (21, ellipsis original). The close juxtaposition of the explicitly described act of reading "half a column" of the newspaper and the kind of judgment the narrator codes, with biting irony, as "the infallible test of appearance" draws a clear link between the two. Like the narrator in Jacob's room, Mrs. Norman regards both her and Jacob's newspapers not as the bearer of signs to be read but as *themselves* signs to be read. They thus do not function as literal texts that impart accounts of the day's current events but as figurative texts that indicate her and Jacob's membership in certain social groups: Jacob is, for Mrs. Norman, the type of person who reads the *Daily Telegraph* rather than the *Morning Post*.[7] This moment makes clear in a way that the scene in Jacob's room does not, however, that one mechanism for this kind of typecasting is Mrs. Norman's disregard of the newspaper's status as an object composed of paper and ink. The way she "look[s] over the edge" of her newspaper underscores this point as it suggests the extent to which the figurative acts of reading themselves overlook the boundaries and edges of the material they are meant to decipher.

The narrator provides a commentary on this interaction: "Nobody sees any one as he is, let alone an elderly lady sitting opposite a strange young man in a railway carriage. They see a whole—they see all sorts of things—they see themselves" (22). As she notes that Mrs. Norman projects her own assumptions and opinions onto Jacob, she describes the kind of relationality that recognizes the other as merely an extension of the self. Indeed, she reflects, "presumably he was in some way or other—to her at least—nice, handsome, interesting, distinguished, well built, like her own boy" (22). The rhythmic string of rather vacuous adjectives illustrates that typing is a hasty, almost reckless process that functions less to contemplate and recognize Jacob than it does to *disregard* him; the equation with "her own boy" makes explicit the way she ultimately looks past Jacob and replaces him with a figure from her own worldview and experience. When the narrator offers a further description of Mrs. Norman's perusal of Jacob, we see another example of this hurried process: "Taking note of socks (loose), of tie (shabby), she once more reached his face. She dwelt upon his mouth.

The lips were shut. The eyes bent down, since he was reading. All was firm, yet youthful, indifferent, unconscious—as for knocking one down! No, no, no!" (21). Much like her treatment of the newspapers, Mrs. Norman here treats Jacob's body and clothes as a text to be read. As the terseness of her parenthetical conclusions indicates, she does not stop to actually observe him as much as she relies on generalized, ready-made criteria that allow her to interpret her perceptions as quickly as possible. She doesn't, that is, *take any time* to really look at Jacob. We might use a term more germane to printing (and Woolf's conception of character) to say that the impression Jacob makes on Mrs. Norman is effectively the impression she places onto him.

We can extend the analogy by noting that the narrator's description of Mrs. Norman's inspection itself proceeds by separate phrases or short sentences that trace Jacob's appearance from bottom to top, which might recall the step-by-step, word-by-word progression by which a reader pieces together the meaning of a sentence. If each of the details of Jacob's appearance thus functions as a figurative letter that Mrs. Norman deciphers to access some more general idea, might the literal act of reading then also rely on the same kind of impulsive impressions at work in Mrs. Norman's attempt to decipher Jacob? Could the reader of a text be rushing to impress discursive meaning onto what we might call the "literal figures" that fill the page? By drawing attention to its own material pages, *Jacob's Room* offers a different fantasy of reading, one that, like the reading of embodiment developed in my discussions of *Ulysses* and *Finnegans Wake*, spends a bit more time thinking about what's involved in deciphering letters on a page. The novel uses the figures of its pages to literally space out the quick drive to cognition and interpretation and exhibit the ways reading itself is embroiled with time's passing. This materially aware and temporally sensitive reading ultimately functions as a model for a relationality that works rather differently from the ways the narrator and Mrs. Norman act.

The narrator's further commentary on Mrs. Norman's report of Jacob—the fact that "one must do the best one can" with it—characterizes this different kind of relationality when she makes an oblique (if unintentional) gesture at the role objects play in intersubjective knowledge. "It is no use trying to sum people up," Woolf writes. "One must follow hints, not exactly what is said, nor yet entirely what is done" (22). Precisely because she cannot "sum people up," the narrator calls for a *larger* view of her characters than just what they say or do. The "hints" she "must follow" thus paradoxically *go beyond* words and actions, those traditional markers of subjectivity that seem to offer themselves up most readily to be epistemologically comprehended and interpreted in an act of reading. Though the narrator leaves it unarticulated, this "beyond" includes the attention to these characters' place in the world of objects, which the novel's play with page and print layout will elaborate in the temporal terms at which I've been gesturing.

II

The attention the novel draws to its pages falls in line with contemporaneous trends in art production of which Woolf had a very intimate knowledge and which she put to work in her own printing practice and literary composition. Roger Fry, one of the high priests of Bloomsbury and a close friend of the Woolfs, had started the Omega Workshops in 1913 to further explore the style of postimpressionism following the exhibitions he had organized in 1910 and 1912 and to provide artists with a cooperative environment that would support them financially. The Workshop was a place in which artists supplemented their fine art activities (such as painting) with work in the applied art of interior design by producing decorated objects such as pottery, picture frames, and furniture. In "Preface to the Omega Workshops Catalog" (1914), Fry describes the project: "The Omega Workshops, Limited, is a group of artists who are working with the object of allowing free play to the delight in creation in the making of objects for common life. They refuse to spoil the expressive quality of their work by sand-papering it down to a shop finish, in the belief that the public has at least seen through the humbug of machine-made imitation of works of art."[8] By lavishing bright colors and loud patterns onto the surfaces of "common objects," the Workshop called attention to individual objects in a way than ran counter to the homogenizing effects of industrialized mass production.[9] In "Prospectus for the Omega Workshop" of 1913, for example, Fry specifies that the Omega artists "endeavour merely to discover a possible utility for real artistic intervention in the things of daily life" (199). These "things" are not in the service of abstract, timeless philosophical tenets; rather they are meant to intertwine themselves into the activities of living—an intertwining that *Jacob's Room* seeks to achieve by underscoring the temporality shared by reader and book.

Significantly the Hogarth Press was, in many respects, modeled after the tenets of the Omega, and not only because Omega's joy in production also finds an analogue in Virginia's own printing practice. ("The fascination is something extreme," she writes to her sister about setting Hogarth's first projects.)[10] Rather, as David H. Porter observes in his short work on the cross-pollination between the two outfits, Fry's emphasis on short, illustrated books in limited editions "foreshadows what [Leonard and Virginia] themselves would seek in many Hogarth Press books."[11]

More specifically both Hogarth's first publication, *Two Stories*, which includes Woolf's first experimental story, "The Mark on the Wall," and the subsequent printing of her later "Kew Gardens" included pictures printed from woodcuts made by Omega artists Dora Carrington and Vanessa Bell, respectively. Woolf was quite drawn to the illustrations; in a letter to Carrington, she observes that the woodcuts "make the book much more interesting than it would have been without [them]" (*Letters* 2:162). She goes on to comment that the woodcuts have shown her and Leonard that they "must make a practice of always having pictures" in their publications; she even proposes, in a letter written to Fry a few days later, the idea of "books of pictures only, reproductions of new pictures" (2:163, 166). Porter traces the persistence in Virginia's mind of this idea of a book of woodcuts through various obstacles (for instance, their original press was not very good with illustrations, and attempts at buying a bigger press were repeatedly stalled) and shows that what he calls this "idée fixe" ultimately resulted in a volume called *Twelve Original Woodcuts*, all by Fry, that came out in 1921, one year before the publication of *Jacob's Room* (26).

Although *Jacob's Room* was Woolf's first unillustrated book for the Hogarth Press, the influence of these woodcuts persists in subtle ways that indicate the novel's alignment with her interest in pictures and Omega's emphasis on objects. At the end of a description of London at night, the narrator appeals to a "picture book" that clearly draws from the illustrated publications that the Hogarth Press had been producing. Interestingly a significant gap on the page (which I preserve below) immediately follows before she launches into an account of Jacob in his city apartment:

> Shawled women carry babies with purple eyelids; boys stand at street corners; girls look across the road—rude illustrations, pictures in a book whose pages we turn over and over as if we should at last find

THE MARK ON THE WALL
By
VIRGINIA WOOLF

Perhaps it was the middle of January in the present year that I first looked up and saw the mark on the wall. In order to fix a date it is necessary to remember what one saw. So now I think of the fire; the steady film of yellow light upon the page of my book; the three chrysanthemums in the round glass bowl on the mantelpiece. Yes, it must have been the winter time, and we had just finished our tea, for I remember that I was smoking a cigarette when I looked up and saw the mark on the wall for the first time. I looked up through the smoke of my cigarette and my eye lodged for a moment upon the burning coals, and that old fancy of the crimson flag flapping from the castle tower came into my mind, and I thought of the cavalcade of red knights riding up the side of the black rock. Rather to my relief the sight of the mark interrupted the fancy, for it is an old fancy, an automatic

Figure 6.   Virginia Woolf, Two Stories (Richmond, UK: Hogarth Press, 1917), 19. Courtesy of Houghton Library at Harvard University, *EC9 W8827 917t.

what we look for. Every face, every shop, bedroom window, public-house, and dark square is a picture feverishly turned—in search of what? It is the same with books. What do we seek through millions of pages? Still hopefully turning the pages—oh, here is Jacob's room.

He sat at the table reading the *Globe*. (77)

As the passage describes an epistemological quest, a search for meaning or significance that functions as an allegory of the kind of reading I examined in the previous section, its repetitive, unanswered questions and the rhythmic phrases draw out the "feverish" speed of this quest only to interrupt it—indeed to interrupt it by drawing attention to the page.

At the same time, however, the passage turns the "pictures" Woolf had wanted to make a habit of including in her publications to metaphorical purpose and slows things down by transitioning from thinking about the page as a metaphor for each of the external world's multiple scenes to attending to the literal leaves of a book. The block of text created by the spacing on the page recalls the square woodcuts that provided illustrations in the previous Hogarth publications, and the deictic "here" makes the obvious double referent of "Jacob's room" more than just a convenient coincidence. Pointing within the narrative to Jacob's lodgings, the close proximity of "here" to the dash that accentuates the space of the page within the development of the sentence suggests that it is also pointing to the page we are now facing. Not only this—and perhaps this is so obvious a point that it barely needs articulating—but the immediate break in the narrative that follows this moment also puts the reader in somewhat of the same position as the narrator. Here, it seems, is also *Jacob's Room.*

This expansion of readerly attention resonates with the general effect of the work produced by the Omega Workshops; in his preface to Isabelle Anscombe's *Omega and After*, the photographer Howard Grey describes how, with Omega art and design, "one looks past the paintings on the walls to the walls themselves," which might also describe how the reader looks past the words on the page to the page itself.[12] In the catalogue for the Second Post-Impressionist Exhibition (1912), Fry offers a more theoretical articulation of this phenomenon that also sheds some light on Woolf's novel: "[Postimpressionist] artists do not seek to give what can, after all, be but a pale reflex of actual appearance, but to arouse conviction of a new and definite reality. They do not seek to imitate form, but to create form; not to imitate life, but to find an equivalent for life."[13] While Fry goes on to appeal to postimpressionism's "logical structure," an abstract and theoretical phrase that seems to belie the painting's own position in the "real world," the emphasis on the creation rather than the imitation of form recalls the Omega Workshop's investment in objects. We thus might read Fry's statement as a description of the way a postimpressionist painting draws attention to its own status as a part of reality rather than simply representing it in paint. The emphasis on real experience rather than mimesis correlates with the temporality that

I have begun to trace, the way *Jacob's Room* is drawing attention to the reader's multidimensional experience of the novel that necessarily takes place in time.

In doing so the novel emphasizes its own status as an object and revises the way we might understand our own turning of the pages. That is, while the description of turning the pages "over and over" describes the habitual action by which we proceed through a novel, the gap in the passage works to break this habit. In this light the "turn[ing] over and over" refers less to our progression *through* this narrative or these pages than to our inspection *of* them. Turning "over and over," that is, could mean that we examine both sides of the page—recto and verso, front and back. As such the page takes on the dimension of depth, an almost sculptural nature that allows it to become an important and perhaps even delightful object in its own right—not unlike an Omega vase. The description of Jacob that follows the gap draws further attention to the multidimensionality of the book but in a somewhat different way: "He sat at the table reading the *Globe*. The pinkish sheet was spread flat before him. He propped his face in his hand, so that the skin was wrinkled in deep folds" (77). The newspaper's pink color makes it of a piece with the skin of his face, whose "deep folds" recall the manipulations a newspaper undergoes in both its production and its consumption. Not only this, but the ephemerality of the newspaper finds an analogue in the suggestion of aging in the image of Jacob's "wrinkled" skin, which aligns this material depth with the sense of temporality at which I have been gesturing and which I will develop further in the next section. The fact that the paper is "spread flat before him" describes the opening of a book that we must also "spread flat" in order to read. The novel thus asks us to recall the way we laid it flat in order to come face-to-face with the page we are reading, an action that presupposes that the novel itself possesses a certain volume and that once again reveals the bodily resonance traced by my discussions of *Ulysses* and *Finnegans Wake*.

Indeed on opening Woolf's novel for the first time, the reader finds her attention drawn to the materials that constitute its format, as Jacob's mother, Betty Flanders, sits on the beach writing a letter: "'So of course,' wrote Betty Flanders, pressing her heels rather deeper in the sand, 'there was nothing for it but to leave.' Slowly welling from the point of her gold nib, pale blue ink dissolved the full stop; for there the pen stuck; her eyes fixed, and tears slowly filled them" (3). As the words Mrs. Flanders is writing lack context and referentiality ("there is nothing" yet for them to refer to, we might say), they effectively act as empty signifiers that, like the welling blot, underscore the ink and letters on the opening page. The fact that her eyes "fixed" suggests the way the page and ink arrest the easy movement from one word to another that could characterize the kind of hurried reading with which I began my argument. While Mrs. Flanders inadvertently allows her gaze to linger over the marks she is making and her eyes fill with tears, the insistent forward-marching progress of that readerly stance transforms into an intensification or deepening of the moment's very passing. As if to suggest an otherwise veiled dynamism, Woolf writes, "The entire bay quivered; the lighthouse wobbled; and she had the illusion that the mast of Mr. Connor's little yacht was bending like a wax candle in the sun" (1).

As the objects in the world seem to take on agency and even vitality, Mrs. Flanders's response is, interestingly, to close her eyes: "She winked quickly. . . . She winked again. The mast was straight; the waves were regular; the lighthouse was upright; but the blot had spread" (3). She thus imposes order and regularity onto the world, so that the objects in it conform to her expectations, to some ideal type, we might say again, by summoning up the standardizing forces of her intellect. A few lines later she shirks this kind of sensitivity altogether when she goes on "scribbl[ing], ignoring the full stop," which contrasts with the earlier "fixed" nature of her eyes (3). It is almost as if she wants to treat the appearance of her letter with the material disregard that the standardization of print normally facilitates.[14] Mrs. Flanders thus stands in direct contrast to Woolf herself, whose work as a printer draws her attention both to her own body and to the much more fluid appearance of words on a page. Woolf complains in a letter that her "back aches with stooping over those infernal trays and tossing 'u's into t boxes and 'y's into 'j's."[15] In another letter she uses language that recalls the "wobbling" that Mrs. Flanders experiences to draw a direct connection between her printing and the inscrutability of her handwriting: "I have just finished setting up the whole of Mr Eliots poem [*The Waste Land*] with my own hands: You see how my hand trembles. Don't blame your eyes" (*Letters* 3: 56). The long stretches of time she spent printing was something that made her all too aware of the appearance of writing. As the rest of this chapter will show, the experiments with print and page layout in *Jacob's Room* have a similar effect. By arresting the reader's eyes and asking her to linger over the material facets of the book in a way that

Betty Flanders refuses to do, the novel explores a dynamic relationality with the phenomenal world of objects based in the very temporality of reading that it works to underscore.

III

The narrator of *Jacob's Room* explicitly enjoins the reader to just such a lingering when she exhorts "Let us consider letters" (71) in the very middle of the novel (an auspicious position for a meditation on a medium). The pun is obvious: let us think about the correspondence we write to each other as well as the alphabetic building blocks of written signification. Her discussion is insistently ambivalent, as she swings back and forth between celebrating letters and perceiving their shortcomings: "Life would split asunder without them. 'Come to tea, come to dinner, what's the truth of the story? Have you heard the news? life in the capital is gay; the Russian dancers . . . .' These are our stays and props. These lace our days together and make of life a perfect globe. And yet, and yet . . . " (73, ellipses original). The phrase "stays and props" points to the structuring effect these letters have, as if they keep our life from "split[ting] asunder" by giving it a rigid scaffolding. The representative quotations from the letters portray this scaffolding as a function of social convention: teas and dinners organize our day in the same way that gossip processes and judges our actions. The perfection of the "globe" thus created is a bit suspect, as the repeated "and yet" casts the benefit of this structure in an uncertain light. Indeed having one's life "lace[d]" together hints at the immobilization of which letters are the purveyors.

It is important to underscore the letters' function as purveyors rather than creators of these immobilizing structures (to which a careful examination of the narrator's declaration points), since the narrator's expansion on her ambivalence also expands on the role played by letters themselves rather than the messages they contain: "Am I doomed all my days to write letters, send voices [via the telephone], which fall upon the tea-table, fade upon the passage, making appointments, while life dwindles, to come and dine?" (73). As the narrator lingers over the communications themselves and emphasizes how the letters "fall upon the tea-table" and how the voices "fade upon the passage," she effectively separates them from the messages they carry. As they "fall" and "fade," words that indicate diminishment and disappearance, the letters and the voices have much more in common with the temporal "dwindl[ing]" of life than they do with the dinner appointments that "lace our days together and make of life a perfect globe." Thus when the narrator states, "Yet letters are venerable; and the telephone valiant, for the journey is a lonely one, and if bound together by notes and telephones we went in company, perhaps—who knows?—we might talk by the way" (73), she introduces subtle but profound changes in the kind of binding at play here. Most obviously, rather than amassing "our days" or "life" in an abstract perfect globe, the letters here bind people together *in their shared temporality*.

This binding of people together through their mutual place in the external, temporal world departs from the disregard for objects—letters and books included—that I've examined in previous examples. It also contrasts with the portrayal of the most traditional figure for interpersonal binding, namely marriage. The narrator says, "Tears . . . made Mrs. Jarvis, the rector's wife, think at church, while the hymn-tune played and Mrs. Flanders bent low over her little boys' heads, that marriage is a fortress and widows stray solitary in the open fields" (3). While the "fortress" of marriage might be meant to protect, this protection commits its own kind of violence, as it is a hemming-in and a confinement that functions to limit and restrict, even to immobilize. The interpersonal relationship thus cuts off relations to the outside world that Mrs. Jarvis views as dangerous and violent.[16] Interestingly it is Mrs. Jarvis who, despite her claim that widows "stray solitary in open fields," ultimately does just that; in the next chapter Mrs. Jarvis, though herself married, "walked on the moor when she was unhappy" (19). In a moment of ambiguous free indirect discourse, the narrator offers a fuller description of Mrs. Jarvis's experiences on the moor that portrays a different attitude to and relationship with the outside world, one in which the reader is allowed to participate as well:

> Yes, yes, when the lark soars; when the sheep, moving a step or two onwards, crop the turf, and at the same time, set their bells tinkling; when the breeze first blows, then dies down, leaving the cheek kissed; when the ships on the sea seem to cross each other and pass on as if drawn by an invisible hand; when there are distant concussions in the air and phantom horsemen galloping, ceasing; when the horizon swims blue, green, emotional—then Mrs. Jarvis, heaving a sigh, thinks to herself, "If only someone could give me . . . if I could give someone . . . " But she does not know what she wants to give, nor who could give it to her. (19, ellipses original)

I quote this passage in full not only for the pleasure of seeing Woolf's lyricism in full force but also because, as the piling up of dependent clauses clearly delays the arrival of a concluding predicate, the passage grammatically encodes Mrs. Jarvis's uncertainty for the reader to experience as well.

More interesting than the simple observation that both Mrs. Jarvis and the reader confront the limits of their knowledge and their ability to penetrate into the situation is the question of what, given these limits, Mrs. Jarvis and the reader *can access*. The descriptions of the natural world surrounding Mrs. Jarvis on the moor hint at an answer. It is not necessarily (or not only) that her experience on the moors indicates to Mrs. Jarvis a larger, more "elementary" relationality that goes beyond the strictures of social convention (what would be a romanticized vision of the landscape and its effect). Rather the explicit emphasis in each of these clauses on constant movement and change points to the fundamentally mobile—indeed fundamentally temporalized—relationship that exists between her and the objects that constitute the outside world. That is, her relationship to the lark, the breeze, or even the ships in the sea is not a static one but one that is inescapably (and pleasurably) dynamic. The reader also experiences some of this pleasure as the insistent rhythm imparted by the repeated commas and semicolons stylistically mimics the very dynamism they are describing. Moreover when the narrator uses an ellipsis to finish Mrs. Jarvis's thoughts at the end of the passage, the novel offers the reader a complementary experience of dynamic movement. As the ellipsis leaves space for the reader to imagine all the possibilities that would finish the sentence (as a concrete predicate would not), it also, startlingly, uses the conventions of print to dissolve the full stops in a way reminiscent of Betty Flanders's opening letter. Here, however, rather than fixing the eye to draw attention to the act of perception, the ellipsis tracks the movement of the eye across the line of type to disclose its mobility in the act of reading. While the book itself might be a static object in a way that the lark, the sheep, or the boats are not, the reader nonetheless experiences the supple dynamism of his own relationship with the page, a situation not unlike the moment in which the narrator observes "Here is Jacob's room."

As this moment brings the issue of temporality and dynamism more clearly to the fore than any of the previous discussions, it allows me to underscore that time is precisely what links the animated human subject and the inanimate world. The rest of this chapter thus continues to develop this temporal imbrication of the animate and the inanimate by looking at the ways the novel repeatedly insists on the mediating role played by the world's dynamic temporality through the figures of its printed pages. For the ellipses come precisely when Mrs. Jarvis is meditating on the exclusively human sociality beyond which the novel allows us to expand. That is, the ellipses and the dynamic, temporalized relationship they both intimate and facilitate supplement the strictly intersubjective terms in which Mrs. Jarvis is thinking. The interaction is not between two human subjects who are giving to each other here but rather between an animate human and the inanimate external world. For the reader of novels more specifically, the page becomes the index of this inanimate world. Importantly this supplementation depends on the blank spaces of the page and in the narrative and on the ellipses and the way they accentuate (even punctuate) those spaces. The novel thus extends the role of printing as a model of a relationship to the external world, since it is precisely the functioning of print that facilitates this temporalized rapport. Indeed standard critical claims for the novel's inherent unknowability seem to resonate more with the fortress-like relations by which Mrs. Jarvis describes marriage than with the actual relationship that the novel sets up between the reader and its printed pages.

IV

The novel provides an even more explicit treatment of this dynamic, printed relationality in the late-night discussion between Jacob and his friend Simeon at Cambridge, a moment that is, without a doubt, one of human intimacy and interpersonal connection. It occurs in the final moment of chapter 3, which is singular in the novel for being one of the few places that includes additional gaps *within* the narration of a moment rather than just between separate moments. I quote the first half of the scene in full:

> " . . . Julian the Apostate . . . ." Which of them said that and the other words murmured around it? But about midnight there sometimes rises, like a veiled figure suddenly woken, a heavy wind; and this now flapping through Trinity lifted unseen leaves and blurred everything. "Julian the Apostate"—and then the wind. Up go the elm branches, out blow the sails, the old schooners rear and plunge, the grey waves in the hot Indian Ocean tumble sultrily, and then all falls flat again.
>
> So, if the veiled lady stepped through the Courts of Trinity, she now drowsed once more, all her draperies about her, her head against a pillar.
>
> "Somehow it seems to matter."

The low voice was Simeon's.
    The voice was even lower that answered him. The sharp tap of a
pipe on the mantelpiece canceled the words. And perhaps Jacob only
said "hum," or said nothing at all. True, the words were inaudible.
It was the intimacy, a sort of spiritual suppleness, when mind prints
upon mind indelibly. (34, ellipses original)

The quoted reference with which the narrator opens the vignette hints
at the basis for the materially sensitive and temporally dynamic reading that I have been trying to develop. As the Roman emperor who
came to power after Constantine in 361, Julian rejected Christianity
in favor of a return to paganism and thus replaced a religion of transcendence based on the word with one based on the importance of
earthly elements. As such he stands as a synecdoche for an embrace of
the worldliness of the material instead of—or at least in addition to—
the abstraction of the linguistic.[17] (When the narrator observes that
"the words were inaudible," she implicitly suggests that this intimate
interaction between Simeon and Jacob does not depend on linguistic exchange.) Moreover the ellipses that frame Julian's name extend
the typographical spacing that borders the vignette into the narration
itself, as the novel highlights the way the worldly material of the page
functions as an agent in the transmission of this scene.

    This emphasis on the page occurs again, this time more obviously,
a few lines later, when the language that the narrator can only just
make out is set off in a way that the rest of the dialogue in the novel
is not. That is, Simeon's comment "Somehow it seems to matter" is
surrounded by the quotation marks that usually indicate speech and
also by the white space of the page that functions as an expansion of
the ellipses around the name of Julian the Apostate. The novel thus
suggests that the blankness of the page itself somehow seems to matter. As opposed to Simeon's "low voice," the space of the page—coming, as I have observed, in the middle of a section of narrative rather
than on its borders—jumps out at the reader and draws attention to
the facets of the book that usually go unnoticed in the act of reading. The pun on "matter" in Simeon's statement should also resound
in the space surrounding its type, since we might think of the blank
lines as an exhibition of an amorphous and deliberately inarticulate
substance, a display of the silent page that flaunts the very opacity
and ultimate inaccessibility that limit the reader's (and analogically
the narrator's) attempts at full comprehension. More than just offering a model of the kind of interpersonal relationship that the reader is

meant to mimic, the novel once again—and even more deliberately—extends these relations to the book itself as the blankness of the page becomes the means by which it engenders a similarly intimate rapport between the reader and the book.

The temporality implicit in the relationship between the reader and the materiality of the page becomes clearer when considered in light of the specific earthly phenomena that the narrator enumerates. The imagery of the wind and the water suggests the elemental mobility of which the world's materiality consists, the constant if sometimes imperceptible motion that highlights the transience to which every material phenomenon is subject. Moreover the fact that the "flapping" of the wind "blurred everything" indicates the lack of distinction between the human and the nonhuman, an indistinguishability that the personification of the "heavy wind" in the "veiled figure" or "veiled lady" makes rather explicit. Even more to the point, the "leaves" that this wind "lifts" quietly evoke the pages to which the typographical layout also draws attention, as if to suggest that, just as Jacob and Simeon's conversation is not occurring in an ideal, timeless vacuum, neither is the reader's awareness of the page separate from the external world's implicitly temporal mobility. Rather it is intimately and inextricably bound up with it.

The narrator's explicit use of a printing metaphor to describe the rather worldly interaction between Jacob and Simeon—she calls it "the intimacy, a sort of spiritual suppleness, when mind prints upon mind indelibly"—offers in condensed form an overt endorsement of the repeated connections that I've been drawing between the functioning of the novel's printed pages and a dynamic, supple mode of relationality. At the same time, the terms of this description fundamentally reimagine the very notion of printing by reframing it in explicit terms of reciprocity and flexibility. In the first place, the preposition *upon* (that most Merleau-Pontean part of speech) grammatically condenses the mutual exchange at play here, the way, for example, the narrator is initially unable to tell Jacob and Simeon apart when she asks "Which of them said that and the other words murmured round it?" Casting Jacob and Simeon's relationship as the kind of pre-positional affiliation in which it is impossible to tell who initiates or dominates the interaction, the narrator extends this mutuality and reciprocity to the action of printing itself. That is, while *to print* is normally a transitive verb in which the object receives the action of the subject—Virginia prints a page—the preposition *upon* suggests the extent to which the ostensibly one-way process of printing might be understood as a reciprocal, two-way action.

As this revised understanding becomes a model for skewing standard ideas of subject-object relations by breaking down the division between the two categories, it paves the way for a consideration of printing as distinctly more supple than the suggestions of fixity with which we usually associate it. Though I will address the significance of this scene's explicitly mental context in a moment, I want to begin approaching this more complex understanding of the printing metaphor—which, for someone like Woolf, whose afternoons with a hand press sensitized her to the subtle dynamics of pressing type to paper, can be neither arbitrary nor insignificant—by returning to the work with woodcuts that so delighted and fascinated Woolf from her first two Hogarth publications onward. Porter reads the multiple references to a book of woodcuts in Woolf's diary and letters from 1917, when she first conceived of the project, to 1921, when she produced Fry's *Twelve Original Woodcuts*, as an indication that "the idea of a book of woodcuts continued to haunt her mind" (24), and I have already suggested that the blocks of text created by the experimental page layout in *Jacob's Room* signal the persistence of the woodcuts in Woolf's imagination. Woolf's description in a letter to Carrington of the problems that she and Leonard had in printing from woodcuts allows us to hypothesize about the extent to which they might have more fundamentally influenced her understanding of the mechanics of printing that she mobilizes in the metaphors: "Our difficulty was that the margins would mark; we bought a chisel, and chopped away, I am afraid rather spoiling one edge" (*Letters* 2:162). In a letter to her sister, Woolf explains more succinctly that Carrington "didn't cut the margins [around each image] low enough" (2:168). Here the cut of the wood all too obviously "seems to matter."

In these comments Woolf shows how receptive she was to the demands of printing with woodcuts, a process that is different from printing with bits of metal type because of the distinct way each is created. With metal type, molten lead is poured into a mold, which creates a surface that is mostly recessed except for the minimal amount of metal jutting out in the shape of a letter. Printing with metal type thus becomes a process of inking and pressing a relatively small surface area into the page. The woodcut, on the other hand, is formed by carving a negative image into a block of wood that leaves a raised pattern to receive the ink, a process in which the Woolfs' stopgap remedy participates rather obviously. This carving process results in a much larger amount of surface area receiving the ink and coming into contact with the paper. Indeed the surface that is used to print with a woodcut is in effect flat with grooves carved *into it*, exactly the reverse of the protruding metal on which letterpress relies. Printing with a woodcut is thus much less about pressing a sharp, refined bit of metal *into* the page than it is about pressing a smooth, flat surface *onto* the page. The shift in preposition signals the way printing transforms from a kind of penetration into a kind of interaction, one that reveals the agency of the paper in the process of producing a mark or image—precisely because the woodcut does not work via an immobilizing bite or, to use vocabulary from earlier in this argument, via an arresting impression.

If I go on at length about the way woodcuts show that, far from being a merely passive or receptive object, paper actually pushes back, it is in order to draw out the material dynamics behind the mental action implicated in the narrator's telling metaphor. The fact that it is two minds printing on each other intimates the extent to which we might consider reading, that intellectual act that explicitly engages with material print, in terms similar to the interaction between type and paper just described. This is not to claim that reading is materially the same as the act of printing, that the reader's mind receives a literal impression. Rather I want to suggest that, in the same way that the characters on the page are produced via an interaction between type and page, these lines are imagining reading as an *analogous interaction*, one that we can explain by thinking about the adverb *indelibly* that describes Jacob and Simeon's reciprocally printing minds. As the *indelibly* suggests their minds remain in contact with each other over time, it singles out temporal extension as what allows them to print onto and influence each other.

It is this indelible temporality that both characterizes the kind of protracted reading that I have been developing and draws out the dynamism or suppleness of print that the discussion of printing's mechanics left more implicit. Since both print and printing depend on and are bound up with the passing of time, they are not nearly as rigid as we might imagine. But, as I have intimated in my readings of Mrs. Flanders and Mrs. Jarvis and as I will continue to develop as I bring this argument to a close, it is only a reading that involves a lingering and maintaining in thought, a "turn[ing] over and over," to use another line from the novel, that can be sensitive to this obscure

dynamism. The "turn[ing] over and over" that previously referred
to the depth of the page, its constitution of a recto and a verso, here
takes on its own metaphorical cast as it describes the mental action
of lingering that might result from the emphasis I have been placing on the physical, perceptual aspects of reading. And it is precisely
these perceptual aspects that, to make another pun, put us in touch
with print, since, just as the reader holds the book in his hand, he also
holds it in his mind, turns it "over and over" in contemplation, rather
than forging ahead with readerly egotism to imprint a fixed meaning
or interpretation onto it.

V

The nexus of reading, time, and the worldly materiality of the printed
page that *Jacob's Room* has allowed me to trace ultimately links up
with the novel's central concern with mortality. In doing so it develops what I have been calling "the death of the book" by pointing to
the living subject's own status as an object, its implicit and ultimately
unavoidable correspondence with the external world's lifelessness. A
scene in which Jacob and his friend Timmy Durant are sailing around
the Scilly Isles off the coast of England makes this particularly clear
by returning us to the skewed division between subjects and objects
entailed in the temporal sensitivity I've been examining. While the
resolute refusal of these kinds of subject-object relations that they
exhibit in the majority of their journey indicates the difficulty of
countenancing this novel's ultimate lesson, the narrator nonetheless
describes the following setting:

> The Scilly Isles now appeared as if directly pointed at by a golden fin-
> ger issuing from a cloud; and everybody knows how portentous that
> sight is, and how these broad rays, whether they light upon the Scilly
> Isles or upon tombs of crusaders in cathedrals, always shake the very
> foundations of skepticism and lead to jokes about God.

> "Abide with me:
> Fast falls eventide;
> The shadows deepen;
> Lord, with me abide,"

> sang Timmy Durant.
>   "At my place we used to have a hymn which began

> Great God, what do I see and hear?"
>   said Jacob. (38–39)

The sight of the external world leads to particularly telling hymn lyrics, however jokingly quoted. Jacob's line, for instance, asks a question that is quite apt for a consideration of the relationship to the page which, with its indented print, we all too obviously see at this moment. Moreover as Timmy's hymn suggests the way visions of the external world have the potential to disarm the critical faculty and cause him to merely "abide" in the experience, it plays on the temporal extension I have been developing and which, I have suggested, the page spacing also asks of the novel's reader. Abiding is itself not so much an action as a restriction of action, an active passivity that describes as much the situation of Timmy and Jacob in the face of these visions as it does the objects they are seeing. The division between perceived objects and perceiving subjects does not apply here, as Timmy and Jacob's "abiding" unveils their place in an inanimate world that is not centered around their own subjectivities. As the description continues, however, and recounts how "the drone of the tide in the caves came across the water, low, monotonous, like the voice of some one talking to himself," it paints a picture of a world—which *The Waves* will take as its center—completely indifferent to Timmy's and Jacob's perceptions of it (39). The hymn that Jacob sings in response—"Rock of Ages, cleft for me; / Let me hide myself in thee"—appeals to a notion of Christian redemption that indicates the extent to which this disclosure of his place in an impersonal, inanimate world is tantamount to a kind of death. At the same time, however, *Jacob's Room* withholds any such redemption for its reader but rather insists that we recognize—and linger over—our own continuity with the inanimate page space that frames the hymns.

With this bookish insistence on death and mortality in mind, it should come as no surprise to see the violence with which Timmy and Jacob treat books—and the external, inanimate world in general. Jacob returns to the book after a brief swim in the sea: "The seat in the boat was positively hot, and the sun warmed his back as he sat naked with a towel in his hand, looking at the Scilly Isles which— confound it! The sail flapped. Shakespeare was knocked overboard. There you could see him floating merrily away, with all his pages ruffling innumerably; and then he went under" (36). At the same time as the frustration caused by the sail flapping disturbs Jacob's view of the islands, the book of Shakespeare suffers a similar—if also more literal—blow. The personification of the book ("ruffling" recalls traditional portraits of Shakespeare with a ruffled collar) adds to the sense that the book itself is drowning. This is a more dramatic version of the difficult reading circumstances described at the beginning of the chapter: "What's the use of trying to read Shakespeare, especially in one of those little thin paper editions whose pages get ruffled, or stuck together with sea-water?" (35). Even before its wholesale destruction, Jacob closes his eyes to the book at precisely the moment when, with its ruffled, stuck-together pages, its materiality becomes apparent. Because it no longer has any use for him, its loss is met with equanimity and irony, as if the loss of these pages is no matter at all.

As the indifference to the book is just a more specific example of Jacob's and Timmy's general orientation to the material world at large, further examination of their actions will throw into greater relief the argument I have been making about the kind of readerly sensitivity cultivated by *Jacob's Room*. Woolf writes, "The Scilly Isles had been sighted by Timmy Durant lying like mountain-tops awash in precisely the right place. His calculations had worked perfectly" (35). The phrasing here recalls the rectifying effect of Betty Flanders's winking that brings the seascape in line with her expectations. Here, however, Timmy does not just use his intellect to bring the world into rigid focus; the pun on *sight* also indicates his belief that the Scilly Isles appear *as a result of* his perfect calculations, as if to suggest his unflagging faith in the autonomy of his own subjectivity. As the Isles' position in "precisely the right place" implies that they obeyed the commands of Timmy's mathematics (and not the other way around), Timmy is able to imagine himself as an omnipotent creator who stands apart from any possible vicissitudes and, even more, imagines the world in petrifying, static terms. When the narrator expounds on such a stance, she explicitly links this attitude to a reading of the world: she describes Timmy "looking sternly at the stars, then at a compass, spelling out quite correctly his pages of the eternal lesson book" (35). While the phrase "eternal lesson book" allies the world with the book, the fact that Timmy is "spelling [it] out" points to the treatment of the world as a set of letters to be arranged in a rigid configuration that anticipates Mr. Ramsey's "alphabetic" conception of knowledge in *To the Lighthouse*.

As she elaborates on the effect of this orientation to the temporal world in her account of the intellectual exchange that Jacob and Timmy base on the latter's "notebook of scientific observations," the narrator subtly points out the pitfalls of such abstract, disembodied thinking. Reporting Jacob's tentative response to Timmy's comment, she offers a clear portrait of the elevated position they are taking that allows them to use the Scilly Isles as a foundation for their discussion: "Only half a sentence followed; but these half-sentences are like flags set on tops of buildings to the observer of external sights down below. What was the coast of Cornwall, with its violet scents, and mourning emblems, and tranquil piety, but a screen happening to hang straight behind as his mind marched up?" (37). The comparison of the coast of Cornwall to a "screen" paints it as an empty canvas on which Jacob can project his ideas, a projection that involves a certain kind of violence, as the military imagery of "marching" suggests. Jacob seems, that is, to be stomping out and flattening the world itself in his attempts to comprehend it. Interestingly it is not only their intellectual but also their affective relationship that distracts them from the sight of the islands (to an almost devastating degree), a distraction described in terms that shift the painting metaphor to a printing one. The narrator relates that "they had quarreled" and then proceeds to repeat the language she first used to describe the "sighting" of the Isles—this time, however, with a significant difference: "The Scilly Isles had the look of mountain-tops almost a-wash. . . . Unfortunately, Jacob broke the pin of the Primus stove. The Scilly Isles might well be obliterated by a roller sweeping straight across" (36, ellipsis original). Once again the ellipsis, an obvious printerly effect, breaks into the line at the same time Jacob breaks the pin on the stove. In the following line the pin becomes a "roller," the hard cylinder used to apply ink to raised metal type, which, in this case, effectively flattens the islands that, like type from metal, protrude from the sea. As the frustration and emotion unleashed by the damage to the stove transfers the destruction to the external world at large, the language also recalls Woolf's letter to Carrington about the difficulty of working with woodcuts, itself a frustrating endeavor. She describes how "the rollers scrape up the wood as they pass," as if to suggest the potential violence of printing (not limited here to the impression of type into paper but also extended to the inking of type itself) implicated in a disregard of the material out of which the world outside the self is composed (*Letters* 2:162).

When Jacob travels to Greece he offers the complement to this scene: he does not so much disregard the world as he discards human relations. The narrator draws an obvious connection between the two scenes: "There are very sharp bare hills on the way to Olympia; and between them the blue sea in triangular spaces. A little like the Cornish coast" (110). Unlike his sailing trip to the Scilly Isles, the world here catches his eye and draws him in with its colors and its geometry, in a way that recalls the designs of the Omega workshop. The narrator reports, "He had never suspected how tremendously pleasant it is to be alone; out of England; on one's own; cut off from the whole thing" (112). The quiet violence of being "cut off" becomes more explicit in the observations with which the narrator ends this section: "To gallop intemperately; fall on the sand tired out; to feel the earth spin; to have—positively—a rush of friendship for the stones and grasses, as if humanity were over, and as for men and women, let them go hang—there is no getting over the fact that this desire seizes us pretty often" (112–13). The overt appeal to isolation anticipates *The Waves*, which Woolf described as a mind's "soliloquy in solitude." Here, however, the feelings of affinity for the world— along with its temporality—not only preclude human relationality but commit an execution: "Let them go hang." The destruction his emotions visited on the Scilly Isles here finds its target in humanity in general, as if Jacob is working in a relational model in which he must choose between two mutually exclusive options: embrace his status as either an omnipotent subject or a nonhuman object.

Yet when Jacob meets Sandra Wentworth Williams, his trip to Greece demonstrates his dual position as a subject and an object by intertwining his connection to the temporal world with a human relationship—an intertwining that the object of the book significantly comes to embody. Jacob gives Sandra his copy of Donne's poems on a nighttime visit to the Acropolis as the scene fades into the dark of a storm that, like the Great War that *Jacob's Room* ultimately commemorates, "passed from east to west," extinguishing the lights of mainland Greece and other "great towns—Paris—Constantinople— London" (124, 125). The narrator observes that, after the storm, "the columns and the Temple remain; the emotion of the living breaks fresh on them year after year; and of that what remains? As for reaching the Acropolis who shall say that we ever do it, or that when Jacob woke next morning he found anything hard and durable to keep forever?" (125). The distinction she makes between the impersonal persistence of the Greek monuments and the transience of human emotion softens, however, in the next lines:

> Sandra Wentworth Williams certainly woke to find a copy of Donne's poems upon her dressing-table. And the book would be stood on the shelf in the English country house where Sally Duggan's *Life of*

Father Damien in verse would join it one of these days. There were ten or twelve little volumes already. Strolling in at dusk, Sandra would open the books and her eyes would brighten (but not at the print), and subsiding into the arm chair she would suck back again the soul of the moment; or, for sometimes she was restless, would pull out book after book and swing across the whole space of her life like an acrobat from bar to bar. She had had her moments. Meanwhile, the great clock on the landing ticked and Sandra would hear time accumulating. (125)

Here the books mediate the ephemerality of human emotion and the durability of the object world as their explicit status as objects (rather than as texts) becomes the spark of Sandra's memories. The chiming of the clock and the accumulation of time that attends her meditations point to the way these books literally embody the passing of subjective time. Despite the fact that she is, in a sense, reading these bibliographic objects in a way similar to the narrator in Jacob's room at Cambridge or Mrs. Norman on the train, the meaning she reaches—"the soul of the moment"—is less a stable, preconceived idea than ephemerality itself. While *The Waves* explores this ephemerality even more extensively, here the books become the index for Sandra's own mortality and transience, the ultimate effect of which is to take on, in death, her own status as an inanimate object.

This emphasis on the inanimate is, in the end, exactly where *Jacob's Room* leaves its reader, with the emphasis it places on pages— or at least paper—in the concluding images that communicate Jacob's death in the Great War. On the last page Jacob's friend Bonamy stands "in the middle of Jacob's room" and observes, "He left everything just as it was. . . . Nothing arranged. All his letters strewn about for any one to read" (143). A few paragraphs later Bonamy is standing at a window, looking out into the city, when "suddenly all the leaves seemed to raise themselves" while, in the next sentence, they "sank down again" (143). The leaves outside the window recall the letters "strewn about for any one to read" and, by extension, the pages we have just finished turning. Bill Brown suggests that the novel "displays the evanescence of the protagonist's life as a relation to the material object world" so that the novel's closing scene "evolves less from the idea of absence (Jacob's death in the war), and more from a lingering presence, the unburied remains."[18] And what remains of the novel that we are finishing but its very pages? The ending of *Jacob's Room* thus recalls the way it begins: it opens itself up and exposes the pages we have been turning. While *The Waves* will explicitly take this turning as the organizational principle shared by its form and format, in *Jacob's Room* this turning leads to a place that seems, for a moment at least, a bit more static. For, as the page spacing in this novel repeatedly asks us to hold our minds open, it uses the machinery of its pages to imprint us with an idea. As we abide and become intimate with the pages in *Jacob's Room*, we are given an impression of the way our own inanimate objecthood entails less a last-minute escape from than an ultimate accession to temporality.

CHAPTER 5

The Binding of *The Waves*

"Now to sum up," writes Virginia Woolf at the beginning of the last section of *The Waves*, which consists entirely of a monologue by the character Bernard that attempts to draw the various strands of the novel together. Like its final section, my reading of *The Waves* also serves as a summing up that gathers together the preceding arguments about the book and our relationship to it. In Bernard's words, "The illusion is upon me that something adheres for a moment, has roundness, weight, depth, is completed."[1] As this feeling of "roundness, weight, depth" speaks to the volumes that I have been analyzing, it characterizes the moment when you turn the last page of a book, close the cover, and feel its heft in your hands. This volume transforms the temporal duration of the reading you have just concluded, the time you have spent engaged with the narrative, into a "solid object," to refer to the title of a short story Woolf published early in her career. When Bernard continues, "This, for the moment, seems to be my life," he expands on the "illusion" of completion that I have been discussing as "the death of the book." As an apt description of the role that, "for the moment," the completed book can play as a material manifestation of the part of your life devoted to reading it, the object you hold in your hands fleetingly indexes the temporal ephemerality in which mortality as such is grounded. While the reader's life extends beyond the covers of the book that contains the text of the *The Waves* in a way that Bernard's does not, Woolf's novel imagines its own paginated and bound format in terms that interrogate the transience that constitutes temporality as such, the very movement of time—common to subject and object alike—that has been at the heart of my discussion.

Woolf hints at this interest in time's impersonal passing in her 1927 essay "The Narrow Bridge of Art," where she critiques what she calls the "psychological novelist" who "has been too prone to limit psychology to the psychology of personal intercourse" (*Essays* 2: 225). In his introduction to the holograph drafts of *The Waves*, J. W. Graham argues that in this essay Woolf was "going beyond the criticism of the Edwardian novel contained in 'Mr. Bennett and Mrs. Brown,' her earlier and more famous speculation about the future of fiction, and is scrutinizing the limitations of her own most recent and successful novels."[2] Woolf herself points out that, with the contemporary novel, "we have scrutinized one part of the mind closely and left the other unexplored. We have come to forget that a large and important part of life consists in our emotions towards such things as roses and nightingales, the dawn, the sunset, life, death, and fate; we forget that we spend much time sleeping, dreaming, thinking, reading, alone" (2: 225). While *Mrs. Dalloway* and *To the Lighthouse* further the investigation of subjective psychology and interpersonal relationships, her enumeration of natural and abstract phenomena here points to an alternative focus that returns to the larger, external world in which she was interested in *Jacob's Room*.[3]

When Woolf describes the composition of *The Waves* in her diary and points out that "the abandonment of *Orlando* and *Lighthouse* is much checked by the extreme difficulty of the form—as it was in *Jacob's Room*,"[4] she deliberately links the two works and hints at the way they form a common project. Whereas *Jacob's Room* draws attention to the way the spaces on its pages contribute to the reader's experience of its narrative, in *The Waves* the pages themselves—or, more specifically, the turning of these bound pages—play an important role in the experience at which that novel is aiming. We can approach this experience by examining the commitment to reality's constant flux implied in the aesthetic ambitions that Woolf describes for her "new novel." In phrasing that Bernard overtly reiterates, she writes that her book will

> dramatize some of those influences which play so large a part in life, yet have so far escaped the novelist—the power of music, the stimulus of sight, the effect on us of the shape of trees or the play of colour, the emotion bred in us by crowds, the obscure terrors and hatreds which come so irrationally in certain places or from certain people,

the delight of movement, the intoxication of wine. Every moment is the centre and meeting-place of an extraordinary number of perceptions which have not yet been expressed. Life is always and inevitably much richer than we who try to express it. (*Essays* 2: 228–29)

The experiences of sensation and emotion, along with the important addition of movement, on which Woolf focuses here all extend across multiple points of space and time; the way life exceeds attempts at its expression has to do with a dynamic progression that reveals any static sense of reality to be bound up with an uncapturable flow. As the continual rather than instantaneous nature of these examples points to Woolf's efforts to investigate the passing of time as such, they also expand on the plans she makes for the work, what she describes as "the stream that I am trying to convey; life itself going on," and, even earlier, of "some continuous stream, not solely of human thought, but of the ship, the night etc., all flowing together" (*Diary* 140, 107).

When Woolf continues her brainstorming and asks herself, "Could one not get the waves to be heard all through?" (*Diary* 141), she suggests that what she eventually calls her "interludes," which periodically interrupt the personal lives her novel narrates with descriptions of depersonalized seascapes, are meant to create a sense of flow by paradoxically *dividing* the human-centered narrative. Her description of the "Time Passes" section from *To the Lighthouse*, the narrative disruption that arguably anticipates the formal experiment of *The Waves*, explicitly yokes this structural rupture with temporal representation: she writes of "this impersonal thing, which I'm dared to do by my friends, the flight of time, & the consequent break of unity in my design" (*Diary* 79). While the interludes that interrupt the novel's monologues formally institute such a sense of temporality, they find an analogue on the level of format in *The Waves*'s own succession of pages. As he traces the tension between the mobile flow of his experience and the paralyzing structure in which he must represent it, Bernard ultimately appeals to the bound pages of the book, which offer less a resolution than a material instantiation of this tension. Mediating between the integrated and the fragmented, the binding of *The Waves* reveals that the object of the book is constituted as much by an accumulation of pages as it is a collection of the divisions between them. At the same time as it thus spotlights the intersection of the temporal and the spatial that has been at the heart of my account of the reader's encounter with these books, *The Waves* helps me to sum up the death of the book that the novels in this study imagine by enacting the inextricably essential role death plays in any kind (which is to say, all kinds) of temporally bound life.

I

While the community of voices that constitutes *The Waves* consists of six personae—three male and three female—Woolf portions out the most significant meditations on their experiences to her male speakers, Bernard, Neville, and Louis. Rhoda's monologues offer a counterpoint to these male voices that reveals the way her extreme alienation from her own body and the object world in which it is situated bars her ability to countenance the progress of time and leads to her suicide. On the other hand, the male figures, especially in the aesthetic development Bernard the novelist undergoes, progressively turn our attention to the binding of the book's pages as the means of coming to terms with the inescapable ephemerality of time's passing. It is Neville, however, who provides the earliest and most explicit account of Bernard's literary ambitions when he states, "Let Bernard begin. Let him burble on telling us stories, while we lie recumbent. Let him describe what we have all seen so that it becomes a sequence. Bernard says there is always a story. I am a story. Louis is a story" (37). The emphasis here is clearly on the construction of narratives that, in these lines, involve the imposition of a sequential order onto visual perception ("what we have all seen"). When Bernard later draws a direct link between narrative organization and subjective agency, however, he indicates that this organizing structure has less to do with the impersonal world than with the erection of his own ego. He states, "I conceive myself called upon to provide, some winter's night, a meaning for all my observations—a line that runs from one to another, a summing up that completes" (115). With its connotations of pregnancy and origination, the use of the word *conceive* suggests that Bernard creates *himself* by connecting up all his experiences. The structure to which he appeals has its origin in his own consciousness.

This subject-centered organization ultimately leads him—along with Louis, Rhoda, and Neville—to an eternal and wholly abstracted realm that has very little to do with phenomenal experience. He expounds further on his narrativizing compulsion: "The bubbles are rising like the silver bubbles from the floor of a saucepan; image on top of image. . . . I must open the little trap-door and let out these linked phrases in which I run together whatever happens so that instead of incoherence there is perceived a wandering thread, lightly joining one thing to another" (49). For the young Bernard writing is a process that allows him to securely grasp his chaotic and frenzied experience. In a move that recalls the idealized abstractions associated with Kleinian paranoia, Bernard transforms the overlapping simultaneities of the boiling bubbles into the sequence of the "linked phrases" and creates a "wandering thread" by which he forces the vagaries of the external world to correspond to a kind of perfect coherence. Here indeed it is not just narrative structure but language itself that also orders and organizes.

When Neville comments on the effect of Bernard's narrative and linguistic ordering, however, he suggests a certain incommensurability between linguistic or narrative structure and the flow of experience—an incommensurability that ultimately leads Bernard to disavow and renounce his coherence-committed ordering habits later in the novel. Using some of the same metaphors as Bernard himself, Neville says, "Bernard goes on talking. Up they bubble— images. . . . When he talks, when he makes foolish comparisons, a lightness comes over one. One floats, too, as if one were that bubble; one is freed; I have escaped, one feels" (38). Bernard's transformation of experience into language seems to liberate him and his listeners from the constraints of the material world. Neville notes that "even the chubby boys (Dalton, Larpent and Baker) feel the same abandonment," as if to underscore the way Bernard's talk allows for an abstraction from the earthbound body's insistent chubbiness. In their drive to become disembodied storytelling minds that exist in a transcendent intellectual realm, these English schoolboys effectively become the classmates of Joyce's Stephen Dedalus, with his headily paranoid denial of the material world.

Louis, however, takes this work of ordering and abstraction to its fullest extent, and a comparison of his and Bernard's projects draws out the will to eternity inherent in their literary endeavors. Woolf writes, "'Now let me try,' said Louis, 'before we rise, before we go to tea, to fix the moment in one effort of supreme endeavour. This shall endure'" (39). As a more extreme version of Bernard's ordering impulse, Louis overlays his own structure onto the flow of experience by trying to grasp the single instant, as if he might immobilize the stream of time and seize the moment for himself. When he goes on to observe, "My shattered mind is pieced together by some sudden

perception. I take the trees, the clouds, to be witnesses of my complete
integration" (39), he amplifies the drive to disembodiment implicit
in Bernard's stories since here physical perception leads to a wholly
mental space out of which Louis can imagine his experience syn-
chronically, excised from the current of life. He makes this even more
explicit when, a few lines later, he says, "Our ring here, sitting, with
our arms binding our knees, hint[s] at some other order, and better,
which makes a reason everlastingly. This I see for a second, and shall
try tonight to fix in words, to forge in a ring of steel" (40). Trans-
muting his experience into the verbal register abstracts the flesh and
blood that form the first ring in these lines; in its place he imagines an
enduring eternality in the figure of a steel ring, whose hardness will
maintain the circular shape that averts any sense of progress or succession. Yet the numerous commas that break up these lines impart
a stop-and-start rhythm and accentuates the way that, unlike a steel
ring, language—no matter how well ordered—unfolds in a temporal
register that Louis cannot elude.

This temporal unfolding is exactly what Louis wants to counter
by appealing to poetry rather than Bernard's stories; in a later scene
that takes place in a crowded restaurant, he describes how the book
he is reading "contains some forged rings, some perfect statements, a
few words, but poetry" (94). It is ultimately poetry, with the clearly
defined rhythms and regular patterns of its "forged rings" and "perfect statements," to which Louis looks to establish control over the
stream of his experience. He elaborates: "I oppose to what is passing
this ramrod of beaten steel. I will not submit to this aimless passing
of billycock hats and Homburg hats and all the plumed and varie-
gated head-dresses of women. . . . And the grinding and the steam
that runs in unequal drops down the window pane; and the stopping
and the starting with a jerk of motor-omnibuses; and the hesitation at
counters; and the words that trail drearily without human meaning; I
will reduce you to order" (95). In a way that Bernard does not, Louis
makes clear that, when aimed at achieving the eternal, literary representation has the potential to commit a certain violence toward the
temporal world, indicated in his language of "beaten" and "forged"
steel that he "opposes" to it. As poetry functions, in his hands, like
an aggressive force that overlays an oppressive framework onto the
world, it suggests that the calls for order that Bernard makes effect a
similar reduction and participate in the same kind of representational
violence. Yet the insistent rhythm created by the repeated *and*s in this

passage seems to suggest the potential for literary representation to share in the flow and mobility expressed by the images of running steam and jerking omnibuses Louis uses to describe the world around him. Indeed as this sentence contains a long string of predicates that precede the subject and verb, Louis's words defer the syntactical closure that might allow the reader to impose a final, ordering meaning on these lines. In a sense his words almost come to "trail drearily without human meaning" and point to a way *other than* "human meaning" that language might intersect with an experience of the object world.

When Bernard ultimately disavows the forms of traditional narrative, he hints at exactly this alternative intersection: "How tired I am of stories, how tired I am of phrases that come down beautifully with all their feet on the ground! Also, I distrust neat designs of life that are drawn upon half sheets of notepaper. I begin to long for some little language such as lovers use, broken words, inarticulate words, like the shuffling of feet on pavement. I begin to seek some design more in accordance with those moments of humiliation and triumph that come now and then undeniably" (238–39). While Bernard's desire for "some little language" has been read as an appeal to the Kristevan semiotic or even the monosyllabic, it might also suggest a limitation of language that reveals other means of communication and transmission at work. The repetition of "feet" in two different phrases suggests that the image is not a random one; indeed it is a standard term used to parse poetic meter. While this sense of the word seems to describe its use in the first case—in the "phrases that come down beautifully with all their feet on the ground"—it takes on another valence in the "shuffling of feet on pavement," where it describes a foundation or base that stabilizes without immobilizing. This use suggests a different kind of literary rhythm and transforms the ordered structure of narrative or poetry suggested by the former phrase into a more mobile, shifting model where words themselves do not stay put. It is this shifting of words themselves—rather than just their sounds—that Woolf's and Bernard's appeal to the object of the book will help us to embody.

Further comparison between Bernard's concluding thoughts and Woolf's description of her novel suggests the increasing influence that the material format of the book comes to have on their respective reconsiderations of literary form. Woolf envisions her new kind of novel as a hybrid combination of prose, poetry and drama; it will, she

proposes, "have something of the exaltation of poetry but much of
the ordinariness of prose. It will be dramatic, yet not a play" (*Essays*
2: 224). Significantly, to the question of what to call this jumbled
genre, she responds that "it is not a matter of very great importance"
and elides the question of generic form altogether by focusing instead
on its format: in the next sentence she calls it "this *book* which we
see on the horizon," as if that object is the means (not to mention
the medium) that brings these varied genres together (2: 224, italics
added). Later, describing the composition process for such a novel,
she writes, "Instead of enumerating details, [the novelist] will mold
blocks. His characters thus will have a dramatic power which the
minutely realized characters of contemporary fiction often sacrifice
in the interests of psychology" (2: 228). The renunciation of "enumerating details" overlaps with the way Bernard ultimately tries to
avoid the imposition of narrative sequence; "mold[ing] blocks" offers
a concrete image for the alternative he comes to pursue. Although this
metaphor of molding recalls the way Louis seeks to "forge a ring of
steel," the "block" that the writer is to produce speaks to the shape
of a book, a "solid object" with which Woolf was quite familiar from
her work for the Hogarth Press. Yet the separate pages of a bookish
solid object mediate between fragmentation and continuity in a way
that diverges from the model Louis proposes. (Interestingly the "solid
objects" on which Woolf focuses in the early story of that name are
almost always some kind of fragment, as if to suggest that, from the
very beginning of her career, she was interrogating the impossibility
of unfragmented wholeness.)

When Neville describes the breakdown of Bernard's stories early in
the novel, he also has recourse to fragmented material drawn from the
object world. As Bernard is speaking, Neville observes, "The sentence
tails off feebly. Yes, the appalling moment has come when Bernard's
power fails him and there is no longer any sequence and he sags and
twiddles a bit of string and falls silent, gaping as if about to burst
into tears. Among the tortures and devastations of life is this then—
our friends are not able to finish their stories" (39). As the "wandering thread" of his story becomes literal and a heavy, earth-bound
sagging replaces the arc of a narrative, the dissipation of sequence
seems to foreshadow death itself. While the "twiddl[ing]" of the "bit
of string" echoes the feeble tailing off of Bernard's sentence and links
the moment of narrative disconnection to the intrusion of the material world, the horror Bernard and Neville experience at this moment

eclipses the way that "twiddl[ing]" also connects with a rhythmic action like shuffling. The "bit of string" thus becomes somewhat of an unheeded hint at the potential of the material world to serve as the basis for the alternative representational model—and an alternative, depressive reaction to finitude—that Bernard comes to desire. Moreover the kind of motion suggested by twiddling and shuffling—which is composed of a series of smaller movements—also describes the way a reader proceeds through a novel incrementally, by the persistent turning of pages, a comparison endorsed by *The Waves* in the metaphor Bernard ultimately uses to characterize his closing summation.

While the impulse to sum up is in line with the compulsion to narrate that Bernard exhibited in his youth, he now observes, "In order to make you understand, to give you my life, I must tell you a story—and there are so many, and so many—stories of childhood, stories of school, love, marriage, death, and so on; and none of them are true" (238). Referring to the incidents that he will rehearse, he proposes an alternative: "Let us turn over these scenes as children turn over pages of a picture-book and the nurse says, pointing: 'That's a cow. That's a boat.' Let us turn over the pages, and I will add, for your amusement, a comment in the margin" (239). Characterizing the monologue that follows as a marginal commentary to the "pages in a picture-book," Bernard distinguishes the narrative summary that he constructs from the content he is summarizing; as he puts it later, "Life is not susceptible perhaps to the treatment we give when we try tell it" (267). Yet by appealing to the way "children turn over pages of a picture-book" (children who, we might assume from the description of the nurse's instruction, do not yet know how to read), he endows the visual image and the sequence of pages with a novel importance, as if they might communicate life in a way that a linguistically constructed narrative cannot. Turning pages thus comes to index and transmit an experience of the very passing of time, which Bernard's stories—not to mention Louis's poetry—can only seek to reduce.

This lack of sensitivity to the passing of time is exactly what Bernard condemns when he launches into another critique of narrative form during his closing monologue. On breaking off from his portrait of himself as a university student, he says, "Here again there should be music . . . a painful, guttural, visceral, also soaring, lark-like, pealing song to replace these flagging, foolish transcripts—how much too deliberate! how much too reasonable!—which attempt to describe the flying moment of first love" (250). In singling out this moment as a

significant one over which he wants to linger, Bernard's appeal to
music, an art form that takes time's passing as its constitutive principle, suggests his simultaneous desire *not* to linger over the moment
or, more precisely, to record the moment *within*, as *part of* a temporal unfolding. He does not so much want to freeze it as to communicate its very dynamism, both the contradictory and fluid emotions he
felt and his experience of the moment's passing, its "flying" momen-
tariness. He goes on to offer a more expansive description of this
moment in a series of sentences that he ultimately interrupts: "—but
what is the use of painfully elaborating these consecutive sentences
when what one needs is nothing consecutive but a bark, a groan?"
(251). This line is often quoted in support of a Kristevan reading,
the "bark" and "groan" serving as examples of the "little language"
Bernard is seeking, but the turn to Kristeva ultimately distracts from
closer examination of Bernard's renunciation of a "too deliberate"
and "too reasonable" sequence. He wants to avoid a sequential ordering because it splits up what is, in experience, a continuity. In this he
echoes Woolf and her ambitions for unity and running all the scenes
together. At the same time, he extends her critique of the genre of
prose to the form of the sentence—even, implicitly, to language itself.
How, Bernard seems to be wondering, can I run all my words together
to communicate continuity rather than sequence?

II

When Bernard takes up the question of expressing what it is that links
his experiences on a deeper, nonlinguistic level, he uses a complicated
and telling description. Echoing Woolf's critical writing again, he proclaims, "It is a mistake, this extreme precision, this orderly military
progression; a convenience, a lie. There is always deep below it, even
when we arrive punctually at the appointed time with our white waist-
coats and polite formalities, a rushing stream of broken dreams, nurs-
ery rhymes, street cries, half-finished sentences and sights—elm trees,
willow trees, gardeners sweeping, women writing—that rise and sink
even as we hand a lady down to dinner" (255). What is interesting
about these lines is the way they signal a "rushing stream" by using
images not of flow or progress but of interruption and the instant, as
if it is precisely *dis*connection that reveals the stream deep below, a
flow that underlies—even as it avoids—any conscious or deliberate
attempts to grasp it. Indeed disconnection was precisely what plagued

Bernard when, as a young man, he tried to "run together whatever happens so that instead of incoherence there is perceived a wandering thread" (49). As I've suggested, *The Waves* performs this tension between disconnect and flow in the descriptive interludes that repeatedly break into the character's dramatic monologues. Portraying consecutive moments in the sun's advance across the sky, these interludes point to the very real temporality in which the performance of these monologues is occurring in a way that accentuates the process of maturation and aging that each of the characters is undergoing. At the same time as they thus organize the intervening monologues in a temporal arc defined less by the conventions of plot than by the rhythms of the natural world, the interludes also tie the book together on a formal level by giving it a recognizable shape and structure. Woolf herself describes this structuring function when she writes in her diary, "The interludes are very difficult, yet I think essential, so as to bridge and also to give a background—the sea; insensitive nature—I don't know" (150). When Graham has recourse to the bibliographic register in his account of the way the work possesses "a structure emphatically modeled on the cycles of day, season and human life, heavily underscored by the spatial and typographical separation of the two 'streams' of the book" (14), he suggests the intimate relationship between the experimental form of the work and its format, as if part of *The Waves*'s "emphatic" structure comes from the pages on which it is printed.[5] And though Woolf's comment refers to the scenes portrayed in the interludes, her description could apply just as easily to the material pages that transmit and constitute a background for them. These inanimate pages themselves belong to the object world and function as a kind of "insensitive nature" that binds the monologues together in the temporally material object of the book.

The novel's opening description of the way an uninhabited seascape gradually becomes visible supports a connection among the natural world, temporality, and the materiality of the book: "The sun had not yet risen. The sea was indistinguishable from the sky, except that the sea was slightly creased as if a cloth had wrinkles in it. Gradually as the sky whitened a dark line lay on the horizon dividing the sea from the sky and the grey cloth became barred with thick strokes moving, one after another, beneath the surface, following each other, pursuing each other, perpetually" (7). As the "not yet" of the first line gestures at the slippery deferral of any present moment, it announces the ungraspable temporality of time's very emergence, an inconceivable dawning figured in the description's imagery of division. Interestingly the divisive creases that temper the initial indistinguishability of sea and sky evoke paper as much as cloth, while the "thick strokes" that bar the surface of the sea conflate the waves with the marks made by a pen. As the description of this seascape's differentiation from the sky also functions as an implicit narrative of the process by which the novel takes shape under the eyes of both the writer and the reader, it links the materiality of the book to the opening up of time itself. Accordingly when the description continues and, in terms that form the sea and sky out of paper-like fibers, relates how "the air seemed to become fibrous and to tear away from the green surface flickering and flaming in red and yellow fibres" (7), it implies that, like time itself, this bookish materiality is as fragmented as it is continuous.

The monologues themselves explore this complex materiality when Neville, who becomes a well-known poet over the course of the novel, describes his reading practices in a way that speaks to the autocratic literary designs of Bernard and Louis. On arriving at school he points out the library, where, he says, "I shall explore the exactitude of the Latin language, and step firmly upon the well-laid sentences, and pronounce the explicit, the sonorous hexameters of Virgil; of Lucretius; and chant with a passion that is never obscure or formless the loves of Catullus, reading from a big book, a quarto with margins" (31–32). Neville's plans involve a slippage from the formal aspects of the classical poets to the "big book" in which he reads them. When he describes reading as "step[ping] firmly," he intimates that his intellectual explorations seek a stability that he hopes to find as much in Latin's linguistic "exactitude" as in the stately quarto format whose margins—no less than Virgil's hexameters—might also be called "well-laid." In highlighting these margins Neville indicates the attention he pays to the organization of the words themselves on the page, as if he organizes and regulates his readerly passion via the structures of both poetic meter and typographical layout. Linking the aspects of poetic form and bibliographic format, these lines overlay the intellectual demands of reading with its sensory demands in a way that distinguishes them from those of Louis and Bernard. While Neville certainly engages with the linguistic structures by which his classmates look to "reduce" and grasp the flux of their experience, his additional sensitivity to the black and white spaces of the page that are themselves part of the stream of his phenomenal experience connects the regularity of poetic meter to the flow of the world in a way that has the potential to soften the violence of Louis.

This sensitivity is quite in keeping with the writers he is reading, since both Lucretius and Catullus explore this very connection
between the intellectual and the physical as they center on the material and the carnal, respectively. Lucretius was one of the first classical writers to explore our phenomenal experience in terms of the
material makeup of the world rather than the divine will of the gods
and expounded a theory of atomism that had great influence on later
writers. As Susanna Rich points out, Lucretius articulated a "materialism that dispatched with gods and superstitions" and argued that
"the soul is corporeal and cannot survive separately from the body
which it infuses."[6] Similarly Catullus's poetry emphasizes the sensual
and the erotic in discussions of love. A lesson Neville might learn
from these two writers would be to invest in the sensuous materiality
of the world; the readerly passion with which Neville approaches the
"big book" might thus recall the AMOUR of Proust's manuscripts or
the intimately physical relationship that Bloom has with his reading
material in *Ulysses*.

Yet Neville shies away from this amorous passion when, picking
up on Catullus's famed homosexual sentiments, he explicitly connects
the object of the book with his angst over "a secret told to nobody
yet . . . whether I am doomed always to cause repulsion in those I
love" (88). The secrecy and repulsion that condition Neville's affective framework suggest that he also imagines the book's materiality
as the means to contain or even obliterate his desires in a way that
recalls Bernard's and Louis's appeals to language to order their experience. Thus Neville returns to Catullus and states, "I do not imper-
sonate Catullus, whom I adore. I am the most slavish of students,
with here a dictionary; there a notebook in which I enter curious uses
of the past participle. But one cannot go on for ever cutting these
ancient inscriptions clearer with a knife. Shall I always draw the red
serge curtains close and see my book, laid like a block of marble, pale
under the lamp?" (87). Once again Neville slips from a discussion of
the exactitude of the Latin language—to which he submits himself
"slavish[ly]," as if he might amplify and borrow its rigor as the basis
for his own self-regulation—to the object of the book that transmits
that language. In this case the book does not so much put him in
touch with the external world as it becomes the means by which he
retreats behind the "red serge curtains" to withdraw from it. As such
it provides a counterexample of the book as a solid object that will
clarify the increasing importance of the separated pages on which I

have been focusing. The block of marble portrays a kind of mono-lithic solidity whose permanence and immutability create a space for his own self-lacerating subjectivity to reign supreme, walled off from any intercourse with the flow of time or the caprice of other people. The violence of cutting into marble recalls the aggression and mate-rial hardness suggested by the "forged ring of steel" by which Louis characterizes poetry.

By surrendering his isolation, however, Neville discovers that opening himself to his amorous desires for Percival also imbues inan-imate objects with heretofore undiscovered affective significance. Waiting for Percival's imminent arrival at his going-away dinner, Neville observes, "Every moment he seems to pump into this room this prickly light, this intensity of being so that things have lost their normal uses—this knife-blade is only a flash of light, not a thing to cut with. The normal is abolished" (119). The prospect of sharing the same space with the man he loves transforms the restaurant into a phantasmagoria that illuminates mundane items: Neville no lon-ger sees the knife as something for him to use in his "slavish" study of Latin but as itself a shining fragment of an "intensity of being." Moreover, at the end of the dinner the knife reappears in a completely different and even more significant guise when it is used to describe the union shared by all six friends, what Louis calls "this common feeling." Neville describes this feeling: "Happiness is in it . . . and the quiet of ordinary things. A table, a chair, a book with a paper-knife stuck between the pages. And the petal falling from the rose, and the light flickering as we sit silent, or, perhaps, bethinking some little tri-fle, suddenly speak" (145). At this moment it is not only Neville's love for Percival but also his connection with all of his friends, their par-ticipation in a common experience, that opens him up to "the quiet of ordinary things," which tellingly includes "a book with a paper-knife stuck between its pages." Here, rather than the knife cutting an inscription, it is wedged into the book, held by it in a way that relieves it of its use value. At the same time, the specification of it as a "paper-knife" also intimates the other kind of holding the book is doing, namely the binding of the pages that the knife has separated from each other.

The subtle transformation in Neville's understanding of the book ultimately speaks to the issues of temporality that seem to vex the group of friends particularly clearly at this moment. For instance, Louis states, "As we rise and fidget, a little nervously, we pray, holding in our hands this common feeling, 'Do not move, do not let the swing-door cut to pieces the thing that we have made, that globes itself here, among these lights, these peelings, this litter of bread crumbs and people passing. Do not move, do not go. Hold it for ever'" (145). The image of the globe, with its suggestion of perfect totality, links Louis and his friends in a static arrangement that recalls the steel rings of his poetry. Precisely because it is so solid and stable, however, the figure of the globe becomes a kind of prison and precludes any possibility of change, development, or individuation. Not only are these relationships fixed in both space and time, but they also obliterate any distinctions among the friends. From this perspective the dispersal of the friends in space or the passing of time is a catastrophe to be avoided since the globe will be irreparably torn apart, the relationships cut to pieces by the door through which Louis and his friends pass. (Louis's anxiety thus once again recalls the Proustian narrator and his paranoid anxiety at his mother's good-night kiss.) The image of the book with the paper-knife, on the other hand, offers a different mode, as it suggests the way the knife cuts the book into pieces that the book's binding nonetheless holds together. A book's pages are both together and separate, so that the book is not the monolithic block imagined by Neville but a collection of leaves that offers a rather astounding material metaphor for the complicated co-implication of space and time. That is, in the paginated book, the pages are bound together in a permanent way (which suggests the simultaneity of space) that does not completely immobilize or homogenize them (which answers to the mobility of time).

This is quite close to the role that the book plays for Bernard when, in an early discussion of his ambitions to one day write a novel, he unknowingly anticipates the pagination of the children's book on which he will ultimately base his closing monologue: "When I am grown up I shall carry a notebook—a fat book with many pages, methodically lettered. I shall enter my phrases. Under B shall come 'Butterfly powder.' If, in my novel, I describe the sun on the window-sill, I shall look under B and find butterfly powder. That will be useful. The tree 'shades the window with green fingers.' That will be useful. But alas! I am so soon distracted—by a hair like twisted candy, by Celia's Prayer Book, ivory covered" (36–37). When the physical world "distract[s]" him from the abstracting process of his novelistic phrase-making, it does so via the object of the prayer book with its ivory covering and the "hair twisted like candy" that echoes the "bit of string" in Neville's description. Looking more closely at these two objects helps to elaborate the way the distinct pages in Bernard's notebook (ordered less by any kind of narrative teleology than by the arbitrary sequence of the alphabet) function as a kind of balm to the "torture and devastation" that beset him when he is not able to finish his story. The stoniness of the prayer book's ivory cover recalls Neville's "block of marble" and suggests a kind of solidity and unity, an impenetrability and totality that share a sense of timelessness and complete comprehension in keeping with the theological nature of the book's contents. Yet the indefinite article in the phrase "a hair twisted like candy" suggests that the hair that distracts Bernard is uprooted and separate from anyone specific. As a piece of physical detritus shed by a body in the daily task of living, it implies the very opposite of the eternal solidity to which the ivory prayer book points. Rather it is a clear signal of a kind of time-bound corporeal dis-integration, the fact, as we saw in *Ulysses*, that the body is not a complete and undivided whole but an assemblage of multiple, interrelated parts.

It is significant, however, that Bernard's notebook combines aspects of both these images. On the one hand, he plans to use it in his project of translating his subjective experience into a series of well-wrought phrases, which will eventually uncover the transcendental meaning of that experience, while, on the other hand, his description of it as "a fat book with many pages" underscores the book's status as an object with which this narrativizing is intimately bound up. And this very objectness depends on the even more literal binding together of its pages, which, at the same time, situates the book as far from the solid and timeless object suggested by either the ivory-covered prayer book or Neville's block of marble. In this case the notebook's constitution of multiple material fragments that cannot all be read at once hints at the succession of pages by which Bernard accesses the book's content. The record of his phrases is thus inextricably involved with the pages' unfolding, an unfolding that approaches the ultimate result around which my arguments have all been revolving: death.

III

The Waves revolves quite literally around the passing of time when the news that Percival has been killed in India comes crashing into the middle of the work and places death center stage. This event has repercussions for all the characters but receives the most extended

treatment from Rhoda, Bernard, and Neville, all of whom react with
a deepened awareness of time's passing and the way it points to the
continual coincidence of life and death. The effect of Percival's death
on Rhoda, the character who is most tormented by the passing of
time, is perhaps most significant. In the account she gives of her temporal consciousness and the changes it undergoes on learning of Percival's death, Rhoda appeals to the material substrate that transmits
written language as providing a pacifying sense of continuity that can
ease her anxiety over her disjunctive experience of temporality.

She articulates this anxiety in explicit terms: "Nothing persists.
One moment does not lead to another. . . . I am afraid of the shock
of sensation that leaps upon me, because I cannot deal with it as you
do—I cannot make one moment merge in the next. To me they are
all violent, all separate. . . . I do not know how to run minute to minute and hour to hour, solving them by some natural force until they
make the whole and indivisible mass that you call life" (130). The
traumatic nature of temporal progress lies in the way she experiences
both time and sensation as discrete rather than continuous phenomena: lacking a protective, equilibrating shield, she feels each moment
and each sense experience as a traumatic encounter with finitude
that she is forced to repeat. For Rhoda life is always a processual living, a successive progression that never stabilizes enough to "hand it
to you entire," as Bernard figures his ambition in his closing monologue. She consequently retreats to the timeless and bodiless sphere of
her fantasy as an escape from the here-and-now. In the middle of a
party she describes this dream space in terms that suggest the idealizations of Klein's paranoid position as much as Bernard's and Louis's
extremes of abstraction: "Draughts of oblivion shall quench my agi-
tation. . . . Let me visit furtively the treasures I have laid apart. Pools
lie on the other side of the world reflecting marble columns. The swal-
low dips her wing in dark pools" (105). The austere geometry of pools
and columns provide a landscape whose location on the "other side of
the world" suggests the opposite of the physical world into which she
is "thrust back to stand burning in this clumsy, this ill-fitting body"
(105).

Perhaps counterintuitively it is Percival's death that allows her
to open herself to and place herself within the time-bound material world. On learning of his accident, she states, "Now I will walk
down Oxford Street envisaging a world rent by lightning; I will look
at oaks cracked asunder and red where the flowering branch has

fallen. . . . Look now what Percival has given me. Look at the street now that Percival is dead" (159). The repeated use of the verb *look* emphasizes that she is reaching out to the traces of the material world around her and drawing support to help her bridge one moment to the next. The word *envisage* also hints at the way she is overlaying these cracks and fissures onto her own face, experiencing the bridging of her own temporal materiality, as the idealized perfection of the pools and columns that filled her fantasy gives way to "oaks cracked asunder" and a "world rent by lightning."

She confirms and explains her newfound tolerance of her own embodiment when she goes on to observe, "I like the passing of face and face and face, deformed, indifferent. I am sick of prettiness; I am sick of privacy. I ride rough waters and shall sink with no one to save me. Percival, by his death, has made me this present, has revealed this terror, has left me to undergo this humiliation" (159–60). Witnessing the ultimate encounter with finitude reveals the traumatic "terror" that has been implicit in each passing moment, so that Rhoda can consciously face the passingness of the present, indicated here by the "face and face and face."

It is significant that, when Rhoda reflects back on her younger days in the aftermath of Percival's death, she does so in a way that connects both an embrace of time and an openness to the world of objects with the pages of a book. Chastising the social order, she proclaims, "How you chained me to one spot, one hour, one chair, and sat yourselves down opposite! How you snatched from me the white spaces that lie between hour and hour and rolled them into dirty pellets and tossed them into the wastepaper basket with your greasy paws. Yet those were my life" (204). Her traumatic experience of time as a discrete phenomenon depends on a belief in the worthlessness of the "white spaces," a disregard of the intervals of "deferral and delay that constitute any event" that leads to a demand for constant and continual significance.[7] Here, however, the emphasis on the "dirty pellets" and the "wastepaper basket" hints at the materiality of these "white spaces" but also explicitly figures them as made of paper. As these paper-based blanks offer an experience of duration that folds the unbridgeable interstices of time into the sensation of space's continuity, they describe a situation drastically different from her early childhood arithmetic lessons that arguably inaugurated her fantasies of idealized and disembodied escape from the world. Early in the novel Louis observes Rhoda and states, "As she stares at the chalk figures, her mind lodges in those white circles; it steps through those white loops into emptiness, alone. . . . She has no body as the others have" (22). The "white circles" of the "chalk figures" serve as a "lodging" house for Rhoda's mind; she approaches them as if she is completely separate from the materiality of the physical world. Thus she finds herself alone in emptiness, disconnected from and frightened of the experience of physical embodiment.[8]

With these image patterns in mind, we readers of *The Waves* might pay attention to the page on which her monologue is inscribed—not to the spaces that allow us to make meaning from the dark marks but to the pages that rend the book into successive parts that constitute the experience of continuity. The latter functions to temper the anxiety of progress that haunts Rhoda as much as Bernard, for whom Percival's death draws out a more nuanced temporal sensitivity. On learning the news, he resists bulldozing ahead and pauses "to save one hour to consider what has happened to my world, what death has done to my world" (153). This suspension allows him to exhibit the kind of attention to time's micromovements for which he calls in his closing monologue. He remarks, "This then is the world that Percival sees no longer. Let me look. The butcher delivers meat next door; two old men stumble along the pavement; sparrows alight. The machine then works; I note the rhythm, the throb, but as a thing in which I have no part, since he sees it no longer" (153). If Rhoda responds to Percival's death via an engagement with the external world that she previously eschewed, Bernard describes a separation from the everyday world that disables his drive to order it according to his own rhythm. Percival's death reveals to him that what he calls "the usual order . . . the sequence of things" covers a different conception of temporality (155). As both Rhoda and Bernard recognize that temporal progress does not rely on their presence but exists apart from their perceiving consciousnesses, they recall the way Klein's depressive position involves a recognition of the independence of the external world. At the same time, they anticipate what Bernard later calls "the world seen without a self" that critics such as Ann Banfield take as the skeleton key of Woolf's aesthetic.

Experiencing the vacillation entailed in the labile idea of the Kleinian position, Bernard observes two pages later that "the sequence returns; one thing leads to another," and returns to his compulsive practice of linking moments into a cognizable linear sequence. As the shock of Percival's death wears off, Bernard understands that this separation is not a transcendence or a permanent renunciation of sequential organization: "Bodies, I note, already begin to look ordinary; but what is behind them differs—the perspective" (154). Learning of Percival's death offers him a window into a different conception of experience itself, one that, as we saw with Rhoda, does not contradict the sequential but exists along with it. This change in perspective, which is replayed even more radically in a central scene at Hampton Court, gives him the "chance to find out what is of great importance" (153). He expands on this statement when he revisits the moment of Percival's death in his closing monologue: "something very important" appears "beneath" his perceptions of the world: "To see things without attachment, from the outside, and to realize their beauty in itself—how strange!" (263). Bernard once again proposes a non-subject-centered account of experience in which the things of the world are not merely objects to be grasped by his consciousness.

In an attempt to prolong this opportunity—for, he comments, "one cannot live outside the machine for more perhaps than half an hour" (154)—Bernard pursues this other perspective by visiting an art gallery, where, he says, "I submit myself to the influence of minds like mine outside the sequence" (155). The pictures that he sees there, he reports, "expand my consciousness and bring him back to me differently. I remember his beauty" (156). Though, at first glance, it seems that the paintings extend the dominion of his subjectivity, as if he might dominate even more of the external world with his habitual ordering, Bernard's elaboration suggests that this expansion is actually an adjustment of his conscious attention. He states, "Here are pictures. Here are cold madonnas among their pillars. Let them lay to rest the incessant activity of the mind's eye, the bandaged head, the men with ropes, so that I may find something unvisual beneath. Here are gardens; and Venus among the flowers; here are saints and blue madonnas. Mercifully, these pictures make no reference; they do not nudge; they do not point" (156). While the description of the bandaged head and the men with ropes portray Bernard's imagined scenario of Percival's death from being flung off a horse, the "incessant" nature of which suggests his inability to pay attention to anything other than his own subjective fantasy, his "mind's eye" not to mention his mind's "I," the alternatives of "pillars" and "madonnas" that they offer him depict a timeless world of geometrical structure that is not so far from Rhoda's fantasies.

Yet, as with Rhoda, this turn to formal structure ultimately breaks down to reveal a nonsubjective return to the everyday world and the objects in it. He wonders, "How shall I break up this numbness which discredits my sympathetic heart?" and indicates that the numb abstractions might relieve him of his own subjective fantasies, but also bypass his affective experience of Percival's death. When he immediately goes on to observe "There are others suffering—multiples of people suffering. Neville suffers. He loved Percival. But I can no longer endure extremities" (158), he describes a return to the world that includes an awareness of other people's experiences as a way to navigate the extremity of a perspective based completely in either his subjective experience or the objective structure of reality. Turning to concrete, solid objects themselves—and one kind of object in particular—he states, "But now I want life around me, and books and little ornaments" (158). Previous comments he makes expand on this nonsubjective engagement with the object world for which the book stands as a synecdoche. He speaks of the "perpetual solicitation of the eye" and states, "I am titillated inordinately by some splendor," as if it is the object world that solicits *him* rather than the other way around. When he describes "the march of pillars," he notices that the static structure to which he had previously attended is subject to the mobility of time and suggests that it is the flux of life that these paintings ultimately reveal to him and that he shares with the other subjects and objects in the world.

It is this common submission to time that ultimately maps out the kind of solidarity that I modeled on the pages of the book and that Neville formulates in his reaction to Percival's death. Opening the central section in which the characters learn this news, Neville transforms the very middle of the novel into a kind of ending when he begins, "All is over. The lights of the world have gone out. There stands the tree which I cannot pass" (151). In the image of the tree Neville recalls a childhood memory of his reaction to hearing a cook speak of a man found with his throat cut, which also characterizes his response to learning of Percival's death. He describes the earlier experience thus:

> He was found with his throat cut. The apple-tree leaves became fixed in the sky; the moon glared; I was unable to lift my foot up the stair. He was found in the gutter. His blood gurgled down the gutter. His jowl was white as a dead codfish. I shall call this stricture, this rigidity, "death among the apple trees" for ever. There were the floating, pale-grey clouds; and the immitigable tree; the implacable tree with its greaved silver bark. The ripple of my life was unavailing. I was unable to pass by. There was an obstacle. "I cannot surmount this

unintelligible obstacle," I said. And the others passed on. But we are
doomed, all of us by the apple trees, by the immitigable tree which we
cannot pass. (24–25)

Neville shares in the experience of stasis and immobility that death
imposes on the man; he cannot "pass by," and the "ripple" of his life
is transformed into the rigidity of the apple tree's static structure. Yet
the fact that "others passed on" indicates that this break in the flow
of Neville's experience, while sparked by the death of *a* life, is not synonymous with the death *of life itself*, a kind of ultimate end. Rather
Neville seems to be describing the paradoxical experience of death's
presence *in* life, the incomprehensible coexistence of these seemingly
mutually exclusive opposites. (As Bernard observes of the simultaneity of Percival's death and his son's birth, "Such is the incomprehensible combination . . . such is the complexity of things" [153].) The
details of the man's death provide a way to grasp this paradox. As
cutting the throat severs one of the main arteries of blood, it violently
interrupts that feature of the body most obviously characterized by
flow. Far from stopping this flow, however, this interruption actually opens it up: as the blood "gurgle[s] down the gutter," it literally
streams into larger currents, as if to suggest the merging of the individual with the surrounding environment. This merging also occurs
on the grammatical level, as Neville's "I" that is "unable to pass"
expands into a "we" who is "doomed, all of us, by apple trees"—from
the confines of an individual experience to the aspects of existence
shared across subjectivities and, even more radically, with the object
world itself.[9]

This becomes even more explicit in Neville's account of the aftermath of Percival's death, which replays the earlier event and recalls
the vocabulary Bernard uses to describe the "little language" he seeks
that would express the flow of his experience: "We are all doomed,
all of us. Women shuffle past with shopping-bags. People keep on
passing" (152). When he continues, however, he directs his statement
to an ambiguous addressee: "Yet you shall not destroy me. For this
moment, this one moment, we are together. I press you to me" (152).
Though the "you" here might most obviously refer to Percival, the
threat of destruction seems to suggest that Neville is addressing mortality itself, the transitory nature of the world. Given the way Percival's recent death uncovers for Neville the presence of death in life,
however, these two options are not necessarily at odds. The together-
ness Neville describes would then be an experience of a kind of death,

a pressing that does not stop the flow of time as much as it seeks, however painfully, to embrace it. Thus he concludes, "Bury your fangs in my flesh. Tear me asunder. I sob, I sob" (152), an imagery of the pressing of bodies and the penetration of flesh that recalls a sexual liaison whose devastating nature destroys his very subjectivity.

IV

This dissolution of subjectivity is ultimately part of the effect intended by *The Waves*'s impersonal interludes, the way they weave the changing aspects of a seascape with the individual voices of the novel's personae. It is also what results from the most explicit communal event the characters share, namely the scene in which, now middle-aged, they repeat Percival's farewell party by meeting at Hampton Court outside London. Neville describes their initial emotions succinctly: "What do we feel on meeting? Sorrow. The door will not open; he will not come. And we are laden. Being now all of us middle-aged, loads are on us. Let us put down our loads. What have you made of life, we ask, and I?" (211). The melancholy sparked by Percival's death bleeds into the recognition of their own aging, the whispers of their own mortality implied by their position as middle-aged. While the question of what they have "made of life" anticipates the attempt Bernard makes in his closing monologue to "hand [my life] to you entire" and suggests a desire to ward off this mortality with more permanent-seeming accomplishments, the shared evening provides an experience of subjective annihilation that allows all the characters to access the kind of "binding" of objective temporality that I have been tracing.

On finishing dinner, Bernard makes an observation, which the rest of the party comes to echo, regarding the way their individual identities seem to slough off: "'Drop upon drop,' said Bernard, 'silence falls. . . . [It] pits my face, wastes my nose like a snowman stood out in a yard in the rain. As silence falls I am dissolved utterly and become featureless and scarcely to be distinguished from another'" (224). The image of the melting snowman suggests the slow softening of the boundaries among the friends and recalls the moment of intimacy that Louis was so anxious to preserve at the end of Percival's going-away dinner. Here, however, the feeling goes beyond their little coterie and indeed beyond human community altogether. In response to this dispersal of self, what he describes as "blunt[ing] the tooth of egotism," Bernard observes, "I reflect now that the earth is only a pebble flicked off accidentally from the face of the sun and that there is no life anywhere in the abysses of space" (225). When Louis repeats this cosmological perspective—"Our separate drops are dissolved; we are extinct, lost in the abysses of time, in the darkness" (225)—he suggests that this dispersal is itself a kind of death, an experience of being swallowed up by the immensity of the universe that reduces consciousness to a bare minimum. This is, in effect, the death of the subject that discloses the radical impersonality of the object world at which my discussion of time's passing has been gesturing.

Despite the dreamlike disembodiment here, the ability to describe the experience of this moment implies that the speakers have somehow survived their own extinction. When Bernard renarrates this moment in his closing monologue, however, he tempers this persistence of subjective consciousness in the face of an imagined disappearance in terms that rely on the mutilation of a faintly bookish materiality: "Half-way through dinner, we felt enlarge itself round us the huge darkness of what is outside us, of what we are not. The wind, the rush of wheels became the roar of time, and we rushed—where? And who were we? We were extinguished for a moment, went out like sparks in burnt paper and the blackness roared" (277). Bernard transforms the spatial movement suggested by the wind and the wheels into a temporal progress that ultimately leads him to visualize his and his friends' eclipse, but he does so in a way that indicates the coincident continuation of time and space. The speakers do not escape—even if they cannot comprehend—the "abysses" of space and time in which they are lost. Rather their dissolution into a pile of charred documents suggests that their extinction leaves only the material remains of the book that has been transmitting their monologues, a brute materiality that serves as an emblem of exactly such intertwined temporal and spatial persistence.

This is, in the end, what Bernard leaves us with in his closing comments, which will allow me, for the last time, to add some volume to the subtle bibliographics that have been driving the entire argument of this book. Declaring the death of time itself when he goes on to claim that, in their experience of annihilation, "past time, past history we went," he paints a picture not of the permanence at which Louis aimed with his poetry but rather of a kind of radical finitude in which the very *passing of time itself* passes by. From this imaginary perspective the "roar of time" that has been pointing to the mortality of the speakers also indicates their *vitality*, the fact that the passing of time implicates as much their dying as their living. Accordingly when Bernard describes how this surpassing of time "lasts but one second. It is ended by my own pugnacity. I strike the table with a spoon" (277), his action underscores his strength and vigor and also suggests the extent to which this time-based vitality is bound up with the object world. Or, to put it more forcefully, the inanimation of the object world itself dismantles the very opposition between mortality and vitality as they take their place in the stream of life while simultaneously lacking any of the attributes that signal life as defined in human terms.

One object in particular showcases this dismantling most clearly, the same object to which Bernard's closing monologue ultimately—though not at first explicitly—appeals in its final renunciations of the phrase-making that has dogged him throughout the novel. Toward the end of his commentary he relates, "The rhythm stopped: the rhymes and hummings, the nonsense and the poetry. A space was cleared in my mind. I saw through the thick leaves of habit" (283). As the buzz of living dies away, Bernard attains a clarity through which he is once again able to perceive in a new way, outside of his routine practices. At the same time, the preposition *through* suggests that this clarity allows him to see *by means of* "the thick leaves of habit," as if the pages or "leaves" that he—like *The Waves*'s own reader—habitually turns reveal something new to him. When he says, "I addressed my self as one would speak to a companion with whom one is voyaging to the North Pole" (283), Bernard effectively splits his self off from his narrating consciousness and makes a kind of object out of it, as if it is ultimately an entity separate from the deliberate phrase-making by which he has tried to access it up to this point.

Indeed when he continues his train of thought, he describes the creation of this object-like self not by means of linguistic construction but in a kind of incremental accumulation that characterizes and subtly recalls the buildup of pages that attends a reader's progress through a book: "I spoke to that self who has been with me in many tremendous adventures . . . the man who has been so mysteriously and with sudden accretions of being built up, in a beech wood, sitting by a willow tree on a bank, leaning over a parapet at Hampton Court; the man who collected himself in moments of emergency and banged his spoon on the table, saying, 'I will not consent'" (283). As the "sudden accretions of being" ultimately result in a self that is able to bang his spoon on the table, these lines link this self to Bernard's physical body and the relationship it has with other material objects on which his life relies. For all Bernard's effort at creating this self out of language, the self does not ultimately—or any longer—speak: "This self now as I leant over the gate looking down over the fields rolling in waves of color beneath me made no answer. He threw up no opposition. He attempted no phrase" (283–84).

This silence sparks a crisis for Bernard: "No echo comes when I speak, no varied words. This is more truly death than the death of friends, than the death of youth" (284). He makes a similar statement a few pages later: "But how describe the world seen without a self? There are no words. Blue, red, even they distract, even they hide with thickness instead of letting the light through. How describe or say anything in articulate words again?" (287). As he views the lack of words as tantamount to death, the representational crisis becomes an ontological crisis. Yet the fact that his narrating consciousness (however self-less) once again persists through this death suggests that his being neither ends nor begins with language. When he finally acknowledges "I have done with phrases" and observes, "How much better is silence; the coffee-cup, the table. How much better to sit by myself like the solitary sea-bird that opens its wings on the stake" (295), he opens his consciousness to the very object world whose support I have been examining. Yet as he asks to be allowed to "sit here forever with bare things, this coffee-cup, this knife, this fork, things in themselves, myself being myself," he accedes to his own status as a physical object that persists through the end of the narrative that has repeatedly exceeded its own pronouncements of closure.

The image of the "solitary sea-bird that opens its wings on the stake" intimates the breakdown of Bernard's subject-centered narrative into the impersonal interludes that underlie it. A few pages earlier he describes, "Day rises; the girl lifts the watery fire-hearted jewels to her brow; the sun levels his beams straight at the sleeping house; the waves deepen their bars; they fling themselves on the shore" (291–92), a description that comes not from the scene of Bernard sitting with his companion in a restaurant but from the interludes that provide a binding background to the novel itself. When Bernard's narrative does ultimately end, when he proclaims, "Against you I will fling myself, unvanquished and unyielding, O Death!," it is the waves of the interludes, the unfeeling world of objects, that take his place. "The waves broke on the shore," Woolf writes (297). Concluding with this breaking of waves calls even this ending into question, since this image itself suggests a kind of perpetual continuation, the persistence of the inanimate world beyond our own consciousness.

But this is not only inanimate persistence at work here: though this might be the end of the novel, it is not the end of the book. There is one more page to turn before we close the cover. And even then the image of the object world with which the novel leaves us finds its own continuation in the object world in which the book takes its place. This is, ultimately, the effect of the curious choice to open and close the novel with these "interludes," a term that denotes precisely connection or continuation. At these points of origin and conclusion, however, there seems nothing within the novel's narrative with which an interlude might connect. In a parallel to both the *Recherche* and *Finnegans Wake*, the final line is ultimately of a piece with the opening interlude, whose description of the way "the sea was indistinguishable from the sky" points to a general lack of differentiation among the objects in the world that also engulfs the book itself.

Yet even as this ending highlights the book's place as an object in the world, the indistinguishability with which *The Waves* leaves us is precisely what my argument has been working to forestall. It should thus come as no surprise that I want to move toward the end of this book by taking advantage of that feature of bookish format on which this chapter has focused—namely the binding that allows me to *turn back* a few pages (which, in temporal terms, is always a move forward) to the moment Bernard begins to narrate his final linguistic renunciation with a vision of his notebook. "My book, stuffed with phrases, has dropped to the floor," he states. "It lies under the table to be swept up by the charwoman when she comes wearily at dawn looking for scraps of paper, old tram tickets, and here and there a note screwed up into a ball and left with the litter to be swept up" (294–95). Though Bernard tellingly ignores the book in his enumeration of the objects that surround him in his approach to his own end, the images to which he compares it here highlight the kind of ephemerality that I have been at pains to draw out. This description can thus allow us to linger, for a final moment, over the way the book gets "swept up" into the larger stream of things in much the same way that the waves of the novel's interludes sweep in and engulf Bernard's narrative. This has, of course, been part of my critical strategy all along, as I have dawdled over the sensory and material aspects of our literary experience of these novels, which, like Bernard at this moment, we must inevitably overlook in our drive to read their texts. By insisting that we take the time to look over these bookish aspects, I have hoped to show how attending to the death of the book can bring it, paradoxically, to life.

Coda

The Afterlives of Reading

The strange concatenation of death and life with which my discussion of *The Waves* falls silent announces the larger implications of the argument about book reading that I have been developing. I have been meditating on the currency of the book at a moment when newer forms of mediation appear to be heralding its obsolescence, but I have not been doing so by drawing out the affordances of the codex in terms of their overlooked similarities with anything like the aesthetic possibilities of film or the seemingly infinite mutability of the digital. On the contrary, the emphasis on temporality and transience that the works of Proust, Joyce, and Woolf root in the object of the book uncover a mutability of a more finite kind: the elementary mutability entailed in finitude itself. Indeed as these works show the way the book indexes or materializes the passing of time, they exhibit the driving force undergirding the obsolete as such. In so doing they allow us to see the way that the category of the obsolete—the status of being outdated, archaic, or even, so to speak, *dead*—is not only an explicit function of local historical circumstances (e.g., the rise of a new technology or practice) but also, and more fundamentally, the implicit condition of the materiality of media forms as such. Following this logic, mediation's material forms are, at least theoretically, always already obsolete, always already bound up with their own supersession. In the more specific terms of my argument, this means that the colloquial understanding of "the death of the book," which would refer to the book's imagined decline in the face of alternative means of textual transmission, is inextricable from, even dependent on the underlying finitude that, in the hands of these novelists, the object of the book makes palpable.

With this in mind, one way to describe the book's persistent contemporaneity is precisely in the way it foregrounds or highlights this condition of finite obsolescence—or, to phrase this in a more punningly metaphorical vocabulary, the way it brings its own death to life. The whisper of the ghostly in this figurative phrasing frames the appeal to the afterlife in the title of this closing coda less as a pledge of eternal existence than as an exposure or *activation* of the bookish death that, in my argument, has been figuring the role time plays in the experience of literary mediation. If reading lives, if in fact it *lives on*, it is only through its imbrication with the very temporality that simultaneously indicates its passing. Accordingly, summoning up reading's afterlife implies that the mode of its continuation is, as my discussion of obsolescence has emphasized, one of continual expiration. At the same time, the rhetoric of the afterlife should also speak to digital forms of textual mediation that position themselves as more or less explicit replacements for the book, technological promises to give reading something like a new lease on life. I thus conclude my discussion by placing it into conversation with some of the various afterlives to which the recent rise of the digital lays claim. Doing so allows me to gesture toward the importance that the old-fashioned bookishness of my argument has for discussions of new media, and it also dates this argument to a very specific historical moment in a way that proclaims its own inescapable entanglement with precisely the finitude it has been exploring. If, some day soon, this argument seems quaintly mired in a passé technological situation, its obsolescence will only be a performance of its point.

Taking a look at one of reading's most highly publicized afterlives will help to materialize my points here. In the August 3, 2009, issue of the *New Yorker*, Nicholson Baker recounts his experience with what was, at the time, amazon.com's newest gadget: the Kindle 2. Baker's account is extensive. He describes the business and technology behind the components out of which the invention is constructed; the hype surrounding its announcement, including its celebration as "an alpenhorn blast of post-Gutenbergian revalorization"; and, ultimately, the mildly successful experience of reading Michael Connelly's mystery novel *The Lincoln Lawyer* after his familiarization with the device. Most interesting for my discussion, however, is the initial difficulty he has in looking past the Kindle's "gray" screen. As he pithily puts it, "It wasn't just gray; it was a greenish, sickly gray. A postmortem gray."[1] The flippant phrasing is all too apt as it connects the material obtrusiveness of the Kindle screen with the very deathliness that has been animating my argument. Yet even as this comment brings what seems to be the never-ending stream of e-readers into line with what I've been calling the death of the book, it does not keep Baker from voicing rather naïve beliefs about digital textuality, beliefs that ultimately elide the very materiality that trips him up. Asserting what, given his previous comments, we recognize as a rather too stark distinction between the Kindle and the traditional book, he writes that, with such a device, "there is no clutter, no pile of paperbacks next to the couch. A Kindle book arrives wirelessly: it's untouchable; it exists on a higher, purer plane" (27).

This fantasy of the digital's purity is only a more explicit articulation of a general readerly disregard of materiality that my argument has been working to contest. Baker's account of amazon.com founder and CEO Jeff Bezos's comments on the more traditional book make this clear. Quoting and paraphrasing Bezos's explanation for the limited public interest in e-books that resulted in low initial sales of the Kindle, Baker writes, "'It's because books are so good,' according to Bezos. And they're good, he explained, because they disappear when you read them: 'You go into a flow state'" (28). Even as Bezos's slightly new-agey idiom stages reading as a kind of zombie-like state between consciousness and unconsciousness that resonates with the life-death dynamic at play in this epilogue, the experience he describes will be familiar to anyone who has been swept up in a mystery novel or a love story. What this account of the book leaves out, however, is exactly what Baker's early dissatisfaction with the Kindle—as well as the readings that have constituted this book—reveal, namely the fact that this flow state is neither constant nor even consistent. My investigation of the ways the novels in my study explore the profoundly sensory experiences with which reading is entwined has aimed at developing the moments when the materiality of our reading platforms flaunt a weighty counterbalance to the idealism behind both Bezos's and Baker's statements. By showing that, in these cases, reading involves as much the book's disappearance as its mode of appearance, this argument implicitly points to the "sickly gray" screen that itself explicitly disputes any notion of electronic "untouchability." Though something like a Kindle might circumvent a pile of paperbacks, my reading of these novels helps us to see that today's growing panoply of digital devices offers a comparable contemporary clutter—as if their plastic and glass components are, in more ways than one, the postmortem materialization of the book's own ghostly afterlife.

In other words, as the Kindle and devices like it come to stand in for the book, they proclaim and indeed embody the death of that medium in material formats that are themselves equally finite. And it is in revealing these deathly continuities that my tenaciously literary argument contributes to what John Guillory felicitously describes as "giv[ing] a better account of the relation between literature and later technical media without granting to literature the privilege of cultural seniority or to later media the palm of victorious successor" (322n3). If in fact, as Guillory claims, the disciplinary division between literary and media studies has been "tacitly supported" by the fact that "literature seems to be less conspicuously marked by medial identity than other media, such as film" (322n3), the ways the novels in my study seem to wear at least part of their "medial identity" on their sleeves works to further flesh out the spaces and modes in which literature abuts other forms of mediation. More specifically, by considering the way these novels more or less explicitly conceive of their own bookish format, this book brings literature's multiple mediums to light and opens up the possibility of a détente in the unnecessary antagonism between so-called high-tech and low-tech forms of mediation.

While this claim might seem somewhat excessive given the narrow scope in which my argument has developed, a return to some of the more expansive work in media studies that I broached in my introduction will amplify the analytical ramifications I'm suggesting. Rounding out the larger critical contours in which my more specific argument can reverberate will also parse, one final time and in larger, disciplinary terms, the connection this project has been asserting between our physical experience of media forms and a sense of temporal progress with which mediation as such is necessarily intertwined. In her book *Writing Machines*, N. Katherine Hayles is interested in reintroducing the notion of materiality into the critical conversation of literature to account for the lives and afterlives of textuality in a digital age. In order to be able to consider the effects of the different formats that a text can take on today, she insists that "the physical form of the literary artifact always affects what the words (and other semiotic components) mean" and provides an especially supple discussion of physical materiality that portrays, in more general terms, the readerly dynamic that these novels have made particularly perspicuous. When, for example, Hayles grounds materiality in "interactions between physical properties and a work's artistic strategies," she describes some of the aesthetic effects—such as the attention that the dim narrative of *Finnegans Wake* draws to its print—that I have been tracing.[2] She goes on to articulate the role played by the reader in these interactions, in ways that recall something like the page-turning of *The Waves*, and discusses materiality as an "emergent property . . . [that] depends on how the work mobilizes its resources as a physical artifact as well as on the user's interactions with the work and the interpretive strategies she develops—strategies that include physical manipulations as well as conceptual frameworks" (33). The three nodes in her discussion, which we might particularize as format, text, and reader, thus work together to produce an aesthetic experience that preserves the emphasis on sensory perception entailed in the Greek root *aisthetikos*.

The central emphasis on perception in this account of materiality points to the way media studies' concerns have sparked and kindled this book's literary argument. For instance, Hayles's interest in making space to address "all the other signifying components of electronic texts, including sound, animation, motion, video, kinesthetic involvement, and software functionality" (for which, she claims, a print-centric view of literature fails to account), is precisely the kind of thinking that has allowed me to articulate an enriched understanding of the visual, haptic, and kinesthetic resources of the printed book itself (20). At the same time, however, the striking sensory experiences provided by the electronic threaten to overshadow the other, equally important aspect of materiality that she mentions, namely its processual constitution, its time-dependent *emergence*. As temporality is precisely the condition that my discussion makes particularly available, it indicates one way this account of the book sharpens our understanding of the materiality of media forms and of the relationship between the study of literature and media more broadly. Indeed an important part of my focus on the particularities of book reading is meant to forestall the simple subsumption of literature and "traditional" literary study into what could seem like an increasingly cannibalistic field of media studies.

While this is not, by any means, the necessary upshot of Hayles's important work, the way she frames the argument for what she significantly calls a "full-bodied understanding of literature" has the effect of tacitly eclipsing some of the critical resources—such as a sense of temporality—that older media forms might afford (26). For instance, despite her assertion "I do not mean to argue for the superiority of electronic media" (33), her insistence on the critical necessity of considering materiality remains firmly motivated by and invested in the digital. She puts her case succinctly: "Without [materiality] we have little hope of forging a robust and nuanced account of how literature is changing under the impact of information technology," as if to suggest that materiality is only an issue for literature now that it must reckon with the computer-based textuality that is becoming ever more ubiquitous (19). Moreover her attempt to expand this claim beyond the particular issues aroused by new media technology only seems to confirm her narrow scope as she points out that "not only electronic literature but virtually all historical periods and genres are affected as print works are increasingly re-produced as electronic documents" (19). The way the continued existence of these various "historical periods and genres" is tied up with their electronic reproduction overlooks that the materiality of transmission is a fundamental, if only implicit issue for literary works across history.

Drawing out the explicit—and explicitly temporal—terms in which the novels in my study reflect on the issue of their own materiality thus gestures at the place older literature and older media forms have within an increasingly expanding media landscape, a way to point toward one specific role traditional literary study plays within a broadened field of media studies. If media studies has provided a perspective that can attend to the sensory experience provided by the phenomenological materiality of the book, then my literary discussion has insisted that such materiality and such an experience are themselves temporal phenomena. What attending to the book—or at least to *these* books—teaches us is that the digital is also subject to the flow of time, is also wrapped up in the inescapable drift toward obsolescence. Although the distinct ways in which the digital intersects with temporality are beyond the bounds of this discussion, such divergence from the book's own particular deathliness in no way undercuts the more fundamental point.

What has ultimately allowed for these considerations and comparisons of literary and media studies is, precisely, my approach to and interest in reading, the way that my meditation on the individual act of taking up a book and coming into contact with the words on its pages positions reading as itself a media experience. This has ultimately been the motivating force behind my choice of a reputedly obsolete critical methodology, my embrace of the rather unfashionable technique of close reading. More than this, it has provided rhetorical justification for the essayistic asides that have been signaling the way my discussion is embedded in precisely the transitory moments of my own textual experiences. When I think back to the beginning of this project, the early drafts written in the blindingly white light of the San Francisco Bay Area, I am struck by the way its final materialization into—what else?—a book has carried these ideas across wide swaths of space and time. Revised and reworked under the heavy snows of several historic Boston winters, the argument embodied in this volume is ultimately the ephemeral record of my reading, my fleeting attempt to give it some kind of passing afterlife.

ACKNOWLEDGMENTS

My primary thanks must go to Elizabeth Abel, who shepherded this project from its early conception to its final bookish form. Her thinking, her criticism, and her support have been invaluable. I sometimes think that the only way I can repay her is by becoming as caring and engaged a teacher and colleague as she has been.

Thanks also go out to the rest of my support network at Berkeley: to John Bishop, whose thinking has remained central to this project even when his physical presence was no longer available; to D. A. Miller, who stepped in as a secondary reader only to become a primary friend; to Kaja Silverman, who arguably sparked this entire intellectual endeavor; to Kevis Goodman, who provided "unofficial" support and advice; to Vicki Mahaffey, who encouraged and advocated for me from afar.

Coming to Tufts I found a set of colleagues and mentors without whose help this project would have languished on the digital files of my old laptop. I am delighted to thank Lee Edelman for his insights, advice, and introductions; Joe Litvak for his guidance and encouragement; Lisa Lowe for taking time to offer some readerly resources in a project that, at first glance, might have seemed far from her own area of interest.

I want to make a special mention of the Dolores Zohrab Liebmann Fellowship, the Tufts Junior Faculty Leave, and the Mesa Vista Santa Fe Writing Retreat, all of which were integral in bringing this project to completion. Additionally I want to thank two journals that published early versions of some of the arguments in this book. Portions of chapter 1 appeared as "Sleeping with Proust: Affect, Sensation, and the Books of the *Recherche*" in *New Literary History* 42.1 (2011): 129–46. A portion of chapter 3 appeared as "Literal

Darkness: *Finnegans Wake* and the Limits of Print" in *James Joyce Quarterly* 50.3 (2013): 675–91.

From a more personal perspective (though, in a career like this one, the categories of professional and personal are often rather difficult to distinguish), I want to thank my dear friends: Katie Peterson, Dan Hantman, Brian Healy, Katy Niner, Brooke Harris, Ben Shockey, Batya Ungar-Sargon, David Divita, Órlaith Creedon, Allegra Love, and the Love-Damm family of Bridget, Justin, Clinton, and Woody.

Finally extreme gratitude and love go out to my parents, Craig and Carla; to my sister, Joanna; to my partner, Arturo; and to my dog, Helios.

INTRODUCTION: OPENING THE BOOK

1. Woolf, *Mrs. Dalloway*, 9.

2. Kittler, *Discourse Networks*, 245.

3. For a broad and diversely historical account of the way knowledge is shaped through its means of transmission, see Chandler et al., "Arts of Transmission." Kittler's argument bears more than a family resemblance to Clement Greenberg's discussion of modernist medium specificity in "Towards a Newer Laocoon," against which my argument is also poised. Greenberg considers "literature" as "subject matter at its most oppressive," where the medium becomes most transparent as poetry "is isolated in the power of the word to evoke associations and to connote" (301, 306). Both Greenberg and Kittler seem to me to have a somewhat narrow understanding of the concept of the medium, which, as we will see, is always and necessarily a multimedium: poetry's words connote at the same time as they are also visible. See Mitchell's "There Are No Visual Mediums". For an example of a study that builds directly on Kittler's work, see Harris, *Mediating Modernity*.

4. Guillory, "Genesis of the Media Concept," 321–22. Guillory's theoretical and historical account complements the argument Hansen makes in his early work for the "robust *materiality* of technology" (*Embodying Technesis*, 4). While the latter's somewhat unconventional reading of Walter Benjamin's discussion of *Erlebnis* helps him to develop "a distinct *postlinguistic* form of mimesis that would restore a crucial dimension of *sensuosity*—a practical, embodied basis—to our contact with the material world" (232), my interest in the way the very language of these novels seeks to draw attention to its material embodiment in the "technology" of the book limits the relevance of his model (which focuses much more deliberately on film) for my argument.

5. Pressman, *Digital Modernism*, 3.

6. Although my use of Wolfgang Iser's idea of the "implied reader" resurrects a rather ancient term (one might even—appropriately enough for an argument about the "death of the book"—call it a "dead" term), situating this phantasmatic reader in the specific media landscape of the early twentieth century attempts to address the critique of an ahistorical universalism

made by book historian Roger Chartier, especially his point that a study like Iser's "in no way depends on the material forms that operate as a vehicle for the text." While Chartier's work is more interested in giving what he calls "an archaeology of reading practices," my approach mines the novels of this historical moment to draw out one particular kind of reading practice that complicates—indeed counters—Iser's insistently disembodied focus on the "virtual" relation between text and reader. Chartier, *The Order of Books*, 10, 22. See also Iser's *The Implied Reader* and *The Act of Reading*.

7. See, among others, Baines and Haslam, *Type and Typography*; Hills, *Papermaking in Britain*; Huss, *The Development of Printers' Mechanical Typesetting Methods*; Legros and Grant, *Typographical Printing-Surfaces*; Southall, *Printer's Type in the Twentieth Century*. In addition to the industrialization of the printing process, a number of other factors contributed to the explosion in printed matter from the nineteenth into the twentieth century, including a marked rise in literacy, the growth of lending libraries, and the creation of a commuter class as people moved out of cities and into the suburbs. See Altick, *The English Common Reader*; David, *Literacy and Popular Culture*.

8. Price, *How to Do Things with Books in Victorian Britain*.

9. The scholarship in this field is extensive, but the most famous exponents of this kind of book history remain Roger Chartier and Robert Darnton, along with other august figures such D. F. McKenzie, Lucien Febvre, and Henri-Jean Martin. See Chartier, *The Order of Books*; Robert Darnton, "What Is the History of Books?"; Febvre and Martin, *The Coming of the Book: The Impact of Printing*; McKenzie, *Bibliography and the Sociology of Texts*. More recently, Andrew Piper's *Dreaming in Books* tells us much about the way romantic literature was formed by and, in turn, helped to form the bibliographic culture that made the format of the book so transparently intelligible to the readers of the nineteenth century and beyond. The wide-ranging sociological discussion of the book's naturalization, however, minimizes the consideration of what it means for a physical object to transmit a text in the first place, a consideration of physical mediation that the experimental novels in my study conduct through their meditations on and play with the practices of book reading. For more general work in material textual studies, which places emphasis on the ways specific formats contribute a determining influence on how and what a text can mean, see "Cluster on Textual Materialism," *PMLA* 125.1 (2010); Bornstein, *Material Modernism*; McGann, *The Textual Condition*; McGann, *Black Riders: The Visible Language of Modernism*.

10. Goldstone, *Fictions of Autonomy*. He offers a wide-ranging, capacious definition of autonomy and writes, "I group under the heading 'aesthetic autonomy of literature' a set of assumptions, doctrines, and themes that have in common an idea of literature as *independent* of some circumstance with which it might otherwise seem to be entangled or as *free* from some obligation or purpose it might otherwise seem to have" (11).

11. Hayles, *How We Became Posthuman*, 5. The novels in my study anticipate the more recent and somewhat more flamboyant exploitations of the

printed book—like Mark K. Danielewski's *House of Leaves*—that help Hayles develop her concept of the "material metaphor," a term that "foregrounds the traffic between words and physical artifacts" (*Writing Machines*, 22).

12. Hägglund, *Dying for Time*, 19. My emphasis on objects offers an expanded perspective on the relationship between modernism and mourning on which a number of recent inquiries have focused. Proposing that, in modernism, the work of mourning spurns ideas of consolation and closure and instead becomes a mode of social and emotional engagement with a world riven by loss and trauma, these projects describe a condition very similar to the one that I am developing here. Yet the subjective experience of sustained loss on which these studies focus is only one, albeit important, part of the experience of modernity; the sense of loss that I am chronicling, however, is rooted in and inextricable from the ephemerality to which objects are, as it were, subject. See Clewell, *Mourning, Modernism, Postmodernism*; Rae, *Modernism and Mourning*; Flatley, *Affective Mapping*; Detloff, *The Persistence of Modernism*; Rosenthal, *Mourning Modernism*. For a more philosophical account of similar issues, see Horowitz, *Sustaining Loss*.

13. Hägglund, "The Arche-Materiality of Time,", 266.

14. Hayles, *How We Became Posthuman, Writing Machines, My Mother Was a Computer, Electronic Literature, How We Think*; Drucker, "Reading Interface," "Intimations of Immateriality," "Humanities Approaches to Interface Theory," "Entity to Event," "The Virtual Codex from Page Space to E-Space," *Graphesis*; Hansen, *New Philosophy for New Media* and *Bodies in Code*.

15. My appeal to periodical studies is meant to use a specifically modernist frame to further articulate the relationship of my argument to the cultural-historical questions asked by book history. Latham and Scholes discuss the emergence of periodical studies in "The Rise of Periodical Studies". In tandem with the development of the Modernist Journals Project, the issue of magazines and modernism has received a number of treatments, including Morrison, *The Public Face of Modernism*; Churchill and McKible, *Little Magazines and Modernism*; Scholes and Wulfman, *Modernism in the Magazines*. Additionally *The Oxford Critical and Cultural History of Modernist Magazines* has been appearing since 2009 with one volume each focusing on Britain and Ireland, North America, and Europe. This more focused consideration of modernist magazines complements larger accounts of the historical and cultural circumstances of modernism's production and reception, such as Willison et al., *Modernist Writers and the Marketplace*; Rainey, *Institutions of Modernism*; Turner, *Marketing Modernism between the Two World Wars*; Dettmar and Watt, *Marketing Modernisms*; Wexler, *Who Paid for Modernism?*

16. The term *remediate*, which refers to the way new forms of mediation (e.g., digital media) take up and refashion previous media forms, comes from Bolter and Grusin, *Remediation*. Gitelman has a chapter on the history of the PDF in *Paper Knowledge*.

17. Latham, "The Mess and Muddle of Modernism," 409. Latham's conception of the book is reminiscent of (if not implicitly indebted to) the theory

of modernism that Jameson develops in *Postmodernism*. Describing the "modernism of the isolated 'genius'" that is organized around the "Book of the World," Jameson details the way Joyce could "singlehandedly produc[e] a whole world" (305, 307). This kind of historicization consequently calls for a tracking of the economic conditions that either allowed for such a fantasy to develop or that point up the impossibility of such a dream; my argument proposes a different way of imagining these works' imbrication into their historical moment.

18. Drucker italicizes only *as*, but I've added emphasis to *interface* to underscore the computer-centric discourse to which she has recourse. It's interesting to note that in her article "The Virtual Codex from Page Space to e-Space" Drucker explicitly indicates the "virtuality" of her conception of book reading when she calls for e-books to stop mimicking traditional books and take advantage of the new material and functional affordances of the electronic: "The traditional book produces virtual *e-space*" (221). Similarly Piper's follow-up volume on the book, *Book Was There*, takes a more "phenomenological" approach to the experience of the book. His argument lightly intersects with mine, but my more focused textual framework provides a more explicit account of the way these novels imagine the book as such, rather than focusing, as he does, on the continuities and discontinuities that book reading, considered across a number of diverse historical eras, has with the kind of perusing we do with contemporary digital media forms.

19. For example, a set of essays like those collected in Harding, *Ford Madox Ford, Modernist Magazines and Editing* delineates the productive exchanges among writers and editors or the economic conditions of the review's management with more detail.

20. Both Price and Christina Lupton have explicitly addressed the book's role as the nonhuman narrator of a more traditional "it-narrative." See Lupton, *Knowing Books*, chapter 2: "What It Narratives Know about Their Authors"; Price, *How To Do Things with Books in Victorian Britain*, chapter 4, "It-Narrative and Book as Agent."

I. THE BOOKS OF THE *RECHERCHE*

1. Proust, *Remembrance of Things Past*, 1: 3.

2. Proust, "On Reading," 116. In *Proust and Signs*, Deleuze offers perhaps the most "spiritually" centered account of Proust's work in the way he traces the narrator's progressive "apprenticeship" in overcoming his "objectivism" and finding transcendental "essences" (see chapters 3 and 4). My account focuses on the privileged place that the object of the book—an explicit bearer of signs that the rest of world carries only implicitly—holds in Proust's work.

3. Beckett, *Proust and Three Dialogues*, 36.

4. Both Gray and Kristeva, for instance, tease out the Oedipal drama and incestuous relationships that form the novel's plot to define the mysterious quality literature takes on for the narrator. See Gray, *Postmodern Proust*, especially chapter 6: "Skipping Love Scenes: Marcel's Repression of Literature"; Kristeva, *Proust and the Sense of Time*, chapter 2: "In Search of Madeleine."

5. The Moncrieff translation omits the phrase, italicized here, "even the title of the book." The original French, however, enumerates the "expedients of nature which had caused a sensation" thus: "bruit de la fourchette et du marteau, même titre de livre, etc" (*À la Recherche du Temps Perdu*, 2266).

6. Bersani, *The Culture of Redemption*, 11.

7. In "The Body of the Text/The Text of the Body," Doubrovsky notes that, in the novel's opening, the narrator's ego "is a pure non-ego" (3), the way it becomes identified with the subjects of the book the narrator is reading as he falls asleep: "a church, a quartet, the rivalry between François I and Charles V" (1: 3).

8. Klein, *The Selected Melanie Klein*, 179.

9. In her essay "Symbol Formation in Ego Development," Klein details the complicated dynamic of infantile sadism that transforms introjected objects into potential sources of dangerous and anxiety-producing retaliation, which in turn causes the infant to identify with ever-new external objects. This ultimately results in the infant's relation to the outside world and reality in general. Here the object to which the narrator turns as a symbol of his mother's fleetingly reassuring presence is Sand's novel.

10. While Proust's manuscripts have provided fodder for a number of genetic studies of his work, I am not interested in describing his creative process in order to reconstruct the development of the specific moments in the work like traditional genetic critics. Compagnon's treatment of the notebooks in *Proust: Between Two Centuries* perhaps comes closest to my approach, as he attempts to read back and forth between the right-hand pages (the location of the novel's development) and left-hand pages (the location of the rare personal note) of the notebooks as a way of discussing the relationship between Proust's novel and his life (see chapter 5: "*Tableaux Vivants* in the Novel," 107–20). I am nonetheless also not engaged in treating the well-examined relationship between Proust's biography and the content of his novel.

11. Lydon, "*Pli selon pli*," 174.

12. For more details on this, see Tadié, *Marcel Proust*, 534–35, 664–65. See also the memoir of Proust's housekeeper Céleste Albaret, *Monsieur Proust*, especially 273–76.

13. Marcel Proust, unpublished manuscripts, Fonds Marcel Proust, n. a. fr. 16686, Bibliothèque nationale de France, Paris, 52v.

14. For a related argument, articulated in more insistently Freudian terms, see Silverman, *World Spectators*, especially chapter 5: "The Milky Way."

15. Cano, *Proust's Deadline*, 60.

16. Ellison, *The Reading of Proust*, 176. See also Kassell, *Marcel Proust and the Strategy of Reading*; Bowie, *Freud, Proust, Lacan*; Ross, "Albertine"; Gray, *Postmodern Proust*. All give a more or less similar argument in varying vocabularies.

17. Sedgwick, "Paranoid Reading and Reparative Reading," 133.

18. Moncrieff translates the last sentence of this paragraph as "In keeping it in front of my eyes" rather than "In keeping her," as if the object of the opening phrase is Albertine's body. Given the fact that *le corps* is masculine

in French, however, the *la* must refer to Albertine herself. I thus deviate here from the standard translation and thank Elizabeth Abel for pointing out this detail to me.

19. Merleau-Ponty, *The Visible and the Invisible*, 134–35.

20. Some prepositions, such as the *in* of sexual penetration, for instance, certainly do not indicate a completely or perfectly reciprocal relationship: the narrator might be *in* Albertine, but Albertine is certainly not *in* the narrator. At the same time, however, while she might not be *in* the narrator, she is nonetheless still in some kind of spatial relationship with him: we might say that she is *outside* the narrator, or *around* him.

21. Bersani, *Marcel Proust*, 79.

22. Merleau-Ponty's emphasis on embodiment uses the vocabulary of subject-object relations to make a similar, less temporally inflected point. In phrasing that describes the interaction between Albertine and the narrator, he writes, "Our body is a being of two leaves, from one side a thing among things and otherwise what sees them and touches them; we say, because it is evident, that it unites these two properties within itself, and its double belongingness to the order of the 'object' and to the order of the 'subject' reveals to us quite unexpected relations between the two orders" (137).

23. Landy, *Philosophy as Fiction*, 96.

2. THE READER OF *ULYSSES*

1. Parandowski, "Meeting with Joyce," 159.

2. See Groden, *Ulysses in Progress*, 37; Moretti, *The Modern Epic*, 183–84. Although Moretti claims that the experiment of the Sirens episode "may be simply regarded as a failure: it is repeated neither by Joyce nor by others" (184), Sirens is one of the most proto-*Wake*an of *Ulysses*'s episodes, as a comparison with my argument in the chapter on *Finnegans Wake* that follows will show.

3. Stainer, "'The Void Awaits Surely All Them That Weave the Wind,'" 326.

4. For the myriad "musically minded" considerations of Sirens, see Levin, "The Sirens Episode as Music"; Bowen, "The Bronzegold Sirensong"; Lees, "Introduction to Sirens and the *Fuga per Canonem*"; Zimmerman, "Musical Form as Narrator"; Mooney, "Bronze by Gold by Bloom"; Fischer, "Strange Words, Strange Music"; Ordway, "A Dominant Boylan." For examples of an emphatically nonmusical approach, see Ferrer, "Echo or Narcissus?"; Rabaté, "The Silence of the Sirens."

5. In *The Odyssey of Style in Ulysses*, Lawrence discusses how the headlines of the Aeolus episode interrupt what she calls the "narrative norm" of the first six chapters (see 55–79). She suggests that the Aeolus episode "can be said to provide the beginning of the middle of the novel we have been reading" and details the way it anticipates a number of the stylistic changes to come (56–57). While the headline "IN THE HEART OF THE HIBERNIAN METROPOLIS" that opens the Aeolus episode certainly comes as a shock to the reader, the fact that it maintains correct orthography and generally follows the rules of English syntax makes it, in my opinion, less of a surprise

than the seemingly nonsensical beginning of Sirens, in which language itself seems to become an object to be broken apart and moved around.

6. Joyce, *Ulysses* (Vintage International, 1990), 256. Subsequent citations are to this edition. Though I prefer the book published by Vintage, the Gabler edition of *Ulysses* corrects a number of errata in the text, including substituting "steelyringing" for "steelyrining" in the first line of Sirens (210).

7. See, in particular, Ordway, "A Dominant Boylan"; Lees, "Introduction to Sirens and the *Fuga per Canonem*."

8. Attridge, "Joyce's Pen," 54; Gottfried, *Joyce's Iritis and the Irritated Text*, 6. Though I consider print more specifically in chapter 3, Gottfried, along with Hugh Kenner, relates this kind of attention to descriptions of Joyce's exacting treatments of *Ulysses*'s printer's proofs. See Gottfried 2–4; Kenner, *The Mechanic Muse*, especially 70–73. For a related discussion of both *Ulysses* and *Finnegans Wake* as "designed assemblages of expressive elements" (8), see Theall, *Beyond the Word*.

9. *Ulysses* has, of course, been a focal point for a number of comparisons between literary and cinematic modernisms that have alternatively found stylistic similarities or important differences between the novel and contemporaneous film. For analogical readings of the representational tactics of *Ulysses* and early twentieth-century film, see Burkdall, *Joycean Frames*; Barzagan, "The Headings in 'Aeolus'"; Briggs, "Roll Away the Reel World, the Reel World"; Baron, "Flaubert, Joyce." For discussions of their differences, see DiBattista, "This Is Not a Movie"; Trotter, *Cinema and Modernism*.

10. Attridge, *Peculiar Language*, 142.

11. Gilbert, *James Joyce's* Ulysses, 116.

12. For a fuller explanation, see Gifford, *Ulysses Annotated*, 45.

13. In his treatment of the presence of Berkeley in Proteus, Vitoux paraphrases the philosopher's position succinctly: "When we see two houses, the actual content of our perception is colors, variously disposed; but we arrange them into definite forms, and if one of those forms is smaller than the other, we conclude that we will have to cover a greater distance to reach it. Stereoscopic vision is not given in, but constructed out of, sensible ideas" ("Aristotle, Berkeley and Newman in 'Proteus' and *Finnegans Wake*," 161). Later he quotes from Berkeley's *New Theory of Vision* and relates this model of perception to language and signs: "We may fairly conclude that the proper objects of vision constitute a universal language of the Author of nature. . . . And the manner wherein [these signs] signify, and mark unto us the objects which are at a distance, is the same with that of languages and signs of human appointment" (167).

14. Joyce, *Portrait of the Artist as a Young Man*, 200.

15. The Vintage International edition has no comma between "No" and "mother," but the standard Gabler edition reinserts one (9) to suggest less a description of not having a mother than a direct address of defiance and resistance.

16. See Kenner, *Joyce's Voices*, 15–38.

17. Recall Stephen's hydrophobia, his reluctance to go swimming in the opening Telemachus episode, and Buck Mulligan's comment that "the

unclean bard makes a point of washing once a month" (15). Part of this
hydrophobia is, perhaps, a reluctance to immerse himself in a medium that
envelops his body so completely and is so different from the "immaterial"
medium of the air.

18. Merleau-Ponty explains, "We see the things themselves . . . [and] at
the same time are separated from them by all the thickness of the look and
of the body. . . . It is that the thickness of flesh between seer and the thing is
constitutive for the thing of its visibility as for the seer of his corporeity; it
is not an obstacle between them, it is their means of communication" (*The
Visible and the Invisible* 135). His description puts into more general terms
the specific relation between reader and book that *Ulysses* makes apparent
at this moment.

19. Benstock, "Printed Letters in *Ulysses*," 423.

20. I am indebted to John Bishop's course lectures on *Ulysses*, specifically on the "psychopathology" of the Lotos-Eaters episode, for much of the
thinking behind this point. For more on letters and masturbation in particular, see Jacques Derrida's treatment of the French slang *s'envoyer* in "Ulysses
Gramophone," especially 303–4.

21. The first part of Lyotard's *Discours, Figure*, entitled "Signification
and Designation," discusses the way that the perceptual field always inhabits
language. He elaborates Émile Benveniste's discussion of deictics to suggest
that these pointing words are where the perceptual most obviously breaks
into the linguistic. See 33–39 for a discussion of deictics specifically and
73–104 for an elaboration of the larger ramifications of this argument.

22. See Ellmann, *James Joyce*, 546–47.

23. Ellman, "To Sing or to Sign," 67.

3. THE DARK PRINT OF *FINNEGANS WAKE*

1. Bishop, *Joyce's Book of the Dark*, 4.

2. Joyce, *Finnegans Wake*, 20.10–13.

3. Rasula, "*Finnegans Wake* and the Character of the Letter," 522. For
arguments about the *Wake*'s treatment of its own textual production, see
Gold, "Printing the Dragon's Bite"; Schloss, "*Finnegans Wake* as History of
the Book."

4. In his treatment of the relationship between *Finnegans Wake* and the
Egyptian Book of the Dead, Bishop discusses how Joyce was able to find "a
cover psychology of sleep" in the bivalent way that the Book of the Dead's
more formal Egyptian title, "Chapters of Coming Forth by Day," can be
read "as the stream of unconsciousness of a man dead to the world, or as the
stream of unconsciousness of a man sleepily dead to the world" (88–89). His
extensive investigation of the "cryptic hieroglyphics of the dynastic Egyp-
tians" shows, in their explanation of how the sun dis- and reappears each
day, that "the phenomenon of the wake turns out to have much to do with
the simple, mundane experience of sleep" (92). This alliance is also in play
in my own argument as I leverage discussions of sleep to ultimately open up
issues of finitude.

5. McLuhan, *The Gutenberg Galaxy*, 27.

6. Derrida, "Two Words for Joyce," 147; Theall, *Beyond the Word*.

7. Connor, "The Modern Auditory I," 223.

8. For examples of this type of discussion, which constitutes the bulk of the writing surrounding the letter chapter, see Kaufman, *Textual Bodies*; McCarthy, "Reading the Letter"; McCarthy, "The Last Epistle of *Finnegans Wake*"; Milesi, "Metaphors of the Quest in *Finnegans Wake*"; Berresem, "The Letter!"; Benstock, *Textualizing the Feminine*; Sailer, *On the Void of To Be*.

9. Beckett, "Dante . . . Bruno," 14.

10. As my analysis suggests, Bishop's virtuosic and far-reaching discussion of *Wake* uses an argumentative method that makes it a paragon of the famous argument made by Joseph Frank in "Spatial Form in Modern Literature" that "the reader is intended to apprehend [modernist authors'] work spatially, in a moment of time, rather than as a sequence," a claim that my argument will explicitly work against (225).

11. Attridge, *Joyce Effects*, 155.

12. He writes that the overturned *E* "means HCE interred in the landscape" (*Letters*, 1: 254).

13. Eagle, "'Our Day at Triv and Quad,'" 321.

14. Crispi, "Storiella as She Was Wryt," 214.

15. While for Attridge the dream is "less relevant" because it is "a largely non-verbal and non-comic text" (*Effects* 148), Shem's example points to the relevance that the specifically visual character of the dream might have for reading the *Wake*'s dark print. This kind of attention to the visual is exactly what is entailed in the exploration of the letter that serves as a kind of intratextual representative of *Finnegans Wake* itself.

16. In her treatment of the letter chapter, "Letters to Biddy," Schaffer discusses another way Joyce temporalizes his letters by turning them into words: *p*'s and *q*'s become "pees" and "kews" (*FW* 119.35–120.1). She writes, "Turning the letters 'awry,' making them into words ('pees' and 'kews'), he has freed them, turned them into texts that can be broken apart, reconstituted, altered, punned," a textualization, she goes on to say, that allows the letters to "flow into a narrative" (627, 628).

17. Liu, "iSpace," 521, 522.

18. The italicized quotation from *Finnegans Wake* can be found at 345.19.

4. THE PAGES IN *JACOB'S ROOM*

1. McDowall, "The Enchantment of a Mirror," 213.

2. See Bishop, "Mind the Gap"; Briggs, *Reading Virginia Woolf*; Marcus, "Virginia Woolf and the Hogarth Press."

3. Woolf, "Mr. Bennett and Mrs. Brown," in *Collected Essays*, 1: 324, italics added.

4. Willis, *Leonard and Virginia Woolf as Publishers*, 16.

5. See Banfield, *The Phantom Table*, which I address in greater length in chapter 5. My account of the reader-book relation adds a reconsideration of readerly consumption to Mao's focus on productive creation in *Solid Objects*.

6. Woolf, *Jacob's Room*, 29.

7. As the editor of the Norton Critical Edition of *Jacob's Room*, Suzanne Raitt glosses the *Morning Post* as a "right-wing daily newspaper, popular with retired officers," while the *Daily Telegraph* was "founded in 1855 as a cheaper rival daily newspaper to the *Times*, aimed at the lower classes" (21).

8. Fry, *A Roger Fry Reader*, 201. Unless cited otherwise, all Fry quotes are from this source.

9. In this the Omega Workshop bears similarities with its closest precursor, the arts and crafts movement of William Morris. However, there were also significant differences between them, in particular Fry's emphasis on present rather than past styles and the lack of a socialist imperative. See Collins, *The Omega Workshops*, 29–31, for details. Additionally the Omega Workshop's emphasis on applied art offers a more object-centered strain in Fry's aesthetics that has been overlooked in favor of a focus on "logical form," which he articulates in later works like *Cezanne* (1927) and in some essays in *Vision and Design* (1920). See Banfield, *The Phantom Table* for a thorough discussion.

10. Woolf, *The Letters*, 2:159.

11. Porter, *The Omega Workshops and the Hogarth Press*, 12.

12. Howard Grey, preface to Anscombe, *Omega and After*, 8.

13. Fry, *Vision and Design*, 167.

14. As Warde writes of the aim of typography, "printing should be invisible" and should aspire to the state of "crystal-clear glass, thin as a bubble, and as transparent" (*The Crystal Goblet*, 11).

15. Woolf, *The Letters*, 3:167.

16. While this description suggests that the "restrictive" relationality of marriage operates along traditional gender lines (the aggressive male doing either the penetrating or the restricting, and the defenseless female being either penetrated or restricted), the example of Mr. and Mrs. Barfoot, both of whom are imprisoned in their own kind of fortress, shows that the restriction of such social conventions cuts across gender lines.

17. For more on Julian, see Murdoch, *The Last Pagan*. Lyotard offers a theoretical articulation of the pagan-Christian relationship at the beginning of *Discours, Figure*: it is "Christianity effectively which occupies the foundation of our problems. . . . It is demanded to deliver oneself from the thick flesh, to close the eyes, to be completely ear . . . that the appearance and depth which permits it be absolved in some way" (10). Drawing on the vision and depth in Merleau-Ponty's phenomenology, Lyotard implicitly emphasizes the interdependence of the discursive and the figural in terms of the pagan (a concept that returns in a more explicit and explicitly political form in *Just Gaming*).

18. Brown, "The Secret Life of Things," 13, 14.

5. THE BINDING OF *THE WAVES*

1. Woolf, *The Waves*, 238.

2. Graham, introduction, 20. During the composition of *The Waves*, Woolf writes in her diary of "books that relieve other books: a variety of

styles and subjects: for after all, that is my temperament, I think, to be very little persuaded of the truth of anything—what I say, what people say—always to follow, blindly, instinctively with a sense of leaping over a precipice—the call of—the call of—now" (*Diary*, 134).

3. For the focus on the construction of subjectivity in *The Waves*, see Stewart, "Catching the Stylistic D/rift"; Lucenti, " Virginia Woolf's *The Waves*"; Katz, "Modernism, Subjectivity, and Narrative Form"; Vandivere, "Waves and Fragments"; Monson, "'A Trick of the Mind.'" In *The Phantom Table*, Banfield offers a nonsubjective account of Woolf's work and views the descriptions of "unoccupied places and times" that occur throughout Woolf's novels—and in *The Waves* in particular—as literary versions of the kind of formal and logical abstraction involved in the work of the Cambridge philosophers to which Woolf was closely connected. Banfield takes a grammatical approach, positing that Woolf represents a thought or sensation not tied to any particular subject via "the elimination of the first person and the representation of a third person privacy" to portray "an absolutely depsychologized reality" (293, 60).

4. Woolf, *A Writer's Diary*, 153–54.

5. See also Lund, "*The Waves*."

6. Rich, "De Undarum Natura," 250.

7. Hägglund, "Arche-Materiality," 265.

8. Stewart ingeniously shows the way that Woolf's style "work[s] to bind and heal these very fissures" by developing what he performatively terms the "transegmental [*sic*] drift," the slippage of a phoneme between two separate words that acts, in English, much like the linguistic concept of *liaison* in French (e.g., the secondary production of the sound "shove" in the voicing of the phrase "rush of"). According to Stewart, this kind of linguistic continuity ultimately reverberates through the body of the reader and, he puns, "serve[s] to flesh out her text" ("Catching the Stylistic D/rift" 459). Patterns like the white spaces (which Stewart reads in deconstructive terms as the aporia that signification can never fully resolve) suggest to me that this "fleshing out" of the text might also extend to the object of the book rather than just the differential function of language.

9. In a scene toward the end of *Mrs. Dalloway*, Woolf offers another example of this phenomenon: "There was an embrace in death" (184).

CODA

1. Nicholson Baker, "A New Page: Can the Kindle Really Improve on the Book?," *New Yorker*, August 3, 2009, 24, 25.

2. Hayles, *Writing Machines*, 33.

BIBLIOGRAPHY

Albaret, Céleste. *Monsieur Proust.* Trans. Barbara Bray. New York: New York Review of Books, 1973.

Altick, Richard. *The English Common Reader.* Chicago: University of Chicago Press, 1957.

Anscombe, Isabelle. *Omega and After: Bloomsbury and the Decorative Arts.* London: Thames and Hudson, 1981.

Attridge, Derek. *Joyce Effects: On Language, Theory, and History.* Cambridge: Cambridge University Press, 2000.

———. "Joyce's Pen." In *Joyce, Penelope and the Body*, ed. Richard Brown. Amsterdam: Rodopi Press, 2006.

———. "Lipspeech: Syntax and Subject in Sirens." In *James Joyce: The Centennial Symposium*, ed. Morris Beja, Phillip Herring, Maurice Harmon, and David Norris. Chicago: University of Illinois Press, 1986.

———. *Peculiar Language: Literature as Difference from the Renaissance to James Joyce.* Ithaca, NY: Cornell University Press, 1988.

Baines, Phil, and Andrew Haslam. *Type and Typography.* London: Laurence King, 2002.

Banfield, Ann. *The Phantom Table: Woolf, Fry, Russel and the Epistemology of Modernism.* Cambridge: Cambridge University Press, 2000.

Baron, Scarlett. "Flaubert, Joyce: Vision, Photography, Cinema." *MFS: Modern Fiction Studies* 54.4 (2008): 689–714.

Barzagan, Susan. "The Headings in 'Aeolus': A Cinematographic View." *James Joyce Quarterly* 23 (1986): 345–50.

Beckett, Samuel. "Dante . . . Vico. Bruno . . . Joyce." In *Our Exagmination Round His Factification for Incamination of Work in Progress.* New York: New Directions, 1929.

———. *Proust and Three Dialogues.* London: John Calder, 1999.

Benstock, Shari. "Printed Letters in *Ulysses.*" *James Joyce Quarterly* 19.4 (1982): 415–27.

———. *Textualizing the Feminine: On the Limits of Genre.* Norman: University of Oklahoma Press, 1991.

Berresem, Hanjo. "The Letter! The Litter! The Defilements of the Signifier in *Finnegans Wake.*" In Finnegans Wake: *Fifty Years*, ed. Geert Lernout. Amsterdam: Rodopi Press, 1990.

Bersani, Leo. *The Culture of Redemption.* Cambridge, MA: Harvard University Press, 1990.

———. *Marcel Proust: The Fictions of Life and Art.* New York: Oxford University Press, 1965.

Bishop, Edward. "Mind the Gap: The Spaces in Jacob's Room." *Woolf Studies Annual* 10 (2004): 31–49.

Bishop, John. *Joyce's Book of the Dark:* Finnegans Wake. Madison: University of Wisconsin Press, 1993.

Bolter, Jay David, and Richard Grusin. *Remediation: Understanding New Media.* Cambridge, MA: MIT Press, 1999.

Bornstein, George. *Material Modernism: The Politics of the Page.* Cambridge: Cambridge University Press, 2001.

Bowen, Zack. "The Bronzegold Sirensong: A Musical Analysis of the Sirens Episode in Joyce's *Ulysses.*" *Literary Monographs* 1 (1966): 247–98, 319–20.

Bowie, Malcolm. *Freud, Proust, Lacan: Theory as Fiction.* Cambridge: Cambridge University Press, 1987.

Briggs, Austin. "Roll Away the Reel World, the Reel World: 'Circe' and Cinema." In *Coping with Joyce: Essays from the Copenhagen Symposium*, ed. Morris Beja and Shari Benstock. Columbus: Ohio State University Press, 1989.

Briggs, Julia. *Reading Virginia Woolf.* Edinburgh: Edinburgh University Press, 2006.

Brown, Bill. "The Secret Life of Things (Virginia Woolf and the Matter of Modernism)." *Modernism/Modernity* 6.2 (1999): 1–28.

Burkdall, Thomas L. *Joycean Frames: Film and the Fiction of James Joyce.* New York: Routledge, 2001.

Cano, Christine. *Proust's Deadline.* Urbana: University of Illinois Press, 2006.

Chandler, James, Arthur Davidson, and Adrian Johns, eds. "Arts of Transmission." Special issue, *Critical Inquiry* 31.1 (2004).

Chartier, Roger. *The Order of Books: Readers, Authors, and Libraries in Europe between the Fourteenth and Eighteenth Centuries.* Trans. Lydia G. Cochrane. Stanford: Stanford University Press, 1994.

Churchill, Suzanne W., and Adam McKible, eds. *Little Magazines and Modernism: Some New Approaches.* Burlington, VT: Ashgate, 2007.

Clewell, Tammy. *Mourning, Modernism, Postmodernism.* New York: Palgrave Macmillan, 2009.

Collins, Judith. *The Omega Workshops*. Chicago: University of Chicago Press, 1984.

Compagnon, Antoine. *Proust: Between Two Centuries*. Trans. Richard E. Goodkin. New York: Columbia University Press, 1992.

Connor, Steven. "The Modern Auditory I." In *Rewriting the Self: Histories from the Renaissance to the Present*, ed. Roy Porter. London: Routledge, 1996.

Conrad, Joseph. "Some Reminiscences." *English Review*, 1–6 (December 1908–May 1909). Modernist Journals Project (searchable database). Brown and Tulsa Universities, ongoing. http://www.modjourn.org.

Crispi, Luca. "Storiella as She Was Wryt: Chapter II.2." In *How Joyce Wrote Finnegans Wake: A Chapter-by-Chapter Guide*, ed. Luca Crispi and Sam Slote. Madison: University of Wisconsin Press, 2007.

Danius, Sara. *The Senses of Modernism: Technology, Perception, and Aesthetics*. Ithaca, NY: Cornell University Press, 2002.

Darnton, Robert. "What Is the History of Books?" *Daedalus* 111.3 (1982): 65–83.

David, Vincent. *Literacy and Popular Culture: England 1750–1914*. Cambridge: Cambridge University Press, 1989.

Deleuze, Gilles. *Proust and Signs: The Complete Text*. Trans. Richard Howard. Minneapolis: University of Minnesota Press, 2000.

Derrida, Jacques. "Two Words for Joyce." In *Post-Structuralist Joyce*, ed. Derek Attridge and Daniel Ferrer. Cambridge: Cambridge University Press, 1985.

———. "Ulysses Gramophone: Hear Say Yes in Joyce." In *Acts of Literature*, ed. Derek Attridge. New York: Routledge, 2002.

Detloff, Madelyn. *The Persistence of Modernism: Loss and Mourning in the Twentieth Century*. Cambridge: Cambridge University Press, 2009.

Dettmar, Kevin J. H., and Stephen Myers Watt, eds. *Marketing Modernisms: Self-Promotion, Canonization, Rereading*. Ann Arbor: University of Michigan Press, 1997.

DiBattista, Maria. "This Is Not a Movie: *Ulysses* and Cinema." *Modernism/Modernity* 13.2 (2006): 219–35.

Docherty, Thomas. "Joyce and the Anathema of Writing." In *James Joyce and the Difference of Language*, ed. Laurent Milesi. Cambridge: Cambridge University Press, 2003.

Doubrovsky, Serge. "The Body of the Text/The Text of the Body." Trans. Elizabeth Richardson. In *Reading Proust Now*, ed. Mary Anne Caws and Eugène Nicole. New York: Peter Lang, 1990.

Drucker, Johanna. "Entity to Event: From Literal, Mechanistic Materiality to Probabilistic Materiality." *Parallax* 15.4 (2009): 7–17.

———. *Graphesis: Visual Forms of Knowledge Production.* Cambridge, MA: Harvard University Press, 2014.

———. "Humanities Approaches to Interface Theory." *Culture Machine* 12 (2011): 1–20.

———. "Intimations of Immateriality: Graphical Form, Textual Sense, and the Electronic Environment." In *Reimagining Textuality: Textual Studies in the Late Age of Print.* Madison: University of Wisconsin Press, 2002.

———. "Reading Interface." *PMLA* 128.1 (2013): 213–20.

———. "The Virtual Codex from Page Space to e-Space." In *A Companion to Digital Literary Studies*, ed. Ray Siemens, Susan Schreibman, and Alan Liu. Malden, MA: Blackwell, 2007.

Eagle, Christopher. "'Our Day at Triv and Quad': Ruskin and the Liberal Arts in *Finnegans Wake*." *James Joyce Quarterly* 46.2 (2010): 321–40.

Ellison, David R. *The Reading of Proust.* Baltimore: Johns Hopkins University Press, 1984.

Ellman, Maud. "To Sing or to Sign." In *James Joyce: The Centennial Symposium*, ed. Morris Beja, Phillip Herring, Maurice Harmon, and David Norris. Chicago: University of Illinois Press, 1986.

Ellmann, Richard. *James Joyce.* New and revised edition. Oxford: Oxford University Press, 1982.

Febvre, Lucien, and Henri-Jean Martin. *The Coming of the Book: The Impact of Printing.* Trans. D. Gerard. London: NLB, 1976.

Ferrer, Daniel. "Echo or Narcissus?" In *James Joyce: The Centennial Symposium*, ed. Morris Beja, Phillip Herring, Maurice Harmon, and David Norris. Chicago: University of Illinois Press, 1986.

Fischer, Andreas. "Strange Words, Strange Music." In *Bronze by Gold: The Music of Joyce*, ed. Sebastian D. G. Knowles. New York: Garland, 1999.

Flatley, Jonathan. *Affective Mapping: Melancholia and the Politics of Modernism.* Cambridge, MA: Harvard University Press, 2008.

Frank, Joseph. "Spatial Form in Modern Literature: An Essay in Two Parts." *Sewanee Review* 53.2 (1945): 221–40.

Fry, Roger. *A Roger Fry Reader.* Ed. Christopher Reed. Chicago: University of Chicago Press, 1996.

———. *Vision and Design.* Ed. J. B. Bullen. Mineola, NY: Dover, 1998.

Gifford, Don. *Ulysses Annotated: Notes for James Joyce's Ulysses.* 2nd ed. Berkeley: University of California Press, 1974.

Gilbert, Stuart. *James Joyce's Ulysses: A Study.* New York: Vintage Books, 1955.

Gitelman, Lisa. *Paper Knowledge: Towards a Media History of Documents.* Durham, NC: Duke University Press, 2014.

Goble, Mark. *Beautiful Circuits: Modernism and the Mediated Life*. New York: Columbia University Press, 2010.

Gold, Moshe. "Printing the Dragon's Bite: Joyce's Poetic History of Thoth, Cadmus, and Gutenberg in *Finnegans Wake*." *James Joyce Quarterly* 42–43 (Fall/Summer 2004): 269–96.

Goldstone, Andrew. *Fictions of Autonomy: Modernism from Wilde to de Man*. Oxford: Oxford University Press, 2013.

Gottfried, Roy. *Joyce's Iritis and the Irritated Text: The Dys-lexic* Ulysses. Gainesville: University Press of Florida, 1995.

Graham, J. W. Introduction to *Virginia Woolf*, The Waves: *The Two Holograph Drafts*. Toronto: University of Toronto Press, 1976.

Gray, Margaret. *Postmodern Proust*. Philadelphia: University of Pennsylvania Press, 1992.

Greenberg, Clement. "Towards a Newer Laocoon." *Partisan Review* 7 (1940): 296–310.

Groden, Michael. *Ulysses in Progress*. Princeton, NJ: Princeton University Press, 1977.

Guillory, John. "Genesis of the Media Concept." *Critical Inquiry* 36.2 (2010): 321–62.

Hägglund, Martin. "The Arche-Materiality of Time: Deconstruction, Evolution, and Speculative Materialism." In *Theory after "Theory,"* ed. Jane Elliot and Derek Attridge. London: Routledge, 2011.

———. *Dying for Time: Proust, Woolf, Nabokov*. Cambridge, MA: Harvard University Press, 2012.

Hansen, Mark B. N. *Bodies in Code: Interfaces with Digital Media*. London: Routledge, 2006.

———. *Embodying* Technesis: *Technology beyond Writing*. Ann Arbor: University of Michigan Press, 2000.

———. *New Philosophy for New Media*. Cambridge, MA: MIT Press, 2006.

Harding, Jason, ed. *Ford Madox Ford, Modernist Magazines and Editing*. New York: Rodopi, 2010.

Harris, Stefanie. *Mediating Modernity: German Literature and the "New" Media, 1895–1930*. University Park: Penn State University Press, 2009.

Hayles, N. Katherine. *Electronic Literature: New Horizons for the Literary*. Notre Dame, IN: University of Notre Dame Press, 2008.

———. *How We Became Posthuman: Virtual Bodies in Cybernetics, Literature and Informatics*. Chicago: University of Chicago Press, 1999.

———. *How We Think: Digital Media and Contemporary Technogenesis*. Chicago: University of Chicago Press, 2012.

————. *My Mother Was a Computer: Digital Subjects and Literary Texts.* Chicago: University of Chicago Press, 2005.

————. *Writing Machines.* Cambridge, MA: MIT Press, 2002.

Hills, Richard L. *Papermaking in Britain 1488–1988.* London: Athlone, 1988.

Horowitz, Gregg. *Sustaining Loss: Art and Mournful Life.* Stanford: Stanford University Press, 2002.

Huss, Richard E. *The Development of Printers' Mechanical Typesetting Methods 1822–1925.* Charlottesville: University Press of Virginia, 1973.

Iser, Wolfgang. *The Act of Reading: A Theory of Aesthetic Response.* Baltimore: Johns Hopkins University Press, 1978.

————. *The Implied Reader: Patterns of Communication in Prose Fiction from Bunyan to Beckett.* Baltimore: Johns Hopkins University Press, 1974.

Jameson, Fredric. *Postmodernism, or, The Cultural Logic of Late Capitalism.* Durham, NC: Duke University Press, 1991.

Joyce, James. *Finnegans Wake.* Introduction by John Bishop. New York: Penguin Books, 1999.

————. *Letters of James Joyce.* Ed. Stuart Gilbert. Vol. I. New York: Viking Press, 1966.

————. *Portrait of the Artist as a Young Man.* New York: Bantam Books, 1992.

————. *Ulysses.* New York: Vintage International, 1990.

————. *Ulysses.* Ed. Hans Walter Gabler. New York: Vintage, 1986.

Kassell, Walter. *Marcel Proust and the Strategy of Reading.* Purdue University Monographs in Romance Languages. Amsterdam: John Benjamins, 1980.

Katz, Tamar. "Modernism, Subjectivity, and Narrative Form: Abstraction in *The Waves.*" *Narrative* 3.3 (1995): 232–51.

Kaufman, Michael. *Textual Bodies: Modernism, Postmodernism, and Print.* Lewisburg, PA: Bucknell University Press, 1994.

Kenner, Hugh. *Joyce's Voices.* Berkeley: University of California Press, 1979.

————. *The Mechanic Muse.* Oxford: Oxford University Press, 1988.

Kittler, Friedrich. *Discourse Networks 1800/1900.* Trans. Michael Metteer, with Chris Cullens. Stanford: Stanford University Press, 1990.

Klein, Melanie. *The Selected Melanie Klein.* Ed. Juliet Mitchell. New York: Free Press, 1986.

Kristeva, Julia. *Proust and the Sense of Time.* Trans. Stephen Bann. New York: Columbia University Press, 1993.

Landy, Joshua. *Philosophy as Fiction: Self, Deception and Knowledge in Proust.* Oxford: Oxford University Press, 2004.

Lane, Jeremy. "Falling Asleep in the *Wake*: Reading as Hypnagogic Experience." In *Re: Joyce—Text/Culture/Politics*, ed. John Brannigan, Geoff Ward, and Julian Wolfreys. New York: St. Martin's Press, 1998.

Latham, Sean. "The Mess and Muddle of Modernism: The Modernist Journals Project and Modern Periodical Studies." *Tulsa Studies in Women's Literature* 30.2 (2011): 407–28.

Latham, Sean, and Robert Scholes. "The Rise of Periodical Studies." *PMLA* 121.2 (2006): 517–31.

Lawrence, Karen. *The Odyssey of Style in* Ulysses. Princeton, NJ: Princeton University Press, 1981.

Lees, Heath. "Introduction to Sirens and the *Fuga per Canonem*." *James Joyce Quarterly* 22.1 (1984): 39–54.

Legros, Lucien Alphonse, and John Cameron Grant. *Typographical Printing-Surfaces: The Technology and Mechanism of Their Production*. London: Longmans, Green, 1916.

Levin, Lawrence. "The Sirens Episode as Music: Joyce's Experiment in Prose Polyphony." *James Joyce Quarterly* 3 (1965): 12–24.

Liu, Lydia H. "iSpace: Printed English after Joyce, Shannon, and Derrida." *Critical Inquiry* 32.3 (2006): 516–50.

Lucenti, Lisa Marie. "Virginia Woolf's *The Waves*: To Defer That 'Appalling Moment.'" *Criticism* 40.1 (1998): 75–97.

Lund, Michael. "*The Waves*: Publishing History and Literary Form." In *Virginia Woolf: Emerging Perspectives*, ed. Mark Hussey, Vara Neverow, and Jane Lilienfeld. New York: Pace University Press, 1994.

Lupton, Christina. *Knowing Books: The Consciousness of Mediation in Eighteenth-Century Britain*. Philadelphia: University of Pennsylvania Press, 2012.

Lydon, Mary. "*Pli selon pli*: Proust and Fortuny." In *Reading Proust Now*, ed. Mary Ann Caws and Eugène Nicole. New York: Peter Lang, 1990.

Lyotard, Jean-François. *Discours, Figure*. Paris: Klincksieck, 2002.

Mao, Douglas. *Solid Objects: Modernism and the Test of Production*. Princeton, NJ: Princeton University Press, 1998.

Marcus, Jane. "Virginia Woolf and the Hogarth Press." In *Modernist Writers and the Marketplace*, ed. Ian Willison, Warwick Gould, and Warren Chernaik. New York: St. Martin's Press, 1996.

McCarthy, Patrick A. "The Last Epistle of *Finnegans Wake*." *James Joyce Quarterly* 27 (Summer 1990): 725–33.

———. "Reading the Letter: Interpreting the *Wake*." In *New Alliances in Joyce Studies*, ed. Bonnie Kime Scott. Newark: University of Delaware Press, 1988.

McDowall, A. S. "The Enchantment of a Mirror." In Virginia Woolf, *Jacob's Room*. Norton Critical Edition. Ed. Suzanne Raitt. New York: Norton, 2007.

McGann, Jerome. *Black Riders: The Visible Language of Modernism*. Princeton, NJ: Princeton University Press, 1993.

———. *The Textual Condition*. Princeton, NJ: Princeton University Press, 1991.

McHugh, Roland. *Annotations to* Finnegans Wake. 3rd edition. Baltimore: Johns Hopkins University Press, 2005.

McKenzie, D. F. *Bibliography and the Sociology of Texts*. London: British Library, 1986.

McLuhan, Marshall. *The Gutenberg Galaxy: The Making of Typographic Man*. Toronto: University of Toronto Press, 1962.

Merleau-Ponty, Maurice. *The Visible and the Invisible*. Trans. Alphonso Lingis. Evanston, IL: Northwestern University Press, 1968.

Milesi, Laurent. "Metaphors of the Quest in *Finnegans Wake*." In Finnegans Wake: *Fifty Years*, ed. Geert Lernout. Amsterdam: Rodopi Press, 1990.

Mitchell, W. J. T. "There Are No Visual Media." *Journal of Visual Culture* 4.2 (2005): 257–66.

Monson, Tamlyn. "'A Trick of the Mind': Alterity, Ontology and Representation in Virginia Woolf." *Modern Fiction Studies* 50.1 (2004): 173–96.

Mooney, Susan. "Bronze by Gold by Bloom: Echo, the Invocatory Drive and the Aurteur in Sirens." In *Bronze by Gold: The Music of Joyce*, ed. Sebastian D. G. Knowles. New York: Garland, 1999.

Moretti, Franco. *The Modern Epic: The World-System from Goethe to García Márquez*. Trans. Quintin Hoare. London: Verso Press, 1996.

Morrison, Mark. *The Public Face of Modernism: Little Magazines, Audiences, and Reception, 1905–1920*. Madison: University of Wisconsin Press, 2001.

Murdoch, Adrian. *The Last Pagan: Julian the Apostate and the Death of the Ancient World*. London: Sutton, 2004.

Murphet, Julian. *Multimedia Modernism: Literature and the Anglo-American Avant-Garde*. Cambridge: Cambridge University Press, 2009.

Ordway, Scott. "A Dominant Boylan: Music, Meaning and Sonata Form in the Sirens Episode of *Ulysses*." *James Joyce Quarterly* 45.1 (2007): 85–96.

Parandowski, Jan. "Meeting with Joyce." In *Portraits of the Artist in Exile: Recollections of James Joyce by Europeans*, ed. Willard Potts. Seattle: University of Washington Press, 1979.

Piper, Andrew. *Book Was There: Reading in Electronic Times*. Chicago: University of Chicago Press, 2012.

——. *Dreaming in Books: The Making of the Bibliographic Imagination in the Romantic Age*. Chicago: University of Chicago Press, 2009.

Porter, David H. *The Omega Workshops and the Hogarth Press: An Artful Fugue*. London: Cecil Woolf, 2008.

Pressman, Jessica. *Digital Modernism: Making It New in New Media*. Oxford: Oxford University Press, 2013.

Price, Leah. *How to Do Things with Books in Victorian Britain*. Princeton, NJ: Princeton University Press, 2013.

Proust, Marcel. *À la Recherche du Temps Perdu*. Ed. Jean-Yves Tadié. Paris: Gallimard, 1999.

——. "On Reading." In *On Reading Ruskin*. Trans. Jean Autret, William Burford, and Phillip J. Wolfe. New Haven, CT: Yale University Press, 1987.

——. *Remembrance of Things Past*. Vols. 1–3. Trans. C. K. Scott Moncrieff and Terence Kilmartin. New York: Random House, 1981.

Rabaté, Jean-Michel. "The Silence of the Sirens." In *James Joyce: The Centennial Symposium*, ed. Morris Beja, Phillip Herring, Maurice Harmon, and David Norris. Chicago: University of Illinois Press, 1986.

Rae, Patricia, ed. *Modernism and Mourning*. Lewisburg, PA: Bucknell University Press, 2007.

Rainey, Lawrence. *Institutions of Modernism: Literary Elites and Public Culture*. New Haven, CT: Yale University Press, 1998.

Rasula, Jed. "*Finnegans Wake* and the Character of the Letter." *James Joyce Quarterly* 34.4 (1997): 517–30.

Rich, Susanna. "De Undarum Natura: Lucretius and Woolf in *The Waves*." *Journal of Modern Literature* 23.2 (1999–2000): 249–57.

Rosenthal, Lecia. *Mourning Modernism: Literature, Catastrophe, and the Politics of Consolation*. New York: Fordham University Press, 2011.

Ross, Kristin. "Albertine; Or, the Limits of Representation." *NOVEL: A Forum on Fiction* 19.2 (1986): 135–49.

Sailer, Susan Shaw. *On the Void of To Be: Incoherence and Trope in "Finnegans Wake."* Ann Arbor: University of Michigan Press, 1993.

Schaffer, Talia. "Letters to Biddy: About That Original Hen." *James Joyce Quarterly* 29.3 (1992): 623–42.

Schloss, Carol. "*Finnegans Wake* as History of the Book." In *James Joyce: The Centennial Symposium*, ed. Morris Beja, , Phillip Herring, Maurice Harmon, and David Norris. Chicago: University of Illinois Press, 1986.

Scholes, Robert, and Clifford Wulfman. *Modernism in the Magazines: An Introduction*. New Haven, CT: Yale University Press, 2010.

Sedgwick, Eve Kosofsky. "Paranoid Reading and Reparative Reading, or,

You're so Paranoid, You Probably Think This Essay Is about You." In *Touching Feeling: Affect, Pedagogy, Performativity*. Durham, NC: Duke University Press, 2003.

Silverman, Kaja. *World Spectators*. Stanford: Stanford University Press, 2000.

Southall, Richard. *Printer's Type in the Twentieth Century: Manufacturing and Design Methods*. London: British Library, 2005.

Stainer, Michael. "'The Void Awaits Surely All Them That Weave the Wind': 'Penelope' and 'Sirens' in *Ulysses*." *Twentieth Century Literature* 41.3 (1995): 319–31.

Stewart, Garrett. "Catching the Stylistic D/rift: Sound Defects in Woolf's *The Waves*." *ELH* 54.2 (1987): 421–61.

Tadié, Jean-Yves. *Marcel Proust: A Life*. Trans. Euan Cameron. New York: Penguin Books, 2000.

Theall, Donald. *Beyond the Word: Reconstructing Sense in the Joyce Era of Technology, Culture, and Communication*. Toronto: University of Toronto Press, 1995.

Topia, André. "'Sirens': The Emblematic Vibration." In *James Joyce: The Centennial Symposium*, ed. Morris Beja, Phillip Herring, Maurice Harmon, and David Norris. Chicago: University of Illinois Press, 1986.

Trotter, David. *Cinema and Modernism*. Malden, MA: Blackwell, 2007.

Turner, Catherine. *Marketing Modernism between the Two World Wars*. Amherst: University of Massachusetts Press, 2003.

Vandivere, Julie. "Waves and Fragments: Linguistic Construction as Subject Formation in Virginia Woolf." *Twentieth-Century Literature* 42.2 (1996): 221–33.

Vitoux, Pierre. "Aristotle, Berkeley and Newman in 'Proteus' and *Finnegans Wake*." *James Joyce Quarterly* 18 (Winter 1981): 161–75.

Warde, Beatrice. *The Crystal Goblet: Sixteen Essays on Typography*. Cleveland, OH: World, 1956.

Westling, Louise. "Virginia Woolf and the Flesh of the World." *New Literary History* 30.4 (1999): 855–75.

Wexler, Joyce Piell. *Who Paid for Modernism? Art, Money and the Fiction of Conrad, Joyce, and Lawrence*. Fayetteville: University of Arkansas Press, 1997.

Willis, J. H., Jr. *Leonard and Virginia Woolf as Publishers: The Hogarth Press, 1917–1941*. Charlottesville: University Press of Virginia, 1992.

Willison, Ian, Warwick Gould, and Warren Chernaik, eds. *Modernist Writers and the Marketplace*. New York: St. Martin's Press, 1996.

Woolf, Virginia. *Collected Essays*. Vols. 1–3. London: Hogarth Press, 1966.

————. *Jacob's Room*. Norton Critical Edition. Ed. Suzanne Raitt. New York: Norton, 2007.

————. *The Letters of Virginia Woolf*. Vol. 2: *1912–1922*. Ed. Nigel Nicolson. New York: Harcourt Brace Jovanovich, 1976.

————. *The Letters of Virginia Woolf*. Vol. 3: *1923–1928*. Ed. Nigel Nicolson. New York: Harcourt Brace Jovanovich, 1977.

————. *Mrs. Dalloway*. New York: Harcourt, 1925.

————. *The Waves*. New York: Harcourt, 1931.

————. *A Writer's Diary*. Ed. Leonard Woolf. New York: Harcourt Brace, 1954.

Zimmerman, Nadia. "Musical Form as Narrator: The Fugue of the Sirens." *Journal of Modern Literature* 26.1 (2002): 108–18.

INDEX